Is the gold you just bought real or is it fake? Did you pa_____ investment? The coin you recently purchased, is it real? Did yo__ _____ _____ ____ ___ ____ investment strategy with respect to precious metals? Should you buy silver coins or gold coins? Should you buy silver bars or gold bars? Should you invest in precious metal ETFs or Mutual Funds and how do these investments compare to owning physical gold or silver? What rate of return can you expect from any precious metal investment in any form and from rare coins? Who do you safely buy from?

I could list questions like these for pages, but I think you get the point. There is so much interest in rare coins and gold and other precious metals in the myriad forms they take. And with this vast array of choices comes uncertainty and the possibility of making a poor decision and being taken advantage of.

Will this book rescue you? I hope so. I am throwing you a lifeline and inviting you to get on board as we journey down this path together. We will explore all the forms gold, silver and platinum take – from coins to bars to rounds to numerous paper forms: ETFs, Mutual funds, ETNs, Futures, Options, Savings Accounts and so much more. We will travel back and look at the return these investment types have generated over the years. I will show you the safest way to buy gold and silver and coins, how to test your products for authenticity, and how to find gold, silver and coins without running around to yard sales, flea markets and estate sales! We will examine rare coins and explain how they relate to the topics mentioned. This book will end with an introduction to coin collecting: learn how to get started and why it is so important to know about coins and how they relate to precious metal investing. We will even look at ancient coins. This journey will begin with baby steps as we cover very basic information then get much more involved with these topics as the book unfolds. The road to success starts with knowledge. **Why did this 1794 Silver Dollar sell for $10.5 million and break all coin records? (Answer at book's end!)**

Gold, Silver and Rare Coins
A Complete Guide To
Finding - Buying - Selling - Investing

By Sam Sommer and Sasha Sommer

eMail Link: Mailing

It is easier than you think!

Copyright, Legal Notice and Disclaimer

This publication is protected under the US Copyright Act of 1976 and all other applicable international, federal, state and local laws, and all rights are reserved, including resale rights: you are not allowed to give or sell this book and the materials contained in it, to anyone else.

Please note that much of this publication is based on personal experience and anecdotal evidence. Although the author and publisher have made every reasonable attempt to achieve complete accuracy of the content in this book, they assume no responsibility for errors or omissions. Also, you should use this information as you see fit, and at your own risk. Your particular situation may not be exactly suited to the examples illustrated here; in fact, it's likely that they won't be the same, and you should adjust your use of the information and recommendations accordingly.

Any trademarks, service marks, product names or named features are assumed to be the property of their respective owners, and are used only for reference. There is no implied endorsement if I use one of these terms. All images in this book are readily available in various places on the Internet and believed to be in public domain. Images used are believed to be used within the author's and publisher's rights according to the U.S. Copyright Fair Use Act (title 17, U.S. Code.)

Finally, use your head. Nothing in this book is intended to replace common sense, legal, or other professional advice, and is meant to inform and entertain the reader.

Copyright © 2014 Sam Sommer. All rights reserved worldwide.

Introduction

Who could have imagined that a routine trip to McDonald's back in the late 50's would start a life long journey into the world of coins and the many forms of gold and silver. My dad took me to this new hamburger joint that he loved, and as always, he handed me the change. As we were leaving and heading for the car, I looked at the coins in my hand and was surprised to find one with an Indian Head on it. I glanced at my dad and showed him the coin. He exclaimed: "That's an Indian Head Penny, you can find them in change, why not keep it and look for more."

Those few words and that neat looking Indian Head got my mind spinning. Could it be so easy to find these different looking pennies? In those days it was! My quest eventually evolved into collecting other coins and precious metal investing.

Coin collecting and searching is quite exciting and very financially rewarding. Our younger generation has little patience for such a pastime, and I fear that it may die out at some point. Who can say for sure?

I am glad we are going on this journey together, and maybe you or someone you know will take up the hobby after this read. I hope you pass on this information and reward yourself in the process. And if precious metal investing is your cup of tea, you are in the right place.

Table of Contents

The Gold Industry

The Silver Industry

The Coin Industry

Gold Has Many Forms

Silver Has Many Forms

Coins: Gold - Silver - Rare

The Relationship (Gold, Silver, Coins)

Finding Gold, Silver, Coins

Is It Silver?

Is It Gold?

Dealing With Coins

Prospecting

Testing Your Gold and Silver

What About The "IRS"?

Important Terminology

Buying: Gold & Silver Coins

Buying: Bars and Rounds

Selling: Gold, Silver, Coins

ETFs, Mutual Funds, Gold Accounts & More

- What To Expect From Your Investment
- Gold vs Silver: Who Wins This Fight?
- Coin Collecting: What Every Investor Must Know
- Coin Collecting: Getting Started (Tools)
- Coin Collecting: Clubs and Terminology
- How To Start Collecting
- Error Coins Can Be Very Valuable
- How To Grade Coins
- How To Handle Coins
- Fake Coins
- Children and Pennies
- Coin Roll Hunting
- Rare Coins
- Special Coins
- Ancient Coins
- Buying Coins
- Selling Coins
- Investment Strategy – Conclusion

The Gold Industry

Gold may be the most recognized object on the face of the earth. Even those who do not know what it is have a fascination with its color and shine, even children. Its beauty and appeal seem everlasting.

I can think of no better place to start this journey than by looking at the gold industry: Where does gold come from? What countries are involved? How much is available and how is it consumed? What is the gold industry worth in dollars and cents? How did we become interested in gold as an investment? Have Americans always been allowed to own gold?

What most people fail to realize is that of all the gold ever mined, almost all of it, is still with us; it hasn't gone anywhere. This is a difficult concept to grasp. If gold has been mined for centuries, even thousands of years, why hasn't it been used up?

You see, gold is only consumed in very small amounts (about 10%), 90% of gold mined each year goes into jewelry and investing, so it is always available in one form or another. Most of the gold ever mined, a staggering figure estimated at 6.5 - 9 trillion dollars worth, is still here. Let's look at the consumption breakdown: (Please note that most charts show metric tons or tonnes. A "tonne" is a metric system unit of mass equal to 1,000 kilograms (2,204.6 pounds) or 1 megagram (1 Mg))

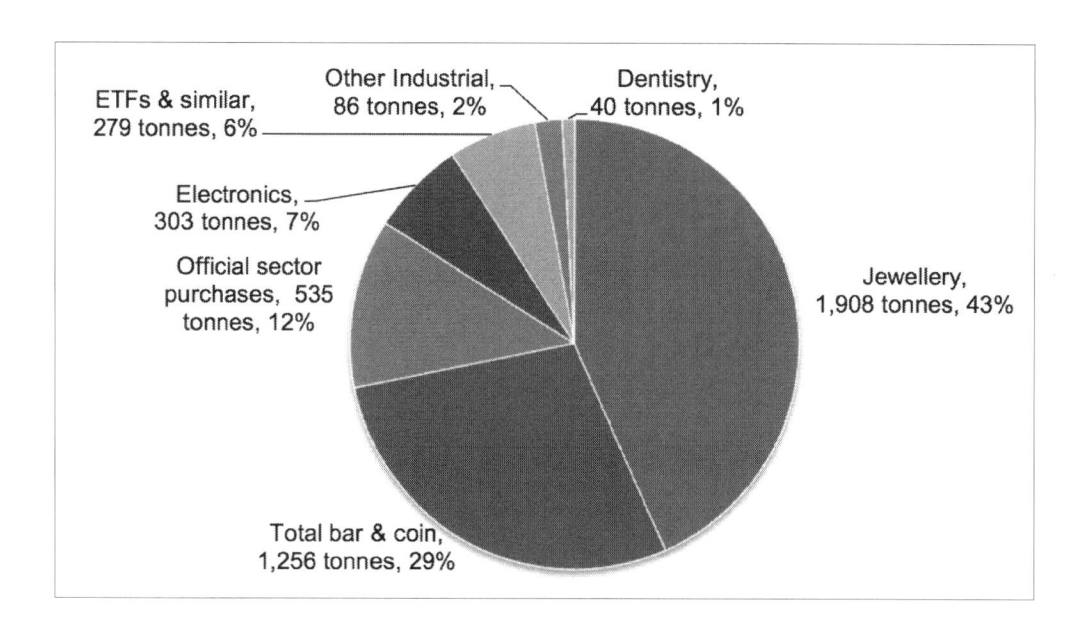

It's easy to understand why most gold is still with us – only 10% goes into technology and much of it can be recycled when no longer needed. Gold mines account for most of the world's gold. Stories of the oceans being rich with the yellow metal are true, but the cost of extraction is currently much greater than the price.

This **list of countries by gold production** is from a report on the U.S. Geological Survey website.

For many years, until 2006, South Africa was the world's dominant gold producer. Recently, other countries with large surface area have surpassed South Africa, including China, Russia, the United States, Peru and Australia.

Rank	Country/Region	Gold production (Metric Tons) in 2013
	World	2,770
1	China	420
2	Australia	255
3	United States	227
4	Russia	220
5	Peru	150
6	South Africa	145
7	Canada	120
8	Mexico	100
9	Uzbekistan	93
10	Ghana	85
11	Brazil	75
12	Papua New Guinea	62
13	Indonesia	60
14	Chile	55
	Rest of the world	700

About 2,700 tons (metric tonnes) are mined each year – 82 million ounces. The value is estimated to be 125 billion dollars. It may seem like a lot of gold is coming out of the ground, but when compared to Walmart's annual sales of $200 billion, the figure appears small. This chart from Morgan Stanley shows current and future supply-demand dynamics. Future gold prices on the chart are estimates.

Morgan Stanley

MORGAN STANLEY RESEARCH
Global Metals Playbook, 1Q13
January 24, 2013

Gold — Global supply / demand

	Unit	2005	2006	2007	2008	2009	2010	2011	2012	2013e	2014e	2015e	2016e	2017e	2018e
Supply															
Total Mine Supply	tonnes	2561	2494	2497	2429	2611	2741	2819	2842	2884	2930	2940	2975	3018	3064
year-over-year chg	%	2.3	-2.6	0.1	-2.7	7.5	5.0	2.8	0.8	1.5	1.6	0.4	1.2	1.5	1.5
Scrap supply	tonnes	902	1133	982	1316	1672	1719	1669	1642	1694	1550	1400	1200	1150	1081
year-over-year chg	%	2.4	25.5	-13.3	34.0	27.1	2.8	-2.9	-1.6	3.2	-8.5	-9.7	-14.3	-4.2	-6.0
Official sector net sales/(purchases)	tonnes	849	289	430	-36	-98	25	-457	-536	-542	-340	-280	-50	-25	-25
year-over-year chg	%	92.6	-66.0	48.8	-108.5	168.7	-125.2	-1953.8	17.3	1.1	-37.3	-17.6	-82.1	-50.0	0.0
Net producer hedging	tonnes	-142	-434	-444	-352	-254	-121	12	-20	-12	55	70	90	110	110
Total Supply		4170	3482	3464	3356	3931	4364	4043	3928	4024	4195	4130	4215	4253	4229
year-over-year chg	%	22.6	-16.5	-0.5	-3.1	17.1	11.0	-7.4	-2.8	2.5	4.2	-1.5	2.0	0.9	-0.6
Demand															
Jewellery	tonnes	2719	2300	2424	2304	1814	2017	1973	1845	1883	1969	2069	2116	2201	2241
year-over-year chg	%	3.9	-15.4	5.4	-4.9	-21.3	11.2	-2.2	-6.5	2.1	4.5	5.1	2.2	4.0	1.8
Electronics	tonnes	286	316	322	311	275	326	330	305	320	325	335	355	380	389
year-over-year chg	%	7.3	10.7	1.8	-3.4	-11.6	18.6	1.3	-7.7	4.9	1.6	3.1	6.0	7.0	2.4
Dental	tonnes	62	61	58	56	53	50	53	53	53	55	55	55	55	55
year-over-year chg	%	-7.7	-2.7	-4.8	-3.6	-5.4	-4.9	4.8	0.0	0.0	4.8	0.0	0.0	0.0	0.8
Official Coins, Medals & Imitation coins	tonnes	149	189	204	262	293	302	333	414	406	392	372	354	338	338
year-over-year chg	%	2.8	26.9	7.9	28.4	11.8	2.9	10.5	24.2	-1.8	-3.5	-5.0	-4.8	-4.7	0.2
Total Fabrication Demand	tonnes	3216	2866	3007	2933	2434	2694	2689	2616	2662	2740	2832	2880	2974	3024
year-over-year chg	%	3.9	-10.9	4.9	-2.5	-17.0	10.7	-0.2	-2.7	1.8	2.9	3.3	1.7	3.3	1.7
Change in ETF Holdings	tonnes	208	260	252	321	617	368	238	285	100	75	25	-50	-50	-50
Bar Hoarding	tonnes	251	233	240	621	498	882	1209	1364	1397	1355	1314	1248	1186	1127
Implied Investment/(Disinvestment)	tonnes	495	123	-35	-519	382	420	-94	-337	-134	25	-40	136	144	128
Total Investment Demand		954	408	197	171	1176	1052	986	1074	1077	1355	1224	1310	1330	1255
Investment as a % of Total Demand	%	22.9	17.7	13.2	12.6	38.1	38.3	33.5	33.4	33.9	34.7	31.4	31.7	30.1	28.5
Total Demand (Fabrication + Investment)	tonnes	4,170	3,274	3,204	3,104	3,610	3,747	3,675	3,689	3,739	4,095	4,055	4,190	4,303	4,279
Gold Price	US$/oz	445	605	697	872	970	1,226	1,546	1,669	1,773	1,845	1,750	1,550	1,400	1,375

e = Morgan Stanley Research estimates Source: World Gold Council, Goldfields Minerals Services, CRU Ltd, Morgan Stanley Research

This Morgan Stanley chart based upon the World Gold Council figures clearly shows that supply is greater than demand: 4000 tonnes vs 3700 tonnes demand for 2013.

However, there is some debate about this supply-demand dynamic. Figures for the gold supply usually come from the World Gold Council, and according to some experts, these figures can be misleading. For example, Eric Sprott, a world gold expert, claims that the demand actually exceeds the supply. This should be mentioned because even though the price of gold (we will look at this topic later) is not determined by the supply vs the demand; this dynamic can influence many market factors that indirectly impact the price of gold.

This is critical to know because it can influence investing decisions. What is important then is not so much demand vs supply, but how gold is consumed. With 43% used for jewelry, 47% used for investing, and only 10% used for consumption, gold ends up being a product that, for the most part, we can do without. When the price was high from 2001 – 2011, the demand for jewelry went down each year. Again, when the price goes way up, investors tend to shy away, feeling that the profit potential is weak.

Gold has always been valued as a form of money and adornment and saved by many for centuries. Gold as an investment is a fairly recent phenomenon. Let's take a look at this.

The worldwide interest in Gold as an investment vehicle, is due in part, to the universal appeal, large number of sales and recognition of the South African Gold Krugerrand

This coin is 22 karat gold and contains 8.33% copper. Its fineness is 91.67% or 92% gold. It was introduced in 1967 to help market South African gold and produced by the South African Mint.

In 1974 the U.S. Government repealed the Gold Reserve Act (we will address this topic later), and Americans could once again freely own and trade gold. As a result, investing in Krugerrands skyrocketed. The U.S. became the biggest market for them, accounting for over 50% of all sales. From 1975 to 1984, 22 million Krugerrands were imported into the U.S..

By 1980, the Krugerrand accounted for 90% of the global gold coin market. The name itself is a compound of "Kruger" (the man depicted on the obverse [rear] and "rand", the South African unit of currency.

During the 1980's some Western countries (including the USA) forbade import of the Krugerrand because of its association with the apartheid government of South Africa.

Investors today owe a debt of gratitude to this coin. Its worldwide sales, amounting to over 48 million ounces of gold, and its association with an apartheid type government provided the impetus for the birth of the Canadian Gold Maple Leaf in 1979, the Australian Nugget in 1981, the Chinese Gold Panda in 1982, the American Gold Eagle in 1986 and the British Britannia coin in 1987.

As mentioned, the repeal of the Gold Reserve Act in 1974, played a key role in the future of gold, especially as an investment asset. Prior to 1974, Americans could not own gold. This was significant. When gold ownership rights were restored, the demand for, and the nature of the gold investment marketplace, began to change dramatically.

The events leading up to the repealing of this Act are momentous and of great historical investing interest. During the great depression Americans hoarded gold. They feared that money might become valueless and the tangibility of gold gave sensible security in a faltering economy.

In an effort to help stabilize a weak economy and stop gold hoarding in 1933, President Franklin Roosevelt issued Executive Order 6102. It made it illegal to own gold coins, gold certificates and gold bullion. The order, shown below, was posted everywhere: magazines, newspapers, post offices, train stations and other public places.

An interesting exception to the Order were gold coins that had numismatic value. In other words, any gold coins that are part of a coin collection were exempt from the order.

As you can see from the Order, criminal penalties were quite severe.

POSTMASTER: PLEASE POST IN A CONSPICUOUS PLACE.—JAMES A. FARLEY, Postmaster General

UNDER EXECUTIVE ORDER OF THE PRESIDENT

Issued April 5, 1933

all persons are required to deliver

ON OR BEFORE MAY 1, 1933

all **GOLD COIN, GOLD BULLION, AND GOLD CERTIFICATES** now owned by them to a Federal Reserve Bank, branch or agency, or to any member bank of the Federal Reserve System.

Executive Order

FORBIDDING THE HOARDING OF GOLD COIN, GOLD BULLION AND GOLD CERTIFICATES.

[Text of Executive Order signed by FRANKLIN D ROOSEVELT, The White House, April 5, 1933.]

For Further Information Consult Your Local Bank

GOLD CERTIFICATES may be identified by the words "GOLD CERTIFICATE" appearing thereon. The serial number and the Treasury seal on the face of a GOLD CERTIFICATE are printed in YELLOW. Be careful not to confuse GOLD CERTIFICATES with other issues which are redeemable in gold but which are not GOLD CERTIFICATES. Federal Reserve Notes and United States Notes are "redeemable in gold" but are not "GOLD CERTIFICATES" and are not required to be surrendered

Special attention is directed to the exceptions allowed under Section 2 of the Executive Order

CRIMINAL PENALTIES FOR VIOLATION OF EXECUTIVE ORDER
$10,000 fine or 10 years imprisonment, or both, as provided in Section 9 of the order

Secretary of the Treasury

The Gold reserve Act was passed a year later. It outlawed most private possession of gold, forcing individuals to sell it to the Treasury. The Act also changed the nominal price of gold from $20.67 per troy ounce to $35. Just before it was passed, the Federal Reserve paid out $20.67 an ounce or $376.58 in today's dollars, based upon the consumer price index. It was a good deal for the U.S. Government. Forcing a sale at $20.67, then raising the price to $35, yielded an immediate paper gain of $2.8 billion, a considerable sum of money in those days.

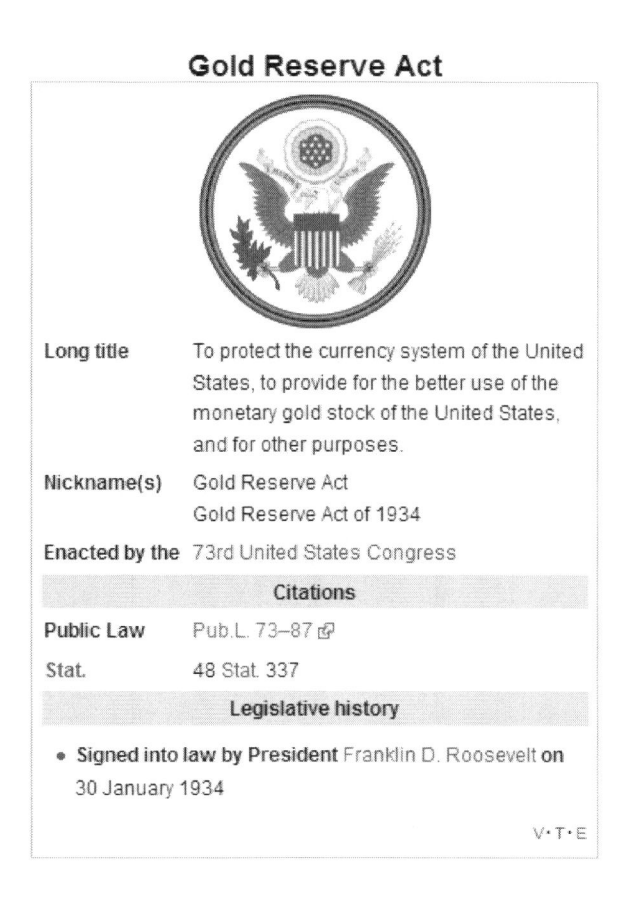

Gold Reserve Act

Long title	To protect the currency system of the United States, to provide for the better use of the monetary gold stock of the United States, and for other purposes.
Nickname(s)	Gold Reserve Act Gold Reserve Act of 1934
Enacted by the	73rd United States Congress
Citations	
Public Law	Pub.L. 73–87
Stat.	48 Stat. 337
Legislative history	

- Signed into law by President Franklin D. Roosevelt on 30 January 1934

V · T · E

With an inventory of gold worth billions of dollars, the U.S. Government decided to build a massive depository inside a fort, and so Fort Knox was born in 1936. Sitting on 42 acres adjacent to Fort Knox Army Base, in Fort Knox, Kentucky, this massive structure held many important documents and historical items over the years, aside from the over $200 billion in gold, currently believed to be housed there. During World War II it is believed to have held over one trillion dollars worth of gold in today's dollars.

During World War II, the depository held the original U.S. Declaration of Independence and U.S. Constitution. It held the reserves of European countries and key documents from Western history. For example, it held the Crown of St. Stephen, part of the Hungarian crown jewels, given to American soldiers to prevent them from falling into Soviet hands. The repository held one of four copies (exemplifications) of the Magna Carta, which had been sent for display at the 1939 New York World's Fair, and when war broke out, was kept in the U.S. for the duration.

During World War II and into the Cold War, until the invention of different types of synthetic painkillers, a supply of processed morphine and opium was kept in the depository as a hedge against the U.S. being isolated from sources of raw opium.

In 1974 the "Privilege" not the "Right", to own gold, was given back when the Gold Reserve Act was repealed. Some say the "Right" to own gold was lost forever.

Even though you can buy and own gold today, many experts argue that the government maintains the right to confiscate gold under certain circumstances:

In a great article by Josephine Mason, called "Gold Confiscation: Legal situation in the U.S." she states: "Although private ownership of gold in the United States was legalized, the power to confiscate gold remains in the hands of the President. At no time during this century has the U.S. government recognized the right of private gold ownership. The Trading with the Enemy Act, which President Roosevelt invoked in 1933 to restrict private gold transactions, remains law. The President still retains the right, under the Emergency Banking Relief Act, to "investigate, regulate or prohibit...the importing, exporting, hoarding, melting or earmarking of gold" in times of a declared national emergency. It is highly unlikely that either the Courts or Congress would successfully argue that confiscatory powers are not implicit in the Emergency Banking Relief Act if a currency crisis or other fiscal emergency prompted the President to, once again, nationalize gold."

It is highly unlikely that gold would again be confiscated, but this information is sometimes used to invoke a sense of fear in investors who often store their gold in other countries. Also, in 1971 when President Nixon ended trading of gold at the fixed price of $35 per ounce, we came off the gold standard, which had allowed governments to sell their gold to the U.S. at that fixed price. Formal links between major world currencies and real commodities were severed as a result.

Once we came off the gold standard, Fort Knox lost most of its appeal. When the "Privilege" to own gold was given back in 1974, gold started to gain momentum as an investment tool, which continues to this day. When asked: "Why still hold gold there?", former Fed Chairman Alan Greenspan said: "You hold onto it because it's the ultimate form of money".

The Silver Industry

Silver production equaled about 26 tonnes in 2013, or about 8 times that of gold. The dollar value of 26 tonnes (800,000,000 ounces) is roughly $16 billion, far less of a value than the $125 billion in mined gold. The top three producing countries are Mexico, China and Peru.

Rank	Country/Region	Silver production (tonnes)
—	World	26,000
1	Mexico	5,400
2	China	4,000
3	Peru	3,500
4	Russia	1,700
5	Australia	1,700
6	Bolivia	1,200
7	Chile	1,200
8	Poland	1,150
9	United States	1,090
10	Canada	720
—	Other Countries	4,300

There are many major differences with respect to gold. When we look at the way silver is consumed and compare it to gold, we see major shifts in usage. The next chart clearly shows this fact:

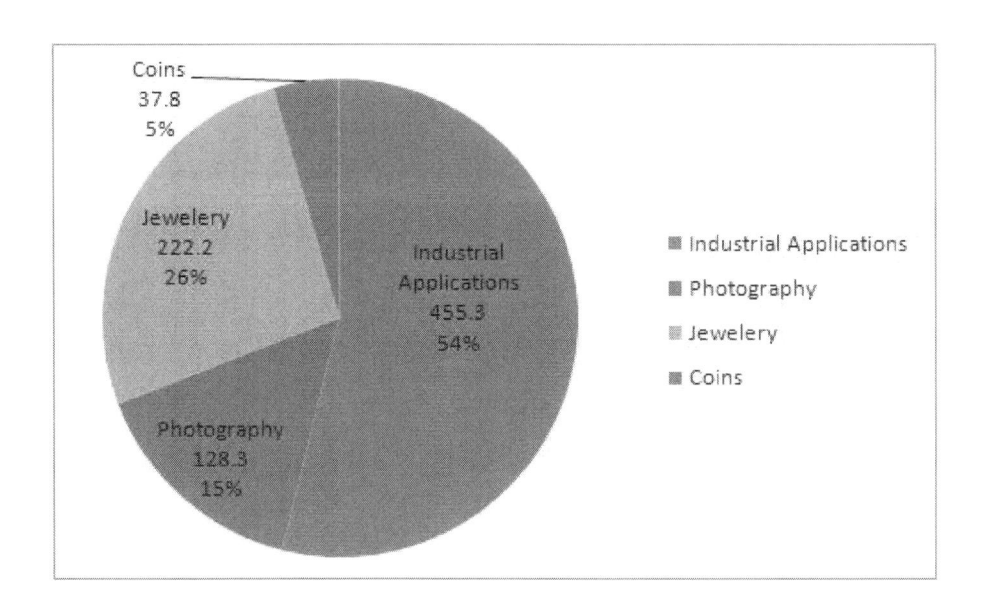

```
Coins
37.8
5%

Jewelery
222.2
26%

Industrial
Applications
455.3
54%

Photography
128.3
15%
```

- Industrial Applications
- Photography
- Jewelery
- Coins

Notice how most need is industrial in nature and not ornamental or investment, like we saw with gold. This implies that over time silver has the greatest investment potential because if supply runs short of demand you have actual need, vs investment and adornment factors found to make up most of gold usage.

In fact, The Silver Institute, a non-profit organization devoted to providing information to those with interest in silver, offers detailed data that clearly shows how the supply vs demand dynamic will continue to put upward pressure on the price of silver. Their chart, which follows, is of interest:

World Silver Supply and Demand (in millions of ounces)	2004	2005	2006	2007	2008	2009	2010	2011	2012	2013
Supply										
Mine Production	613.6	639.7	641.7	668.1	683.1	713.8	750.6	754.6	792.3	819.6
Net Government Sales	61.9	65.9	78.5	42.5	30.5	15.6	44.2	12.0	7.4	7.9
Scrap	198.6	202.5	206.0	202.9	200.7	199.7	225.5	258.7	252.6	191.8
Net Hedging Supply	-2.0	45.9	-11.6	-24.1	-8.7	-17.4	50.4	12.2	-47.0	-41.3
Total Supply	872.0	954.1	915.6	887.3	905.7	911.7	1,070.7	1,037.6	1,005.3	978.1
Demand										
Jewelry	187.1	187.9	176.0	183.2	178.2	177.3	190.6	183.4	181.4	198.8
Coins & Bars	53.0	51.5	48.7	51.2	187.7	87.9	146.1	212.6	139.3	245.6
Silverware	68.1	69.4	63.2	61.3	59.5	54.2	52.6	48.1	44.6	50.0
Industrial Fabrication	608.9	637.1	645.2	656.7	651.3	540.2	643.2	624.8	589.1	586.6
...of which Electrical & Electronics	191.8	211.1	223.1	239.8	245.5	203.1	272.6	260.6	237.0	233.9
...of which Brazing Alloys & Solders	48.9	52.4	54.4	58.1	61.3	53.3	60.6	62.4	60.3	62.4
...of which Photography	178.8	160.3	142.2	117.0	100.2	78.4	68.8	61.7	54.4	50.4
...of which Other Industrial	189.4	213.2	225.4	241.9	244.4	205.4	241.2	240.0	237.4	240.0
Physical Demand	917.1	945.9	933.1	952.3	1,076.7	859.5	1,032.6	1,068.9	954.4	1,081.1
Physical Surplus/Deficit	-45.1	8.2	-17.5	-65.0	-171.0	52.2	38.1	-31.3	51.0	-103.0
ETF Inventory Build	0.0	0.0	157.8	54.8	101.3	153.8	132.6	-24.0	55.1	1.6
Exchange Inventory Build	-20.3	15.9	-9.0	21.5	-7.1	-15.3	-7.4	12.2	62.2	8.8
Net Balance	-24.8	-7.7	-166.3	-141.3	-265.2	-86.3	-87.1	-19.4	-66.3	-113.3

Notice the supply figure of 978 million ounces for 2013. Then take a look at the demand side. Physical demand is 1,081 ounces, leaving a net deficit of -113 million ounces. When we look at how silver is used in some detail you will realize how significant these figures are. If demand is greater than supply, how does the supply keep pace? Some supply comes from recycled scrap silver and some from inventory. Let's take a look at how silver is used:

Silver is the best electrical conductor of all metals - making it an absolute must in conductors, switches, contacts and fuses. Silver use in electronics is due to its unique chemical properties: low contact resistance, mechanical wear resistance, chemical stability, low polymer formation, a long functional life and the highest electrical and thermal conductivity of any metal. It is an important element in many types of batteries. Quartz watch batteries contain a silver oxide cell to increase power and battery lifespan. Aside from rechargeable batteries, disposable batteries also use silver.

In the medical field silver is utilized for its antimicrobial properties. Due to its ability to inhibit microbial growth, it is used for wound dressings, gowns, catheters, stethoscope diaphragms, implants and other medical equipment. Silver sulfadiazine is topically applied to burn victims to prevent infection, and silver nitrate is utilized to inhibit the herpes simplex virus (type 1). Silver nanoparticles are also grafted into textiles to manufacture antimicrobial bedding and clothing.

In air travel and the military, silver is employed as a dry lubricant in giant engines with high speed parts that otherwise run the risk of oil interruption and serious damage. It is also a component of coated bearings in jet engines.

In brazing and soldering, silver produces a smooth leak-tight and corrosion resistant joint. Purified water tanks possess silver to prevent bacterial growth and silver tin solders are used for bonding copper pipe in homes to eliminate lead and provide built in antibacterial action. Silver alloys provide a strong bond for ceramic to ceramic joints, silicon chips to metallic surfaces and surface mounted electronic components soldered to print circuit boards.

Silvers unique chemical properties make it the ideal component for an extensive list of manufactured materials. It is used in handles for stoves, key tops for computers, electrical control knobs, domestic appliance components, electrical connector housings, and in Mylar tape.

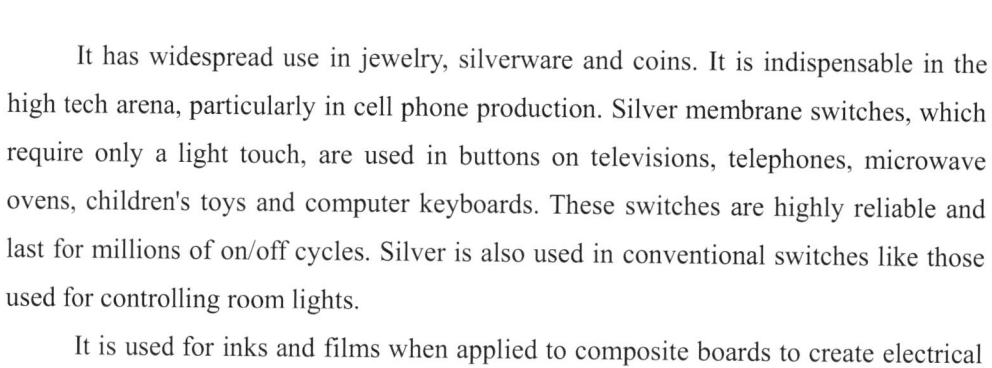

It has widespread use in jewelry, silverware and coins. It is indispensable in the high tech arena, particularly in cell phone production. Silver membrane switches, which require only a light touch, are used in buttons on televisions, telephones, microwave ovens, children's toys and computer keyboards. These switches are highly reliable and last for millions of on/off cycles. Silver is also used in conventional switches like those used for controlling room lights.

It is used for inks and films when applied to composite boards to create electrical pathways which are used in hundreds of millions of products to prevent theft.

The Coin Industry

The coin industry is valued at $10 billion in America. Worldwide figures put the total at $100 billion. As you can see, it is quite substantial. Did you know that many international financial heavy weights invest in the U.S. rare coin market? Why do you think that is?

The coin industry has many components:

- Governments that mint coins
- Companies that buy and sell coins
- Companies that appraise coins
- Companies that make and sell coin supplies
- Companies that hold coin auctions – eBay and Amazon e.g.
- People and institutions who collect coins
- People who save coins
- People and companies who invest in coins

It is very hard to get a handle on the exact size and scope of the coin industry because there is no central gathering tool or facility to reference. In other words, no one keeps track of what goes on. By rough estimates there are over 5000 coin dealers in the U.S. To get a sense of the size and scope of the coin marketplace, a major auction house (called Heritage Auctions, we will look at them later on in the book) had a sale in January 2014, that brought in $75,000,000. Two of the lots being sold went for over $5,000,000.

The "rare coin market" has fueled interest in coins for a number of reasons; not the least of which are investment returns averaging over 11%.

There are at least ten companies with sales exceeding $100,000,000 per year. Heritage Auctions alone touts annual rare coin sales of over $500,000,000. The Professional Numismatic Guild has around 300 members, most of which have large annual sales of numismatic material. There are also quite a few mass marketing companies with annual sales over $100,000,000. These companies specialize in modern and world coins.

The worldwide sales of gold and silver coins from government mints are in the tens of billions of dollars. The U.S. Mint publishes an annual report showing sales figures. Here is a link to the figures; some are listed below:

http://www.usmint.gov/about_the_mint/?action=annual_report

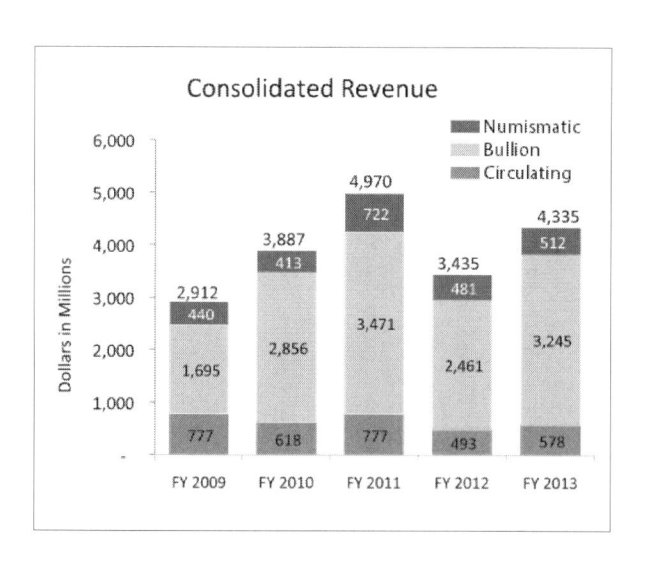

Consolidated Revenue

Year	Circulating	Bullion	Numismatic	Total
FY 2009	777	1,695	440	2,912
FY 2010	618	2,856	413	3,887
FY 2011	777	3,471	722	4,970
FY 2012	493	2,461	481	3,435
FY 2013	578	3,245	512	4,335

(Dollars in Millions)

Notice the 3.2 billion dollars in the chart above and below for bullion (gold-silver-platinum) coins in 2013.

BULLION COINS (dollars in millions)

	2013	2012	2011	2010	2009	% Change 2012 to 2013
Gold oz. sold (thousands)	1,218	788	1,235	1,839	1,418	54.6%
Silver oz. sold (thousands)	44,644	34,152	44,048	33,983	26,148	30.7%
Platinum oz. sold (thousands)	–	–	–	–	25	–
Sales Revenue	$3,244.6	$2,460.9	$3,471.4	$2,855.4	$1,694.8	31.8%
Gross Cost	$3,185.3	$2,432.5	$3,405.6	$2,800.2	$1,662.1	30.9%
Cost of Goods Sold	$3,159.0	$2,407.6	$3,378.8	$2,778.4	$1,650.0	31.2%
Selling, General & Administrative	$ 26.3	$ 24.9	$ 26.8	$ 21.8	$ 12.1	5.6%
Net Income	$ 59.3	$ 28.4	$ 65.8	$ 55.2	$ 32.7	108.8%
Bullion Net Margin	1.8%	1.2%	1.9%	1.9%	1.9%	

The U.S. Mint states that 140 million people have invested in the new state quarters. You do not need any special knowledge or skill to get involved with coins, and almost no money. By book's end, you will have all the knowledge you will need to not only start collecting coins, but to invest in bullion coins, bullion bars and other precious metal forms.

Gold Has Many Forms

When you mention gold what usually comes to mind? Most people think of some form of physical gold:

- Bars and rounds
- Jewelry
- Scrap gold
- Gold objects
- Gold coins
- Nuggets

Gold, however, can come in other forms – investment forms. Some are listed below:

- ETFs
- Mutual funds
- Gold certificates
- ETNs
- Futures
- Options
- Gold related stocks

We will look at all the forms as this book unfolds. Jewelry, gold nuggets, gold electronics and dental work all posses scrap gold that can be recycled. Scrap gold accounts for 20% of all the gold used each year.

Physical gold can be in the form of a round or bar:

This picture (above) of gold bars and rounds (also called medallions) comes from the Perth Mint in Australia and shows various gold products made of 99.99% pure gold. As you can see there is a wide range of sizes and weights.

This chart shows some of the sizes and weights you can buy from gold suppliers:

Typical Gold Bar Dimensions

All dimensions are in millimetres. To convert to inches, divide by 24.

Weight	Length	Width	Depth
400 Ounce	200	80	45
1 Kilo	80	40	18
500 Grams	65	32	14
250 Grams	55	25	10
100 Grams	55	31	3
50 Grams	45	25	2.3
1 Ounce	42	24	2
20 Grams	39	22	1.3
10 Grams	31	18	1
5 Grams	23	14	0.7
1 Gram	15	8	0.4

To help visualize sizes and weights: (Source: demonocracy.info)

From left to right – 1 Gram, 5 Grams, 10 Grams, 20 Grams, 31 Grams (One Troy Ounce)

From left to right: 50 Grams (1.76oz), 100 Grams, 250 Grams, 500 Grams, 1KG (35oz)

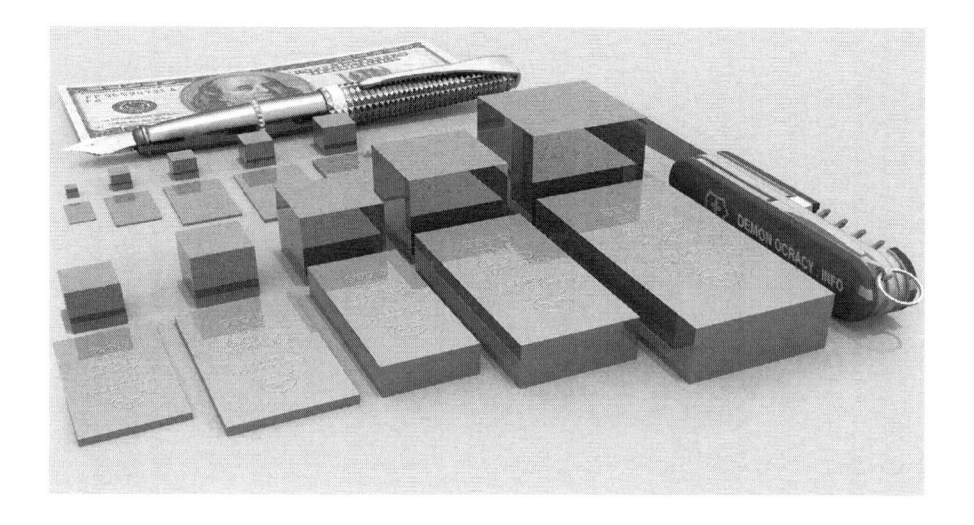

Gold nuggets are found in the ground or near the surface using sight and metal detectors. Some time ago, prospectors used to find nuggets the size of potatoes lying on the ground near Prescott, Arizona. The nuggets displayed below were found in Arizona:

Gold coins have been part of monetary systems for over 2,500 years and used in trade. The Roman Empire had a vast amount of gold coins that can still be found and purchased today. This gold coin of Titus was minted just 80 years after the death of Christ!

Many governments mint gold coins and have been doing so for hundreds of years. Purchasing gold coins is now very popular with investors. The U.S. Mint started making gold coins for circulation in the mid 1800's. In 1933 it stopped making gold coins and most of the coins minted that year were melted down. This is a picture of a rare 1933 Gold Double Eagle that survived. Perhaps one of only a dozen or so in existence:

We mentioned Order 6102 issued by President Franklin Roosevelt and how it made it illegal to own gold in any form, including coins, unless part of a collection. When this Act was issued the U.S. Mint melted all the coins it had made that year. It is important to remember this point and we shall see why later. After 1933 the U.S. Mint never made a gold coin again that was part of the general circulated coinage. Gold coins were only made for special sets such as commemoratives and coins sold in limited quantities via the U.S. Mint and through special distributors. In other words, gold coins are no longer put into the coin supply like pennies, nickels, dimes, quarters, halves and dollars are.

You don't have to buy physical gold to have a stake in the gold precious metal market. There are ways to have exposure to gold and the gold marketplace without actually buying the physical metal and holding on to it.

What's so nice about the investing marketplace of today is the wide variety of ways you can invest in precious metals, like gold, but never get your hands dirty. Just a play on words to indicate that you never have to touch the precious metal and yet you can own it either directly or indirectly. Let's briefly look at some of the options and later we will cover this subject in more detail.

An obvious way to invest in the gold industry is by owning gold stocks. For example, there are mining stocks: companies that own gold mines, exploration companies, gold processing companies. Most investors prefer a more balanced approach where they invest in a wide variety of gold related companies to provide safety. There are also ways to own gold in a group setting - you own a piece of the action. Many investors pool together and own a large block of gold.

Let's briefly look at options, futures, mutual funds and ETF's. Later we will explore these and other types of investments in much greater detail. For now we just need to know that many investment forms are available to us with regard to precious metals, like gold, and here are some examples:

A "future" is a financial contract obligating the buyer to purchase an asset such as gold or for the seller to sell an asset at a predetermined future date and price. Options are similar to futures but they differ in that the holder of an option has the right to buy or sell the underlying asset at expiration. A futures contract requires the terms to be fulfilled. However in real life, the actual delivery rate of the underlying goods specified in the futures contracts is very low. This is a result of the fact that the hedging or speculating benefits of the contracts can be had largely without holding the contract until expiry and delivering the good(s).

An exchange traded fund or ETF, is an investment fund traded on stock exchanges. It holds assets such as gold and is attractive because of its low cost, tax efficiency and stock like features. By owning an ETF, you get the diversification of an index fund as well as the ability to sell short, buy on margin and purchase as little as one share.

Another advantage is that the expense ratios for most ETFs are lower than those of the average mutual fund. There are gold related ETFs, such as; short gold ETFs, double ETFs and reverse gold ETFs.

A Mutual Fund is an investment vehicle that is made up of a pool of funds collected from many investors for the purpose of investing in securities such as stocks, bonds, money market instruments and similar assets. Mutual funds are operated by money managers, who invest the fund's capital and attempt to produce capital gains and income for the fund's investors. A mutual fund's portfolio is structured and maintained to match the investment objectives stated in its prospectus, such as a precious metal, like gold.

A Gold Fund is a mutual fund or exchange-traded fund (ETF) that invests primarily in gold-producing companies or gold bullion. The price of shares within a gold fund should correlate very closely to the spot price of gold itself, assuming the fund holds the majority of its assets in bullion or in the stocks and bonds of gold miners and manufacturers.

Silver Has Many Forms

Everything mentioned in the last chapter on gold applies to silver as well (physical and paper forms: ETFs, Mutual Funds, etc...). There are a few slight differences. Silver nuggets cannot be prospected like gold. Silver is tied up with other minerals and has to be mined and extracted. It can be found in nugget form, but this is an extremely rare event. A picture, like this of a silver nugget, is a very unusual occurrence:

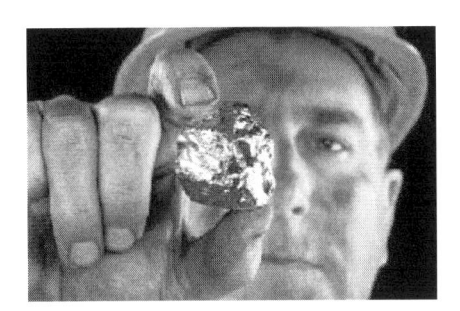

Another difference is how easily silver can be recycled and how many billions of silver coins exist vs fewer gold coins. Because so many ornaments are made of silver and there is so much silver jewelry, recycling - turning scrap into silver, is a really big business. Also there are many billions of silver coins in circulation and they can be found in change. Gold coins are few and far between and much harder to find and are not in circulation.

Typical sizes for silver bars from U.S. Sources:

1 oz Silver Bars and Rounds. One ounce silver bars are the smallest, and because of that, they typically carry the highest premium over spot price as it costs the mints the most in fabrication costs per ounce of any sized bar.

5 oz Silver Bars. Five ounce silver bars are the next smallest, but they actually carry roughly the same premiums as 1 oz bars because they are a bit less common than 1, 10 or 100 oz bars.

10 oz Silver Bars. Ten ounce silver bars are some of the most widely traded on the market, and are produced by nearly every silver bar manufacturer out there. The premiums start to get more reasonable at this size.

1 kg Silver Bars. One kilogram silver bars are more of a specialty bar, and aren't produced by many of the major manufacturers. You will likely have to look long and far to find these, and because of that, you'll usually pay an inflated price.

100 oz Silver Bars. The largest commonly traded form of silver bar is the 100 oz bar, which is about the largest bar that can be held comfortably in your hands (and that might even be pushing it). Nearly every provider produces 100 oz bars.

Like gold there are metric sizes as well: Left to right 5 grams, 10 grams, 1 Troy ounce, 28.35 grams, 100 grams, 250 grams (8.82 oz)

Steve Mitchell, KTXK general manager, holds the 100 ounce silver bar that was given to the station by an anonymous donor to cover the cost of needed repairs for damage that silenced the station for several days. Just days after Texarkana College's radio station repaired a $3,000 part to get KTXK back on the air, an anonymous donor dropped off a present of equal value. (December 2011 – price of silver was around $30 an ounce).

Silver coins are abundant and can be found in change, if you know how to locate them. I will tell you how. Let's take a look at the many types of gold, silver and rare coins that can be purchased and found.

Coins: Gold - Silver - Rare

Gold and silver have many forms. Besides physical bars and rounds and investment forms there are gold and silver coins. In this chapter we will briefly examine them. What comes to mind when you mention the word "investing" with respect to precious metals? Certainly gold and silver coins are at the top of the list. However, "rare coins" are also considered a great investment opportunity, even though they may not be made of silver or gold. Rare coins can be classified as an investment because they are scarce and have value. Rare coins that are in exceptionally good condition can hold higher value. The rate of return on rare coins ranks as one of the highest investment assets over time.

Gold coins are coins that have some amount of gold in them. It could be over 99% or a much smaller amount, say less than 20%. No coin is 100% gold. Gold always has some impurity in it. Gold coins made by the U.S. Mint up until 1933 were available to the general public as part of the circulated coin supply, just like pennies and quarters were.

Executive order 6102 made ownership of gold illegal so coins minted that year were melted down. A few survived. Prior to 1933 some of these coins were melted, but most survived and many ended up in Europe. The Europeans loved to hoard gold, and American coins were available to them. Millions of pre-1933 coins still exist today.

In 1986 the U.S. Mint started minting a few types of gold coins again, but they were not part of the circulated coin supply. These coins are only sold through authorized distributors, and some of them are only available from the U.S. Mint directly.

Gold coins are not an exclusively U.S. product. Coins were made of gold for thousands of years. Coins are made in many countries, like Canada. Ancient Roman coins were sometimes made of gold.

Silver coins can have over 99% silver in them or as little as 10%. Most U.S. minted coins for circulation contained 40% - 90% silver. Starting in 1965, the U.S. Mint stopped making silver coins for circulation, (the exception to this rule is the 40% silver Kennedy Half Dollar minted from 1965-1970) but they continued to make silver coins in special issue sets. Like gold, starting in 1986 a few select silver coins were offered through a distribution network and the U.S. Mint. The 1 oz Silver American Eagle Dollar is an example of a silver coin offered via this network. It is in high demand because it is 99.9% pure and can be purchased in small quantities. A total of 337,031,982 of these coins were minted from 1986 – 2012.

Prior to 1965, dimes, quarters and half dollars were made of 90% silver and billions were made. Some war time nickels had silver in them. From 1965 – 1970 half dollars had 40% silver, as just mentioned. There are currently over one billion 40% silver halves in circulation, and these coins can be found in change.

The reason the U.S. Mint stopped making silver coins for circulation in 1964 has, in part, to do with cost. The U.S. Mint used the equivalent of 67% of today's total worldwide silver mining production to mint 1964 dimes, quarters and half dollars for everyday use. This should tell you why they stopped making silver coins. The silver value of the 549,549,066 ounces in those coins (at $19.35 an ounce) is worth more than $10.5 billion.

Many silver coins come from other countries as well. Investors love 1 oz Canadian Silver Maple Leafs because of their purity (.9999 vs .999 for the 1 oz American Eagle) and lower cost. They can sometimes can be purchased for $1 less than the American Eagle, and they have a $5 face value vs $1 for the Eagle. According to data released by the Royal Canadian Mint, there were 28.2 million Silver Maples sold in 2013. This is an astonishing figure as it was a 56% increase over the 18.1 million ounces sold in 2012.

Let's talk about "rare coins" for a few minutes. This subject is very complex, but let's looks at some basics for now. Rare coins that are incredibly valuable only have this value because they are in high demand. Coins that are old can be rare, (only a few minted) but not of great worth because the demand is not strong. People that have old coins and claim they have value are misinformed. For example, I have seen 200+ year old pennies worth only several dollars. The point is that old age does not necessarily mean more value.

Coins that are old but in pristine condition generally are worth much more money than similar dated coins in average condition. We will look at this subject in great detail when we examine coin collecting and investing. For now, here is a good example: A 1793 penny in average condition is worth about $2,500. However, one in excellent condition sold for $632,500 at auction in 2008.

Examples of coins that are in great demand (and often made part of an investment portfolio) are pre-1933 U.S. minted gold coins in high grades or in pristine condition. Are they a good investment? No! They are often referred to as rare and valuable. Here is a picture of some pre-1933 Gold Double Eagles:

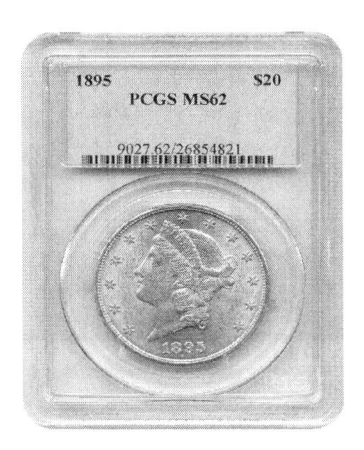

A pre-1933 $20 Gold Double Eagle (dated 1895) that is in a very high grade or condition (62 out of 70) is shown above. These types of coins are often over sold. To suggest that they are valuable and rare and a good investment is not true. They are not rare, not valuable and not a good investment. I will show you why in future chapters.

Real valuable and rare coins come in many forms, such as highly sought after pennies, like this 1909 S VDB Lincoln Cent, which sold for $900:

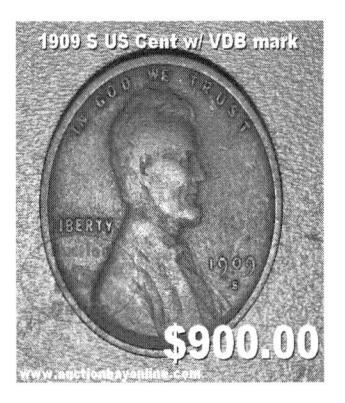

This can be considered a rare and valuable coin, unlike the pre-1933 Gold Double Eagles. The Gold Double Eagles are worth their gold content, but not more than that. This 1909 penny, however, is worth **90,000 times its face value**.

The Relationship (Gold, Silver, Coins)

The purpose of this book is to convey information that will make it easier for you to find, buy, sell and invest in gold, silver, and coins, including gold and silver coins and rare coins (certainly a wide range of topics). I have noticed that interest seldom focuses on just one of these topics, for example gold bullion (bars, rounds or gold coins). All of these topics seem to overlap on many levels, so it is imperative to include them all in one document. Coin collectors usually have silver and gold coins and also invest in gold and silver bars and rounds and continue to buy rare coins and coins made of gold and silver, it is ongoing. Gold and silver investors, on the other hand, usually invest in all types of silver and gold, including coins, but they do not know enough about the coins they invest in and they often pay too much for them.

Investment houses usually suggest at least a 5% portfolio exposure to some form of precious metal, and some even suggest as high as 20%. As you can see, it's hard to limit yourself just to gold or just to silver or just coins, there is too much overlap. Because the condition of coins has a profound effect on their value and because coins over time have demonstrated to be one of the best investments, it is important to cover all of these topics together. You have to draw comparisons. You can't just look at paper investments like ETFs or Mutual Funds.

Another way of looking at this is to realize that many investors have exposure to the gold and silver coin market yet do not understand anything about coins. If you are trained in this topic you can make much better decisions with regard to your financial future. Also, coin collecting is a hobby that is being lost, as young people seldom have interest in it. Need proof? Just go to a coin club meeting; if you are 50 years old, you feel out of place because you are so young compared to the old timers present.

If you have children, getting them into this hobby costs little and can end up being rewarding on many levels (it improves their math skills, helps them save for the future and teaches them how to make money by investing in their collection).

To illustrate how important it is to have a better understanding of rare and valuable coins and how they can impact your bottom line, let's take a look at one of the most unusual and the biggest treasure finds in U.S. history. This event occurred right in some ones back yard. I am speaking about the Saddle Ridge gold coin find of 2013 in Northern California. A total of 1,427 gold coins were found in a couple's back yard valued at over $10 million, as of July 2014! Part of this hoard was auctioned on Amazon, in their new Coin Collectibles category.

Yes, this is an unusual find, but don't you think knowing about coins can serve a useful purpose. This point will become very clear as more information is revealed throughout the book. The next picture shows part of the actual Amazon auction. Notice the 14 finest coins selling for $2,750,000.

Finding Gold-Silver-Coins

This topic: **"finding gold and silver and coins"**, when mentioned, often results in an unusual response: "How do you find gold and silver and coins? No one can imagine that finding these valuable assets is a possibility. Yet, coin collectors and investors all use a technique that will be described in this chapter, to find and buy gold, silver and coins. In order to get a handle on this concept you have to factor several variables into the equation.

First of all there are large numbers of people who have coins and gold and silver jewelry and other forms of these assets and need money, but do not know how to sell them, and get the best result. Also, the demographics of our population illustrates that tens of millions of baby boomers are getting older and passing away, often leaving coins and precious metals behind to someone who knows little about them, but would rather have their dollar value than the actual asset itself.

Before we look at this technique to find these valuable assets, let's address a common problem that often prevents people from using the tools needed to acquire precious metal assets from other people. In particular, the challenge many of us face is the issue of how to buy precious metals, including coins, if we do not have extra money or disposable money (as some describe it).

With this topic in mind it will be advantageous to spend a few minutes talking about an investment strategy. First of all everyone should have an investment strategy. Even though most people live pay check to pay check (76% do), visualizing an improvement in one's financial picture is advantageous. How then can we take advantage of this book material if we do not have extra money? There are two ways to look at this, start saving or just give up. Let's assume you will not give up.

One way to budget money and set some aside each month, is to use a grocery list (20% of food shopping is impulse). So, if you spend $150 per week on food by the end of the month you can save $120 by cutting your weekly bill by 20%. Cut out alcohol, cigarettes, candy etc…Turn off lights, turn off the computer, the cable box, modem, when you leave the house. Also turn the thermostat down when leaving for a few hours or more. Here are some more ways to save and make extra money:

Go through your house and set aside every item you no longer want and then knock on your neighbors doors and ask them flat out if they have anything in the house they no longer need. I guarantee you that you will end up with dozens of items that you can sell on eBay. Hit every yard sale on Friday morning and look for cheap items that you can also sell on eBay. Almost every type of item imaginable can sell on line.

One way to save lots of money and few people think of this, is your hot water heater, mine is electric. Buy a new one when the time comes and pay for a more expensive digital one, such as a Whirlpool Model: ES40R92-45D (Lowe's Item #: 345706). Yes, it costs $150 more than the cheap ones but I have saved over $200 a year with it and the digital dial lets you set the water temp in a few seconds. And it comes with a 9 year guarantee.

You will need some money to get started finding and buying gold and silver and coins. I apologize for getting off target a little, talking about saving money, but it upsets me when I hear that someone has no extra money to invest, when in reality they can be saving. Okay, then what is the best way to get started?

There is a system that you can use to start your investing that has worked for many coin collectors and I want to share this information with you. It is called the poor man's system for finding gold-silver-coins. Remember all gold, silver and rare coins have value, getting your hands on them at a fair price is a good investment strategy. How can you do this?

Believe it or not I have acquired thousands of dollars worth of silver and gold jewelry, silver and gold coins, and rare coins with a simple method. Please note this is one of many investment strategies that I have used and you should know about this one in particular.

I run ads looking to buy gold, silver, gold coins, silver coins, rare coins and jewelry. Here are the steps to follow:

First invest in a cheap business card. This helps establish credibility. The business card should have your name, phone number and business name and some slogan such as "Cash For Gold, Silver, Coins, Jewelry" on it. If you do not have a business name, make one up (take your last name and add "& associates" to it). In addition to your name, add you wife's name if you are a man and if you are a woman ad your husband's name. If not married, ad a male or female name of any one you know. Why?

It is very important to build some trust with someone so they will be willing to work with you. For example, if you meet someone at the library to see a coin they want to sell and you hand them your card, the information on the card reassures them. So before running ads and looking for gold, silver and coins, you must establish credibility. Having references written down also helps.

Okay you have a business card, now what? Place fliers everywhere you can and run ads everywhere you can. If you don't have the time for fliers don't worry, just run ads. Fliers can be placed in the library, post office, church, senior center, supermarket, laundromat and any other wall you can think of.

Ads that work best can be placed on Craigslist and any other place that lets you run ads for free (Backpage, local classified, etc...). Also go around to yard sales every Friday or Saturday morning with your business card. Talk to everyone there, including the yard seller, and let them know what you are looking for.

Here are a few other ways to find gold, silver, coins and jewelry. Look for ads from anyone wanting to sell their coins or gold or silver or jewelry. Look in the newspaper for legal notices. Sometimes estates or items left over from deaths have to be sold and the public is invited when bank owned collections acquired from loan debt are being sold. These were loans taken out against a coin collection as collateral and the bank took the collection in when the loan was not paid, and now has to sell it.

Churches are often given coins and other items. Let them know who you are and that you will buy them. Senior centers are the best place to post ads and speak with groups about your interest in buying coins and old jewelry. Also coin clubs have auctions. Join your local coin club and get involved. Detailed info on this subject will come in the chapters on coin collecting.

Why is this method so valuable? Why use it? First of all, it works, and many people use this system. Just to give you an example of how many people are out there who have valuable coins and jewelry but do not know what to do with them, an investment adviser told me that 1 in 15 people he consults with, have, as part of their assets, rare coins and gold and silver but need help in trying to get rid of them. And they have no idea of their value or what to do with them.

A very important point to make is not to worry if you have absolutely no knowledge of coins, jewelry, gold and silver. By the end of this book you will know exactly how to be successful at this!

Let's take a look at some typical ads that have worked well for me and others: "**Cash For Coins, Gold, Silver or Jewelry - Immediate Payment**" or "**Let me sell you coins and jewelry on eBay**" or "**Cash For Coins**" or "**Free Coin Evaluation**" or "**Free coin and jewelry evaluation**" or "**We Buy Coins and Gold and Silver**"

Place both names in the ad, such as "John and Sally Smith". Protect yourself and provide credibility. Always meet people in a neutral place for your protection and to make them feel secure: library, coffee shop, mall, senior center, book store etc…Tip: If someone sounds fishy or you gut says no, back off.

When someone responds to your ad and you are able to speak with them on the phone, a good response is: "Thank you Mrs. Smith for responding to my ad. My name is John Watson and my wife and I and our three beautiful children have lived here in ………….. for 20 years. I am a Deacon in our local church (name of church) and have had the pleasure of collecting coins for over 40 years! I would love to learn more about what you have? You can see the wisdom of this easy going, yet informative approach.

When interviewing them you must gather some basic information. First you need to find out what they have. Get some details. If they have lots of coins ask them how they acquired them and what types of coins they are? Do they have pennies for example. How old are they? Are they in coin books? Just get all the details so you can decide if these items are worth pursuing.

Let's look at some more situations that may come up when you run your ads. These I consider Red Flags. Someone contacts you and says "I have a very rare coin that was passed down in my family". This is probably a fake coin they are trying to get rid of. A single valuable coin is not something people usually have unless it is a gold coin.

Another Red Flag: I have many old coins in a jar or box that I have been saving for many years and they are valuable because they are old. Probably a bunch of worthless coins but worth asking more questions: How many coins? How old? What denominations? Let's look at some of the opposite situations, not red flags:

- I have an old coin collection passed down to me.
- I have some gold and silver coins that my husband saved.
- I have boxes of old coins that my wife saved since she was a child and she is 80 years old now.
- I have a bunch of Indian Head Pennies I saved over the years.
- I inherited some coins and jewelry.
- I have old jewelry that I no longer want.
- I have my husbands rolls of coins that he started buying over 60 years ago.

Keep in mind, many people need money and they may want to sell their coin collection and other items.

Okay, so you might be thinking that you do not have enough experience to do this. What do you pay for gold or coins or silver or jewelry on the spot and how do you tell if the gold or silver is real? Let me reassure you, this is really easy, and I am going to show you how. Some inexpensive tools needed to make all this work are listed below. These and other tools will be explained in more detail in a later chapter, particularly how to buy them, but for now you will need to understand how they are used:

- A powerful magnet: Gold and Silver are not magnetic, if it sticks to a magnet the gold or silver item is not made of a precious metal ($5)

- The current edition of "The Red Book": This book lists every U.S. Coin minted and shows what they are worth and their weight ($10)

- A magnifying loupe or jewelers loupe is used to examine coins and look for stamps on gold and silver ($5)

- A gram scale: Used to weigh coins and silver and gold (bigger scale might be needed for heavier silver items) ($10)

- A non glazed ceramic plate or tile: the smooth surface is used to rub gold onto to check color – gold color means item is gold ($5)

- A gold and silver testing kit ($15)

The Red Book (fully titled, *The Official Red Book - A Guide Book of United States Coins*) provides the retail value of every U.S. coin minted. So when you look up a coin and it says it is worth $10, then offer the seller $5 (50%), never more. The condition of the coin is important, and the Red Book lists values based upon condition. The loupe lets you see a coin close up and see stamp marks on gold and silver. The scale is used to weigh certain coins and weigh gold/silver. Please note - the Red Book tells you the weight of each coin. You must weigh every gold and silver coin and use the magnet test. This helps verify authenticity.

When it comes time to meet with someone and see what they have, you must have your tools with you so you can easily determine the weight of the coin or object and look it up in the Red Book (Don't let them see the Red Book – put a cover on it). If they have gold or silver in bulk, or jewelry, you need to weigh it (Small gram scales usually only go up to about 8 ounces).

Okay, it is now time to negotiate a price for an item or items that the seller wants you to make an offer on. First and foremost do what the master does. Did you ever watch Rick from the "Pawn Stars TV Show". Notice how he looks at an item and then says: "What are you looking to get for it?" He never makes an offer first. The reason he does this is simple. Suppose someone is looking to get $50 for a coin and Rick knows it is worth $200 and he is willing to pay $100 for it. That being said, the $50 the seller is asking is a good deal for Rick, so he buys it at that price even though he would have gone as high as $100. Remember you have to make a profit. If you are unable to agree on a price take the eBay route.

A situation may come up where you do not have enough money to buy the item(s), so rather than walk away from the deal I suggest: Offer to sell the items for them on eBay. Tell them you will take the pictures, create each listing and package and insure the items and the seller can watch the auction happen and they hold onto the pieces until they sell. As I said before, a 40% commission after expenses is fair. Explain the eBay fee structure to them.

The eBay fee structure is subject to change but eBay takes 10% of the total sale (item and shipping). PayPal takes 2.9 % of the total sale plus 30 cents. The maximum amount eBay takes is $250 per item, so if your item sells for more than $2500 you only pay $250. We will revisit this topic when we discuss selling (Amazon is another selling venue to consider).

With eBay in mind, a situation may come where you are looking at a very valuable coin or coin collection and you feel the eBay route will not get the best return for the seller. Another option exists. There are some very reputable coin auction companies that can appraise the coin(s) and for a percentage of the sale, auction them for you. These are typically better coins, those worth many thousands. So what you can do is tell the seller that the best bet for them is to have them auctioned by a professional dealer and you can make all the arrangements.

The two most recognized auction companies are:

Heritage Auctions: http://coins.ha.com/
and
Stack's Bowers: http://www.stacksbowers.com/Home.aspx

I suggest you contact them and find out what their policies are with regard to referrals (You refer a good customer to them). In other words, do they pay a referral fee or finders fee. If not, I suggest you draw up an agreement with the seller so you can get a piece of the sale. Without you, they would never know about these auctions companies who get top dollar. It's win win for both parties. Never tell them the names of these two auction companies.

Many coin shops are now willing to pay spot or close to spot for gold and silver in the hopes that it will increase in value over time so they can make a profit. Spot refers to the actual price of gold or silver at the time of the sale, so you may find yourself competing with them. If you offer 50% of the spot value you may loose the sale. So I like to make my offer (50%) and see if they bite.

If they bite, close the deal. If they hesitate then you know they have gotten another quote or have a sense of what the item is worth. That's why it is good to ask up front what they want for it. You can always counter, but do not go to actual spot price because if gold or silver goes way down you will be sitting on the item for a long time.

A few final thoughts. Never argue with someone. If you disagree, it is better to agree with them first, and then tell a story as to why you do not agree. Suppose they say: "Well I was offered $500 for the gold necklace, why are you offering me $200?" Your answer: To be honest, I weighed it and it only has $200 of gold in it so that's all I can pay. Here's $200 cash. Hold it in front of them. You have no way of knowing if they actually got a $500 offer, and when they see the cash, they may just take it.

It is important to mention a few more tips so you can use this method successfully. When someone responds to your ad you should be prepared to meet them with cash in your pocket. You need to close the deal on the spot. Give them time to think and you will loose. Never pay more than 50 cents on the dollar for any item you buy. Only pay 50% of what you think it is worth. Otherwise you will not make any profit. Trust me, most coin shops, pawn shops etc.. only pay 50%. Some say they will pay spot, but I have serious doubts about it.

Because you will have cash it is important to go as a team and meet in a neutral place. When speaking to someone suggest several places to meet: Starbucks, the library, the mall, the senior center, somewhere where you both feel safe and secure.

Let's go over certain situations that may arise and you have to know how to handle them. If the person you meet knows the value of what they have and insists on 100% value payment you remind them that they will never get 100% at a coin shop, pawn shop or anywhere else.

A good way to handle this is if they insist on more than you are willing to pay is to offer them a percent of the sale.

What a percent of the sale means is that you will pay them say 60% of what you sell the item for. If you auction it on eBay offer them 60% of the profit (after all fees come out). Tell them that you are doing the work: the listing, shipping, etc... and they reap most of the reward, and they hold onto the item until you sell it. You will need pictures of the products. They can follow your eBay listing so they feel they are not being cheated and can see the results. I have used this approach before and it works. Never go below 40% and even consider a 50-50 split. Trust me, I helped a friend out once and only took 20% for myself, but in the end the $200 I made hardly covered the weeks of work. He had many silver coins that I sold for him on eBay and it was very time consuming.

When people respond to your ads they usually have coins to sell, but in the event they have a silver item, it is important to have a complete understanding of how to tell real silver from fake silver, which we will look at first. Then we will look at gold verification and then how to deal with coins.

Is It Silver?

A good YouTube video from Rick of the TV show "Pawn Stars", illustrates how he evaluates silver items:

http://www.history.com/shows/pawn-stars/videos/certified-silver

Having a list of purity stamps that may appear on a silver piece makes it easy to understand what you are looking at. This list illustrates various levels of silver purity that you may come across as stamps on a piece and also shows coin silver values:

These values are percentages, such as 925 sterling silver, which means 92.5 % pure silver

999.9 (four nines fine) Ultra-fine silver used by Royal Canadian Mint in the Canadian Silver Maple Leaf

999 (Fine silver or three nines fine) Used in Good Delivery bullion bars

980 Common standard used in Mexico ca.1930 - 1945

958 e.g., Britannia silver

950 e.g., French 1st Standard

925 (Sterling silver)

900 (one nine fine or "90% silver") e.g., all 1892-1964 U. S. silver coins

835 A standard predominantly used in Germany after 1884

833 A common standard for continental silver especially among the Dutch, Swedish, and Germans

830 A common standard used in older Scandinavian silver

800 The minimum standard for silver in Germany after 1884; Egyptian silver; Canadian silver circulating coinage

750 An uncommon silver standard found in older German, Swiss and Austro-Hungarian silver

720 e.g., many Mexican silver coins

When you are confronted with a silver item and do not see a purity or silver stamp on it, such as 92.5 for sterling silver, what do you do? While most items you come across will be silver plated and not worth much, some items that do not have stamps of purity can however, be solid silver, and quite valuable. Remember, some silver plated items are collectible and also have value.

A good way to become familiar with marks you may come across is by investigating the silver encyclopedia web site:

http://www.925-1000.com/

This silver encyclopedia site will show you the marks on silver pieces that indicate genuine silver when a percentage mark may not appear. Also as a rule of thumb, stamps that will most likely appear and mean real silver, are:

Sterling, Ster, 925 are the most common indicators

Other silver indicators:

'999'	'950'	'900'
'0.999'	'STG'	'850'
'Fine Silver'	'COIN SILVER'	'835'
'9854'	'COIN'	'800'
'BRITANNIA SILVER'	'PURE COIN'	'750'
'CONTINENTAL SILVER'	'STANDARD'	'VERMEIL'

The marks 'silver' or 'silver' followed by the name of a country may mean silver but some mark this way, and it is not silver. Some marks clearly indicate that the item is not silver:

'silver plate'	'old Sheffield'	'EPB'
'sterling inlaid'	'old Sheffield plate'	'EPC'
'afghan silver'	'German silver'	'EPCA'
'nickel-plate'	'Austrian silver'	'EPGS'
'nickle silver'	'wolf silver'	'EPMS'
'Mexican silver'	'Venetian silver'	'AA'
'British silver'	'Yukon silver'	'EP'
'1000'	'Sterline'	'18/10'
'ARG1000'	'EPNS'	'silverware'
'English silver'	'EPWM'	'pewter'
'Sheffield plate'	'EPBM'	

Valid Platinum marks: 'PLAT' 'PT' '850PLAT' '800PT 150IRID' (This means that it has Iridium in it – another precious metal).

Once you determine that the item in question is silver you can go on line and calculate its value. Calculating silver scrap is easy. There are many silver scrap calculators on line. Coinapps.com is a good on line silver calculator. This is the direct link to it:

http://coinapps.com/silver/scrap/calculator/

Let's look at it: In this example below you can see that the unit of measure selected was ounces and the item weighed 5ozs. The item is sterling silver or 92.5 % pure. The calculator keeps track of the current price of silver, so it is able to calculate that 5ozs of sterling silver is worth $79.88.

The total silver value is calculated based on the currency amount shown in the **Silver Price** text box. The current silver spot price is updated frequently during normal trading hours. The silver price can be changed to any value of your choice.

1. Select the Unit of Measure(Weight Type):

   [Ounces ▼]

2. Enter total weight of the scrap silver:

   [OZ] Total Weight in Ounces: [5]

3. Select silver purity from list or enter percent:

   [.925 - Sterling ▼] Silver Purity = [92.5] %

4. (Optional) Change silver price or leave as is:

   Silver Price: $ [18.95] per Troy Ounce

   Currency: [USD - U.S. Dollar ▼] [Update Price]

   Silver Spot Price Data Last Updated:
   6/6/2014, 7:27:53 AM

5. (Optional) Enter a price spread or leave as is:

   Price Spread: [5] %

Resultant values will be rounded to two or more decimal places depending on length.
Calculator only figures the total value and weight of the silver portion of your items. Does not include any other metals used if silver scrap is an alloy.

Total Silver Value:
(USD - U.S. Dollar)

$79.884

[Reset/Clear Calculator]

Total Silver Weight
Grams:	131.12
Kilograms:	0.13112
Grains:	2,023.44
Pennyweight:	84.31
Ounces:	4.625
Troy Ounces:	4.2155
Pounds:	0.28906
Troy Pounds:	0.35129

5% Price Spread (USD)
Bid Price: $75.889
Ask Price: $83.878

Is It Gold?

Silver is the most common form of jewelry and coin you will encounter when you run ads, but having knowledge of gold jewelry is helpful. Most gold is stamped with a gold carat value. Typical carat readings on jewelry are as follows:

Correlation between carats and fineness (gold)

24 carats = .999 fine or above

23 carats = .958 fine

22 carats = .917 fine (the UK gold coin standard)

21 carats = .875 fine

20 carats = .833 fine

18 carats = .750 fine

16 carats = .667 fine

14 carats = .583 fine

10 carats = .417 fine

The fineness is often converted to a percent, as well. If a gold coin or ring has a fineness of .900, then it is 90.0% pure gold. If it has a fineness of .850, then it is 85.0% pure.

Some gold stamps may not be easy to recognize:

Here are a few stamps which signify the piece is NOT gold:

- **14K 1/20** (1/20 gold is basically gold-filled)
- **14K G.F.** (gold-filled)
- **14K G.P.** (gold-plated)
- **14K H.G.E.** (hydrostatic gold electroplating)
- **14K G.E.P.** (gold electroplating)
- **.925** (sterling silver)

Anything with one of these stamps is not gold. It is made out of a different metal with a very thin gold layer that will wear off over time. These pieces do not have any real metal value and most gold buyers won't purchase them from you (with the exception of sterling silver).

Stamps that mean your piece IS gold:

- A plain **14K** stamp
- **14K P** (The "P" stands for plumb gold)
- **14K** with a company logo after such as **14K <3**
- **417** (10K, means 41.7% gold)
- **585** (14k, means 58.5% gold)
- **750** (18K, means 75% gold)
- **917** (22K, means 91.7% gold)
- **999** (24K, means 99.9% gold)

That being said, **even if your piece is stamped "14K" you cannot be 100% sure it is gold**. There are a number of fake stamps out there and the only way to be 100% sure is to test the metal with a gold tester using nitric acid. On the other hand, even if there is **no stamp** it could **still be gold**.

(Information: Jewelry Gold Blog)

Remember that most jewelry should be stamped and keep in mind that many fake pieces are also stamped. We will learn how to test for authenticity later. Some jewelry is real but has no stamp on it, why?

- It is very old
- The stamp has worn off
- The item has been modified and in so doing the stamp was covered over or removed
- The stamp is behind something – under a stone or inside a watch for example

Locating the gold stamp can be problematic at times, especially if it is very small and hidden. It is important to inspect every square inch of the item for the mark. If you do not find the mark, don't worry. I will show you how to determine the gold content later on. Keep in mind that gold can come in many colors: white, yellow, red, green, pink, rose. It depends upon the base metal content. Let's assume the item is real and you find the mark – then what?

First let's use the weight of the item and its carat content to determine it's value (we will assume for now the item is real gold) and you know the weight. A simple on line calculator tells you the value. Most jewelry is stamped, such as 20 carats. Please note that if it is not stamped it can still be real, for example when rings are re sized they often loose their metal stamp, as mentioned earlier. Go to this web site again and click on the Gold calculator:

http://www.coinapps.com

Let's look at it and see how it works on the next page:

1. Select the Unit of Measure(Weight Type):

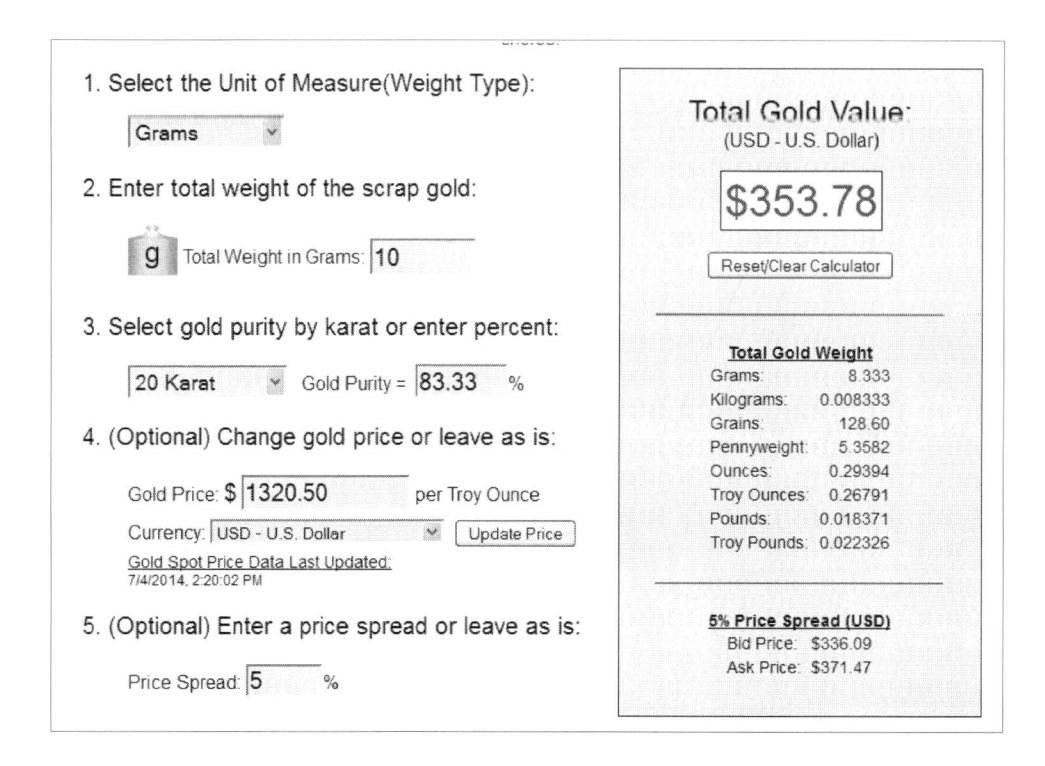

   Grams

2. Enter total weight of the scrap gold:

   g Total Weight in Grams: 10

3. Select gold purity by karat or enter percent:

   20 Karat   Gold Purity = 83.33 %

4. (Optional) Change gold price or leave as is:

   Gold Price: $ 1320.50   per Troy Ounce
   Currency: USD - U.S. Dollar   Update Price
   Gold Spot Price Data Last Updated:
   7/4/2014, 2:20:02 PM

5. (Optional) Enter a price spread or leave as is:

   Price Spread: 5 %

Total Gold Value:
(USD - U.S. Dollar)

$353.78

Reset/Clear Calculator

Total Gold Weight
Grams: 8.333
Kilograms: 0.008333
Grains: 128.60
Pennyweight: 5.3582
Ounces: 0.29394
Troy Ounces: 0.26791
Pounds: 0.018371
Troy Pounds: 0.022326

5% Price Spread (USD)
Bid Price: $336.09
Ask Price: $371.47

In this example we put 10 grams of 20 carat gold into the on line calculator and it tracks the current spot price of gold and tells us that the gold in question is worth $353.78.

Please remember that some items may be gold plated or have very small amounts of gold in them but may be worth money as collectibles or ornaments that are in high demand. eBay is a good way to check the value of items. Do a picture search and see if you find matches on eBay or other sites for the item. A very important point to make concerns children's jewelry and adult bracelets. Sometimes the charms on them are all fake except for one or two that are real gold or silver. Check each one carefully.

Dealing With Coins?

This was stated before, but it bears repeating: The Red Book (fully titled, *The Official Red Book - A Guide Book of United States Coins*) provides the retail value of every U.S. coin minted. So when you look up a coin and it says it is worth $10, then offer the seller $5 (50%), never more. The condition of the coin is important, and the Red Book lists values based upon condition. The loupe lets you see a coin close up and stamp marks on gold and silver. The scale is used to weigh certain coins and weigh gold/silver. Please note - the Red Book tells you the weight of each coin. You must weigh every gold and silver coin and use the magnet test.

Let's imagine someone calls you and wants to sell 2 gold coins they have. You have no coin experience so you wonder how to handle this situation. Well it is really easy. Look up the coin date in the Red Book and you will see the value of the coin and the Red Book will tell you if it is gold. You will then want to be sure it is not a fake (this topic will be covered in more detail in the coin sections).

The easiest way to do this is by weighing the coin. The Red Book tells you the weight of each gold coin. If the weight is correct it is probably gold. Also you can place the coin next to your magnet. If it sticks, it is not gold. There are some more tests that I will show you later.

Let's say that someone wants to sell two coins: Liberty Head Gold $20 pieces. These were minted from 1849 -1907. There are fake versions out there that weigh the same and we will look at this subject later on but for now, using the magnet and weight test is a pretty reliable way to determine authenticity (most fake coins will not pass the magnet or weight test). The next picture from The Red Book shows this coin's detailed information:

LIBERTY HEAD (1849–1907)

This largest denomination of all regular United States issues was authorized to be coined by the Act of March 3, 1849. Its weight was 516 grains, .900 fine. The 1849 double eagle is a unique pattern and reposes in the Smithsonian. The 1861 reverse design by Anthony C. Paquet was withdrawn soon after being struck. Very few pieces are known.

Designer James B. Longacre; weight 33.436 grams; composition .900 gold, .100 copper (net weight: .96750 oz. pure gold); diameter 34 mm; reeded edge; mints: Philadelphia, Carson City, Denver, New Orleans, San Francisco.

VF-20 Very Fine—LIBERTY on crown bold; prongs on crown defined; lower half worn flat. Hair worn about ear.
EF-40 Extremely Fine—Trace of wear on rounded prongs of crown and down hair curls. Minor bagmarks.
AU-50 About Uncirculated—Trace of wear on hair over eye and on coronet.
AU-55 Choice About Uncirculated—Evidence of friction on design high points. Some of original mint luster present.
MS-60 Uncirculated—No trace of wear. Light blemishes.
MS-63 Choice Uncirculated—Some distracting contact marks or blemishes in prime focal areas. Impaired luster possible.
PF-63 Choice Proof—Reflective surfaces with only a few blemishes in secondary focal areas. No major flaws.

Without Motto on Reverse (1849–1866)

Mintmark is below eagle.

1853, "3 Over 2"

The Red Book provides a clear picture of the coin and describes conditions that it may be in and shows the weight and metal composition. Notice the weight is 33.436 grams. Any coin you look at should be very close to this weight. Slight differences can occur if the coin is worn down.

This list below for gold purity, has some good coin reference information in it. Notice it lists many foreign coins not found in The Red Book. So if you find a coin not listed but know its gold purity, you can weigh it and determine its metal value.

999.999 (six nines fine) The purest gold ever produced. Refined by the Perth Mint in 1957.

999.99 (five nines fine) The purest type of gold currently produced; the Royal Canadian Mint regularly produces commemorative coins in this fineness

999.9 (four nines fine) E.g., ordinary Canadian Gold Maple Leaf and American Buffalo coins

999 (24 carat, also occasionally known as three nines fine) E.g., Chinese Panda coins

995 The minimum allowed in Good Delivery gold bars

990 (two nines fine)

986 (Ducat fineness) Formerly used by Venetian and Holy Roman Empire mints; still in use in Austria and Hungary

958.3 (23 carat)

917 (22 carat) Historically the most widely used fineness for gold bullion coins; currently used for British Sovereigns, South African Krugerrands and American Gold Eagles

900 (one nine fine) Mostly used in Latin Monetary Union mintage (e.g. French and Swiss "Napoleon coin" 20 francs)

833 (20 carat)

750 (18 carat)
625 (15 carat)

585 (14 carat)

417 (10 carat)

375 (9 carat)

333 (8 carat) Minimum standard for gold in Germany after 1884

The condition of a coin can improve its value. The better the condition, the more it is worth (detailed information on this topic and more coin information will appear later). Please keep in mind that foreign coins are valued for their metal content and not condition, so if you come across foreign gold or silver coins they will not appear in the Red Book. Also, you can always go to eBay and see what they are selling for.

In addition to "The Red Book" there is a web site similar to coinapps.com, called coinflation.com:

http://www.coinflation.com/silver_coin_values.html

Coinflation has charts that show you the current value of gold and silver coins based upon the current spot price of silver and gold. Coinapps.com also has this feature.

Let's look inside coinflation.com: The next image shows the silver value of most U.S. Coins minted for circulation.

Description	Face Value	Silver Value
1942-1945 Nickel *	$0.05	$1.0566
1892-1916 Barber Dime	$0.10	$1.3585
1916-1945 Mercury Dime	$0.10	$1.3585
1946-1964 Roosevelt Dime	$0.10	$1.3585
1892-1916 Barber Quarter	$0.25	$3.3963
1916-1930 Standing Liberty Quarter	$0.25	$3.3963
1932-1964 Washington Quarter	$0.25	$3.3963
1892-1915 Barber Half Dollar	$0.50	$6.7926
1916-1947 Walking Liberty Half Dollar	$0.50	$6.7926
1948-1963 Franklin Half Dollar	$0.50	$6.7926
1964 Kennedy Half Dollar	$0.50	$6.7926
1965-1970 Half Dollar (40% silver)	$0.50	$2.7774
1878-1921 Morgan Dollar	$1.00	$14.5253
1921-1935 Peace Dollar	$1.00	$14.5253
1971-1976 Eisenhower Dollar (40% silver) **	$1.00	$5.9388
1986-2013 Silver Eagle (.999 Silver)	$1.00	$18.7612

Notice the last entry on the list, for **Silver Eagles**. These coins are 99.9% silver and were made available to the general public though U.S. Mint selected distributors. They are sold at a premium each year (above spot price) and many investors include them in their precious metal inventory.

The image below shows gold values for coins minted for circulation. Notice how 1933 was the last year the U.S. Mint produced gold coins for general circulation. Special gold coins however, are now available. We will look at this later in detail. These charts are in real time so when you come across a silver or gold coin you can look it up and determine its precious metal value only. Its value as a collectible can only be determined by looking at The Red Book and on line.

U.S. Circulated Gold Coins

Gold coin values below are based on the bid price at the CME. These coins were in standard circulation until gold was removed from all circulating coinage in 1933. The values below only reflect the gold value, not rarity or numismatic value. All values shown in USD.

Coin value calculations use the 11:32 PM EDT gold price for June 04, 2014:
Gold $1244.00/oz ↑ 0.60

Description		Face Value	Gold Value
	1849-1854 Liberty Gold Dollar Type 1	$1.00	$60.17
	1854-1856 Liberty Gold Dollar Type 2	$1.00	$60.17
	1856-1889 Liberty Gold Dollar Type 3	$1.00	$60.17
	1840-1907 Liberty Quarter Eagle	$2.50	$150.44
	1908-1929 Indian Quarter Eagle	$2.50	$150.44
	1839-1908 Liberty Half Eagle	$5.00	$300.88
	1908-1929 Indian Half Eagle	$5.00	$300.88
	1838-1907 Liberty Eagle	$10.00	$601.78
	1907-1933 Indian Eagle	$10.00	$601.78
	1849-1907 Liberty Double Eagle	$20.00	$1203.57
	1907-1933 Saint Gaudens Double Eagle	$20.00	$1203.57

To sum up, the coinflation and coinapps web sites tell us which coins are gold and which are silver. These sites even list many foreign coins. The Red Book also tells us this (U.S. Coins) and in addition, provides clear pictures and the metal composition of precious metal coins. For example: Morgan Silver Dollars are very common and people often want to get rid of them. So how much are they worth? There are fake versions out there that weigh the same as real Morgans and we will look at this subject later on, but for now, using a magnet (silver and gold coins are not magnetic) and weight test is a pretty reliable way to determine authenticity (most fake coins will not pass the magnet and/or weight test). The next image from The Red Book shows this coin's detail:

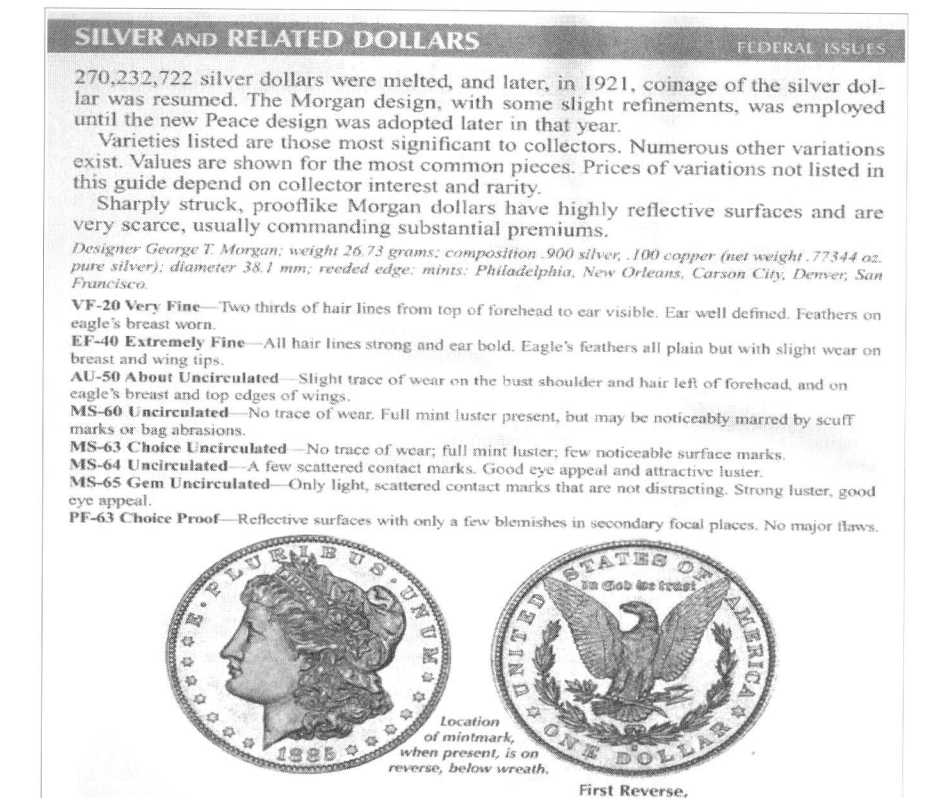

SILVER AND RELATED DOLLARS — FEDERAL ISSUES

270,232,722 silver dollars were melted, and later, in 1921, coinage of the silver dollar was resumed. The Morgan design, with some slight refinements, was employed until the new Peace design was adopted later in that year.

Varieties listed are those most significant to collectors. Numerous other variations exist. Values are shown for the most common pieces. Prices of variations not listed in this guide depend on collector interest and rarity.

Sharply struck, prooflike Morgan dollars have highly reflective surfaces and are very scarce, usually commanding substantial premiums.

Designer George T. Morgan; weight 26.73 grams; composition .900 silver, .100 copper (net weight .77344 oz. pure silver); diameter 38.1 mm; reeded edge; mints: Philadelphia, New Orleans, Carson City, Denver, San Francisco.

VF-20 Very Fine—Two thirds of hair lines from top of forehead to ear visible. Ear well defined. Feathers on eagle's breast worn.
EF-40 Extremely Fine—All hair lines strong and ear bold. Eagle's feathers all plain but with slight wear on breast and wing tips.
AU-50 About Uncirculated—Slight trace of wear on the bust shoulder and hair left of forehead, and on eagle's breast and top edges of wings.
MS-60 Uncirculated—No trace of wear. Full mint luster present, but may be noticeably marred by scuff marks or bag abrasions.
MS-63 Choice Uncirculated—No trace of wear; full mint luster; few noticeable surface marks.
MS-64 Uncirculated—A few scattered contact marks. Good eye appeal and attractive luster.
MS-65 Gem Uncirculated—Only light, scattered contact marks that are not distracting. Strong luster, good eye appeal.
PF-63 Choice Proof—Reflective surfaces with only a few blemishes in secondary focal places. No major flaws.

Location of mintmark, when present, is on reverse, below wreath.

First Reverse, 8 Tail Feathers

The Red Book explains that the coin weighs 26.73 grams and is 90% silver. Various types of condition are described and this helps determine coin value. By looking at a coin you can match it with the condition listed in The Red Book and see where it fits. The higher the grade, the more it is worth. Notice the condition list above (VF-20 for example). So when you buy silver dollars and pay the silver value of the coin, it may be worth much more because it is in a high grade or condition!

Prospecting

What exactly is prospecting? Most of us are familiar with gold prospecting: That age old story of the miner who searches the land for signs of yellow metal on or in the ground, looking for "The Mother Load". When I think of prospecting today, I think of sophisticated equipment, like metal detectors, that can find valuable objects in the ground and provide a drawing of the object, such as a half dollar. So as far-fetched as it may seem to you, metal detecting is a great way to locate precious metal in any form, and you can do it anywhere, even in big cities.

The beauty of it all is that it no longer matters where you live: the country, the city, the desert, you name it; you can find valuable objects anywhere in the world. Suppose you live in or near a big city. Where and how do you locate treasure? It's simple. Any place that people gather or have lived or gathered in the past or present has collected coins (old and current), jewelry (rings mainly) and other objects that a metal detector can identify. A simple stroll on the beach can also yield great results, especially after a storm.

Spending a fun day on the beach looking for buried treasure

Associated Press photo of ancient Roman gold coins found using a metal detector

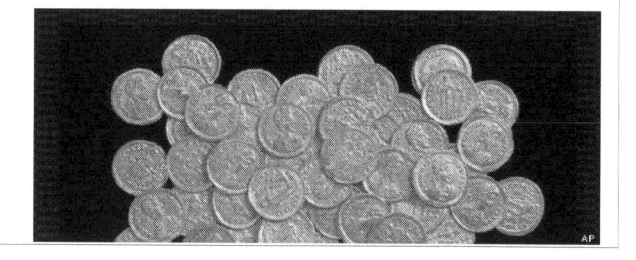

Here's a list of places that will produce metal detecting results:

- Walking trails – running trails
- Beaches
- Ball parks
- Park fields where people play and hang out
- Gold sites – by water and by land that has gold (Arizona – Ca)
- By rivers where people swim
- In the water
- Old battlegrounds
- Known historical sites
- Abandoned places where people once lived – old towns e.g.

If you would like to learn more about prospecting I suggest you locate forums in your area and join them to start learning. I belong to these two:

http://www.treasurenet.com/forums/gold-prospecting-forum/

http://www.nuggetshooter.ipbhost.com/index.php?showforum=7

For a list of prospecting clubs in your area follow this link:

http://www.goldminershq.com/clubs/gold1.htm

The link below is a great article on buying gold nuggets on eBay:

http://www.gold-nuggets.org/how_not_to_get_ripped_off.htm

There are several things you need to know with respect to these forums. First, they are free. Upon joining, announce yourself and say something nice. For example, "My name is John Doe, and I just joined and am eager to learn from the experts. Thank you for putting up with a newbie!" Proceed very slowly with questions and comments.

If you consider buying a metal detector, then ask the members what works best for your part of the country, and what it is you are looking for: gold or silver or coins. Remember this important point: the value of a gold nugget depends upon how much gold is in the nugget. Did you know that gold nuggets average anywhere from 60 to 98% gold, depending on where they came from?

I would not buy a metal detector without extensive research. If you plan on taking it seriously, and spending quality time, then I suggest you invest in a better detector (over $500). Here is a link to a product supplier that has a good reputation:

http://www.kellycodetectors.com/metaldetectors/topselling/?gclid=CNfo_dH-474CFRRsfgodXDUAHA

Testing Your Gold and Silver

In order to take full advantage of the information presented here, necessary tools include:

- A powerful magnet ($5)
- The current edition of the Red Book ($10)
- A magnifying loupe or jewelers loupe ($5)
- A gram scale ($10)
- A non-glazed ceramic plate or tile ($5)
- A gold and silver testing kit ($15)

We spoke about these tools before. There are some simple inexpensive ways to verify that the item in question is gold or silver and what carat gold it is. Most jewelry stores use the acid test (we will look at it in detail in this chapter), to determine the value of an item. The acid test along with some others, can ensure success. Let's start with the most basic test you can use for gold and silver verification: the magnet test.

The magnet test is very easy. Using a good quality (not small refrigerator magnet) you simply hold the gold or silver item up to the magnet. If it sticks, it is not gold or silver. It could however be gold or silver plated with a base metal underneath that is not magnetic so be careful. Even though it may not be solid gold or silver it could be very valuable as a collectible.

This method is not fool proof. Some gold looking items are made of non-magnetic material, and you can be fooled into thinking it is gold or silver because it does not stick to the magnet. This is a very basic test and needs to be followed up with more accurate tests. If it does stick to the magnet you know it is not solid gold or solid silver.

When you examine a piece of gold or silver you will want to find the stamp or marking on it that indicates carat of gold or silver purity. The jewelry loupe is now used to look closely at the piece so you can find the mark. Finding the mark is helpful in the process of determining if the item is gold or silver. If you find the mark, then you must test further because many fake items have fake marks on them. And some real items have no marks for reasons mentioned earlier: worn off or hidden. So do not rely on the purity mark as a final way to determine authenticity.

Another reliable way to test an item for gold is to rub the gold piece on the surface of a non-glazed ceramic plate or tile. Rub it where you will not notice any mark this may leave on the item, and for items that have extreme value, be careful. After rubbing the gold on the plate a mark will be left on the plate. Gold colored means the item is gold. A dark mark means no gold.

Another way to test for gold, and again, this can damage the item, is to press a sharp object against the gold piece. If a mark appears, it is gold. Gold is soft and easy to dent. But again, fake items will mark as well because they may have lead under gold plate.

Believe it or not many experts can spot gold just by looking at it. Also if a gold item is worn out in spots, look at the worn marks. If you see gold under them, you can be pretty certain it is real gold. If you see another color under the gold plate, then the item is gold plated and has a base metal under it. Remember, gold is very heavy. So if you pick up a piece that you suspect is gold, and it seems very heavy, then it probably is gold. Another simple and easy test is to take the gold item and try to scratch glass with it. Gold is soft and will not scratch glass.

The density test can also be used to test the item. Even though it requires some patience and practice, is very accurate. It can be used for both gold and silver. Let's explain how to do it with gold:

- First, weigh the gold in grams.
- Next, fill a vial with water – mark the level with tape or marker.
- Place the gold in the vial – note the new water level with tape or marker. Measure the difference in milliliters (ml). (1 milliliter = 0.3937 inch)
- Density = mass/volume displacement.

A result close to 19 g/ml indicates either real gold, or a material with a density similar to gold

Here is an example calculation: the gold item weighs 38 g, and it displaces 2 ml of water. Using the formula of [mass (38 g)] / [volume displacement (2 ml)], the result would be 19 g/ml, which is very close to the density of gold (24K).

Bear in mind that different gold purity will have a different g/ml ratio:
- 14K – 12.9 to 14.6 g/ml
- 18K yellow – 15.2 to 15.9 g/ml
- 18K white – 14.7 to 16.9 g/ml
- 22K – 17.7 to 17.8 g/ml
- 24K – 19.2 g/ml

The test used by jewelers (produces the best results) is the nitric acid test. There are two versions of it. No doubt, you have heard of the term "acid test". This phrase comes from the gold test using nitric acid. Nitric acid is caustic and should only be handled with gloves, eye and mouth protection.

With respect to gold, you simply place the gold in a stainless steel pot and place a drop of the acid on it. Most gold (14kt and above) will not be damaged by the acid. Cheap gold may show a mark. If there is no reaction from the acid, then the item is gold. A green color reaction indicates a base metal under the gold. A milk colored reaction indicates gold plate over sterling silver.

Below are more detailed reactions to look for when using the straight nitric acid method.

- 10 KY (Yellow GOLD) - Brown color
- 14 KY - Very slight brown color
- 18 KY - No color change
- 10 KW (White Gold) - Dark brown, after 20 seconds the acid starts to fizz
- 14 KW - Slight brown
- 18 KW - Faint brown
- Sterling Silver - Milky whitish color with some faint brown
- Pot metal - Grey color, no fizzing
- Base Metal - Fizzes green, smokes (brass or copper present) see base metal plated bangle below

(See the green residue present on the test below - this fake was stamped 14k)

Another way to use Nitric Acid on jewelry is to rub the item on a rubbing (slate) stone (make sure you use the correct stone so no damage results). When you rub the gold or silver on the stone, a mark is left behind. Next you will use the correct acid marked for the carat mark on the gold item. If the mark on the stone does not change after dropping some acid on it, then you know the item is the carat that is marked on it. If the mark disappears, then test again using lesser strength acid for lower quality gold. Each test kit has instructions.

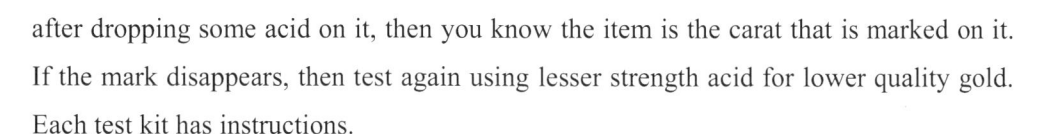

If the acid bubbles up or turns green or smokes, this indicates base metal, not gold.

Let's take a look at an inexpensive silver and gold testing kit that I recommend you buy on eBay.

http://www.ebay.com/usr/goldtestempire

The next two images show what the test kit looks on the eBay site:

This kit has six bottles of acid, tests for silver and gold and has a rubbing stone. For under $15 with free shipping, you can't go wrong. The seller has a pretty good track record with some negative feedback, but I feel confident this kit will work as advertised.

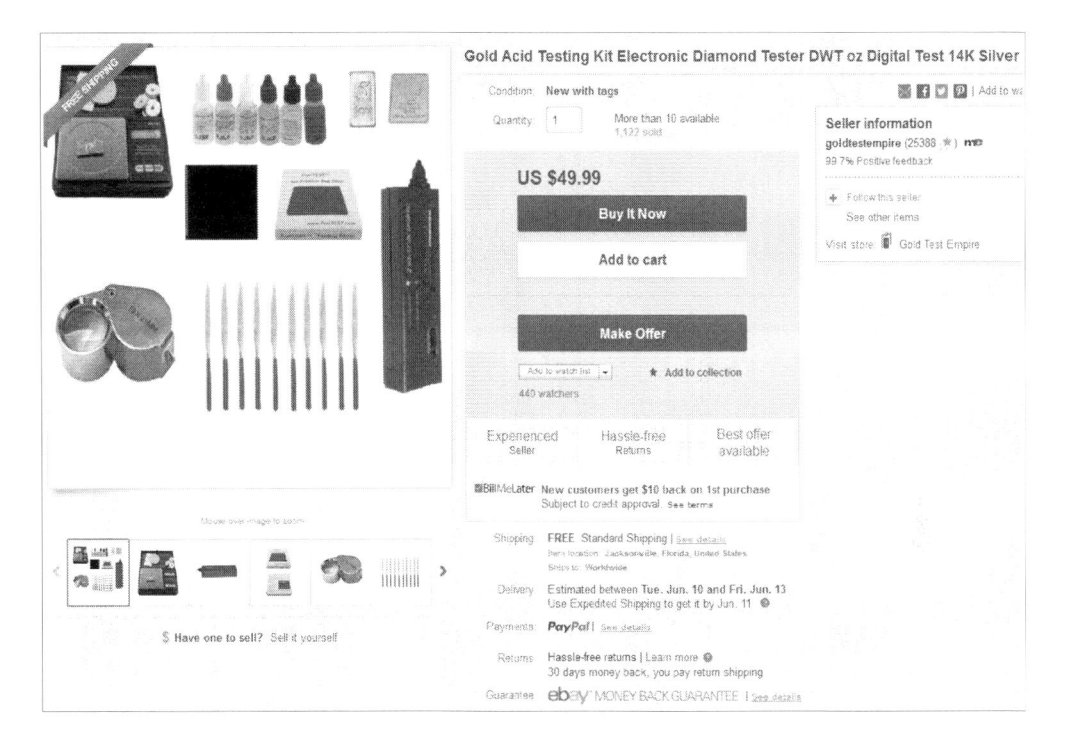

This kit tests for gold, silver and diamonds. It includes a gram scale, jewelry loupe, and some other items.

Let's talk a little about silver, and checking for authenticity. Quality silver usually has a stamp of purity or the word sterling on the back or bottom: such as .800 or .925 (sterling silver – 92.5%) as mentioned earlier. Most silver looking jewelry, plates and cups and other serving items are silver plated. If they are very old, they may have value as a collectible.

Silver has such a high conductivity rate that when you place an ice cube next to a piece of silver it will start to melt almost immediately. This test works well for coins and bars. To test silver, you can also tap on the silver piece with a coin to listen for a bell ringing sound, meaning silver. Don't tap on the exposed part of an item.

The testing kit is the best method for testing silver. I recommend one that comes with a rubbing stone so you can rub your silver or gold on it (which should not cause any damage) and then test the residue left on the stone, since acid directly on the silver can damage it. Acid placed on a coin will damage the coin. So, if you must place a drop of acid on a coin, use the coin edge only.

Here are typical silver color results from placing acid on a mark left on the rubbing stone. Each kit may differ, so refer to kit instructions:

COLOR SCALE OF YOUR SPECIFIC SILVER TEST	
Bright Red	Fine Silver
Darker Red	925 Silver
Brown	800 Silver
Green	500 Silver
Yellow	Lead or Tin
Dark brown	Brass
Blue	Nickel

A great short and entertaining you tube video from the Pawn Stars TV Show is worth watching. Rick shows you how he tests for silver:

http://www.youtube.com/watch?v=e6mqbQtr9DM

What About The "IRS"?

Mention the letters "IRS", and everyone gets nervous. The fact of the matter is, the IRS does not care about coins or bullion you purchase or sell, per se. What they care about are the amounts of money involved in the transactions and more importantly, what form the money takes, the number of transactions that occur in a short time period and the type of product you are selling or buying. For example, some bullion coins are exempt from government reporting, no matter how many you purchase.

What is so unfortunate is that aggressive sales people tell you that certain purchases are not subject to government reporting, when in reality they have no idea of what they are talking about. While there may be some truth to what they say, they do not convey the whole picture.

Several things must be kept in mind when buying and selling any form of gold or silver or any coin type. Before you do, make sure you understand what you are liable for with respect to taxes, and what the company you buy from, or sell to, is required to report as a result of the sale. Some sales and amounts are reportable and some are not. Also keep in mind that laws change over time, therefore before making any large purchase or purchases consult an accountant first. Remember you may not be aware of what the company you buy from or sell to, is doing behind your back. Don't worry; I am going to explain this subject to you. It is really very basic.

Selling: With respect to selling bullion, and this means selling to a dealer, the dealer has to file a 1099B when the following thresholds are met:

LIST OF REPORTABLE BULLION

Bullion Type	Minimum Fineness	Minimum Reportable Amount
Gold Bars	.995	Any size bars totaling 1 Kilo (32.15 troy ounces) or more.
Silver Bars	.999	Any size bars totaling 1,000 troy ounces or more.
Platinum Bars	.9995	Any size bars totaling 25 troy ounces or more.
Palladium Bars	.9995	Any size bars totaling 100 troy ounces or more.
Gold 1 oz. Maple Leaf	As minted	(25) 1 oz. coins
Gold 1 oz. Krugerrand	As minted	(25) 1 oz. coins
Gold 1 oz. Mexican Onza	As minted	(25) 1 oz. coins
U.S. 90% Silver Coins	As minted	Any combination of dimes, quarters, or half dollars totaling $1,000 face value or more.

Why is it only these items and why these quantities? The types and forms of bullion that trigger reporting are related to the regulations that are placed on brokers. The brokers are required to report some of the proceeds from stock and bullion transactions. For example, regularly traded items on the commodities exchange used to be 1,000 oz Comex bars, or 1 Kilo gold bars. This is why the 1099B report is triggered at those levels.

Gold Coins That Do Not Trigger IRS Reporting:

Gold Eagle:

American Gold Buffalo:

Austrian Gold Philharmonic:

American Gold Eagles, American Gold Buffaloes and Austrian Gold Philharmonics do not require any 1099 IRS reporting. You can sell as many as you want and no 1099B will be reported to the IRS.

Silver Coins That Do Not Trigger IRS Reporting:

American Silver Eagle:

Canadian Silver Maple Leaf:

Austrian Silver Philharmonic:

American Silver Eagles, Canadian Silver Maple Leafs and Austrian Silver Philharmonics do not trigger any 1099B IRS reporting. You can sell any quantity of these coins you want and bullion dealers are not required to report it to the IRS.

Please keep in mind that sales tax laws differ from state to state, so when buying, make sure you know what applies. Some states have sales tax exemptions for bullion purchases. However, there may be minimum purchase requirements in order to qualify for this exemption. If you live in such a state, it may make sense to save your money until you're able to buy in bulk, rather than buying a single coin at a time.

Buying: In most cases, bullion and rare coin transactions are not reportable. If you pay with a personal check, credit card, or bank wire, there are no reporting requirements. If you pay with cash, money orders, cashier's checks, or travelers checks, and the purchase price is at least $10,000, it must be reported to the government.

The dealer is required to submit IRS Form 8300, "Report of Cash Payments Over $10,000 Received in a Trade or Business". This document is required for all cash transactions over $10,000 in the United States, not just precious metal purchases. It requires information such as your name, address, and social security number.

Given the $10,000 price at which IRS reporting becomes mandatory, some investors try to skirt the rules by making multiple smaller purchases. This is known as "structuring," and doing so is not legal. $10,000 in related transactions must still be reported, even if the purchases occurred in separately in one day or even on separate days.

If you wish to avoid the IRS reporting requirement, consider using a payment method that does not require reporting, such as a bank wire. There are other reporting requirements for precious metal dealers. The Suspicious Activity Report (or SAR), part of the 2001 Patriot Act, requires financial institutions (which includes coin dealers) to report suspicious transactions. However, there are no firm rules about which transactions should be considered suspicious.

Know the rules, but keep in mind that most purchases and sales are not subject to any form of reporting because they are either too small or because of the method used to pay for them. The company you buy from or sell to should be able to help you with this.

These links do a really good job in helping to explain this in detail. But remember, before buying or selling in quantity, consult an accountant:

http://www.coinweek.com/news/industry-insider-irs-reporting-rules-for-cash-transactions-and-precious-metals/

http://www.cmi-gold-silver.com/gold-confiscation-1933/

http://goldsilver.com/article/irs-1099-gold-reporting-private-gold-private-silver-bullion/

Important Terminology

Uncirculated:

Because so much of what we have, and are going to speak about, has to do with coins (whether in the form of coin bullion or rare coins), it is important to define some words and terms that will help us better understand this subject matter, especially if you are new to coins.

A word that is used often when speaking about coins, but not well understood, is "uncirculated". A coin that is considered to be uncirculated is a coin that was issued but never got into the coin supply and has no wear on it. Now here comes the tricky part. Some coins have been handled or touched by people but can still be considered "uncirculated". As an example, you go to the bank and ask the teller for a roll of new pennies. The teller says you are in luck; we just got these rolls in. The U.S. Mint just made the coins, rolled them and put them into the money supply.

So, in this case the roll has 50 brand new pennies, never touched, put into the roll when minted. These are "uncirculated" coins. Okay, let's say you go home and open the roll and pour them out onto the table and exclaim: "Wow, these coins are brand new; I am going to save them." So you put them back into the roll and set them aside. My question to you is: Are these coins still uncirculated? The answer is, yes! The coins still have no signs of wear at all. Please note, a coin can still be considered "uncirculated" even if it has a few blemishes on it.

With this in mind, some coin sellers use the term: "Brilliant Uncirculated", BU for short. What does this mean? It really means nothing at all. The pennies we just described were brand new and shiny and even though they were dumped out of the roll they were not blemished in any way. They are considered uncirculated and BU, too (still shiny). So a BU coin and an "uncirculated" coin are basically the same thing. When sellers use the term "BU" they are trying to dress the sale up, make it seem like a better product even when it is not.

It is advantageous to ask the dealer you are buying coins from what condition they are in. For example, American Eagles should be "uncirculated" when you buy them because they have never been handled (perhaps only touched for repackaging purposes). Dealers that say their coins are uncirculated, while others are not, may be practicing questionable sales techniques.

Bullion vs Bullion Coins:

Bullion refers to a precious metal, such as a silver bar.

Bullion Coins are also a precious metal, but in the form of a coin, like a silver or gold coin, for example.

Other Terms:

Gold   A precious yellow metallic element (Atomic Number 79) that is resistant to oxidation and is highly ductile and malleable.

Silver   A soft-white lustrous metal, silver (Atomic Number 47) has the highest electrical and thermal conductivity of any metal and occurs both in minerals and in free form (rarely).

Platinum   A heavy, malleable, ductile, precious, gray-white metal, platinum (Atomic Number 78) is resistant to corrosion. Platinum coins and bars are now very popular investments.

Palladium   A rare silver-white metal of the platinum group, palladium (Atomic Number 46) resembles platinum chemically and is primarily used as an industrial catalyst and in jewelry.

Pure Gold A term sometimes used, but is very misleading. There is no such thing as 100% pure gold or silver. To be considered "pure," gold, silver and palladium products must be at least .999 fine (99.9% pure), and platinum products must be .9995 fine (99.95% pure).

Coin Grades The condition or grade of a coin helps push its value up in most cases. We will address this subject in detail later, but for now it should be mentioned that higher grade coins are very desirable and often become part of one's investments, either in the form of old coins or new coins with high grades. "Uncirculated" coins are high grade coins and usually start at MS60 and go can go higher (grading scale 1 – 70) "MS" means mint state. MS70 is a perfect coin.

It is very important to mention that because a coin has been certified and the grading is very high, let's say MS66 out of a grade of 1 – 70, logic dictates that MS66 is very high on the scale and suggests that a coin in this condition may have much higher value than a coin with the same date in lower condition, this is not the case! A coin with a high grade may not be worth much more than a coin of the same date in a lower grade. For example, if there are many thousands available of a coin that is in a high mint state, the coin is really considered common, in some sense of the word, and has no greater value because of the condition it is in, because there are so many of them available.

On a practical level what this translates to is the fact that if you are being told a coin has great value because of its condition, and therefore, you should pay a premium for it, you are getting a marketing pitch and not the whole truth. Examples of this will follow in future chapters.

Numismatic Coins Coins whose prices depend more on their rarity, condition, dates and mint marks than on their gold or silver content, if any.

Certified Coins Coins that have been graded by a grading company (such as PCGS or NGC). The company assigns a value to the coin in terms of its condition. In theory, the better the condition of the coin the higher the value. Graded coins are placed in a sealed case once they are certified. The case is labeled as to the grade, name of company that certified it, and date of coin.

Obverse The front of a coin.

Reverse The back of a coin.

Slabbed Coins Coins encapsulated in plastic for protection against wear. Slabbed coins are graded by an independent grading service (certified coins and slabbed coins mean the same thing).

Proof Coins Specially made coins that are only made by and sold by the U.S. Mint. They have a polished mirror like surface and come in their own container. They are never touched and should never be touched (oils from your hands can damage them). If they need to be handled, only an expert should do so by wearing cotton gloves.

For a complete list of words and terms with respect to investing and coin investing please refer to this link:

http://www.apmex.com/glossary#a

Certified Silver and Gold:

Let's look at gold and silver bars or rounds with respect to certification. An extremely important topic that needs to be examined is certification. We know that certified coins have been slabbed; they have been graded and certified by a coin grading company. Certified coins are genuine coins because in order to obtain certification, they must be inspected to verify that they are not fake.

A very similar situation exists with respect to gold and silver. Gold and silver can be certified. Certified gold is gold that is issued or minted by an entity, such as the U.S. Mint, to grade and purity. The certification process will include an analysis of the metal for weight and purity, meaning its ore composition. The process is not complicated, but must be completed by a licensed certified appraiser. The key difference between regular bullion and certified, is that the question of content is eliminated. Unlike a bar of bullion of unknown origins, certified gold or silver will be stamped and accompanied by a letter of certification stating, in no uncertain terms, the content and weight. The only thing certified metal leaves to question is the actual value, meaning its worth if sold for currency. This amount cannot be certified as the price per ounce is constantly changing.

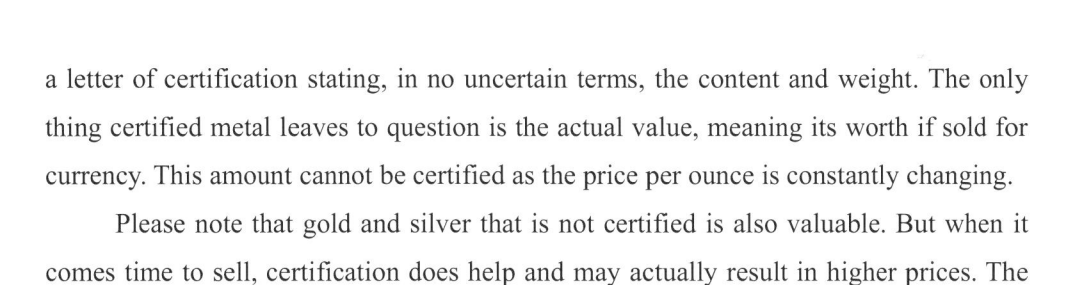

Please note that gold and silver that is not certified is also valuable. But when it comes time to sell, certification does help and may actually result in higher prices. The flip side also holds true, when you buy certified product it can cost more.

Buying - Gold & Silver Coins

Past chapters focused on buying from individuals who responded to advertising so we could buy low and sell high, to make profit. What about buying gold, silver and coins through direct purchase from companies and auction sites? We need to take a close look at how to buy gold and silver bars or rounds, gold and silver coins and other coin types. Many people are taken advantage of when they purchase coins and metals, so this information will prove very valuable. Hopefully, after reading, you will be protected.

As you can imagine, there are many companies that sell gold, silver and coins. Companies range from big to small and domestic to international. Not all companies are created equal. There are many companies selling fake gold and silver bars and rounds and fake coins.

A fake gold bar:

Deviously crooked companies will purchase real gold bars that are certified with serial numbers and papers. They then hollow out the bars and sell the removed gold. The hollow bars are filled with tungsten, and then the bar is closed up. That is a sophisticated operation!

High quality fake silver coins and small fake silver bars are also being produced in high volume in China. In particular, there are fake Silver Eagle coins being struck and distributed and priced as low as 50¢ a piece (with capacity of wholesale production lots of 100,000+ pieces).

Above: Image of fake Silver Eagle coin factory in China.

Fakes come in many forms. There are plated gold and silver coins and bars, consisting of a thin layer of gold or silver covering base metal alloys underneath. Then there are hallowed out gold and silver bars and coins with thicker covers of gold and/or silver, filled with tungsten, lead, copper, and/or nickel. Many of these elements are not magnetic so the magnet test would fail.

How do you prevent this from happening? **There is only one way.** Buy from the dealers that have a long positive track record. Since there are a variety of gold, silver and coin types, some companies will only sell a limited selection, while others may carry all forms of gold or silver or coins.

Let's take a close look at buying coins, and how to safely do this. Some coins can only be purchased directly from the U.S. Mint. Some coins can only be purchased from U.S. Mint certified dealers. Most coins, however, especially older coins, can be purchased just about anywhere. To gain a better understanding of this topic, the U.S.

Mint has issued this statement (this applies to bullion coins, not older coins):

"Congressionally authorized American Eagle Bullion coins provide investors with a convenient and cost effective way to add a small amount of physical platinum, gold, or silver to their investment portfolios. The American Eagle Bullion program was launched in 1986 with the sale of gold and silver bullion coins. Platinum was added to the American Eagle Bullion family in 1997.

A bullion coin is a coin that is valued by its weight in a specific precious metal. Unlike commemorative or numismatic coins valued by limited mintage, rarity, condition and age, bullion coins are purchased by investors seeking a simple and tangible means to own and invest in the gold, silver, and platinum markets. American Eagle Gold Bullion Coins are available in four denominations: one ounce, one-half ounce, one-quarter ounce, and one-tenth ounce while the American Eagle Silver and Platinum Bullion Coins are only available in the one ounce size.

How to Buy American Eagle Bullion Coins. Aside from the proof version, the United States Mint does not sell American Eagle Bullion coins directly to the public. Instead, the Mint distributes uncirculated bullion coins through a network of wholesalers, brokerage companies, precious metal firms, coin dealers, and participating banks, a network known as Authorized Purchasers.

This method provides effective and efficient distribution, which maximizes the availability of the coins in retail markets as well as major investment markets. For more information about American Eagle Bullion Coins, call 1-800-USA-GOLD."

Coins sold through "Authorized Distribution"

American Eagle Gold Bullion Coin Obverse (4 Sizes) 1/10oz 1/4oz 1/2oz 1oz $5-$10-$25-$50
.9167 or 22 Karat

American Eagle Gold Bullion Coin Reverse

American Eagle Silver Bullion Coin Obverse

American Eagle Silver Bullion Coin Reverse
99.9 Pure

American Eagle Platinum Bullion Coin Obverse

American Eagle Platinum Bullion Coin Reverse

Coins sold only through "Authorized Distributors" are illustrated above. You may find these coins being sold in a variety of ways. If you buy from "Authorized Distributors" you greatly lesson your chances of fraud and deception. Notice the four sizes for the Gold Eagle.

What is so nice about the coins shown above, is the fact that, they can become part of your IRA. The U.S. Mint states: "American Bullion coins are considered investment-grade bullion coins and are the only official investment-grade coins in the United States. As such, these coins can be used to fund Individual Retirement Accounts (IRAs). Major investment markets around the globe also accept them. Additionally, the Internal Revenue Service (IRS) exempts them from IRS 1099 reporting, which provides the investors with an added level of privacy."

In addition to these three American Eagle Series coins, there is also the 1oz gold American Buffalo coin with a face value of $50 that can be purchased from some "Authorized Distributors". It is 24kt gold (.9999) and became available in 2006 in an uncirculated version (instead of a proof version) due the great demand for a gold coin of this fineness. The coin was created in order to compete with foreign 24kt gold bullion coins. Since investors sometimes prefer 99.99% pure gold over the 91.67% gold used in the American Gold Eagle, many were choosing non U.S. coins, such as the Canadian Gold Maple Leaf, to meet their bullion needs.

The picture above of the Gold American Buffalo is a 4th U.S. Mint bullion coin, often not mentioned because the emphasis is placed upon the Eagle Series.

There is actually a fifth bullion coin that is part of the U.S. Mint bullion offering that is often overlooked by investors: The America The Beautiful 5oz Silver Coin.

This coin weighs 5 ounces, has .999 per cent fine silver and measures 3 inches across. It is available from distributors in a circulated version and from the mint in a better uncirculated condition, for more money. Distributors often sell the uncirculated version as well. I don't think there is any real difference between what is referred to as uncirculated and circulated. However, some coins grade much higher than others and come in protective cases. These coins never really touch any hands. Technically they are all uncirculated but some grade higher than others. The U.S. Mint explains why this coin was issued:

"The United States Mint America the Beautiful Quarters Program is a multi-year initiative to honor 56 national parks and other national sites in each state, the District of Columbia and five U.S. territories—Puerto Rico, Guam, American Samoa, U.S. Virgin Islands and the Northern Mariana Islands. Under this program, five new reverse designs will appear on the quarter-dollar each year beginning in 2010 and through 2020, with one final coin in 2021.

The United States Mint will also mint and make available for sale silver quarter-dollar uncirculated coins that replicate the designs of the United States Mint America the Beautiful Quarters. These coins are made of .999 fine silver, have a diameter of three inches and weigh five ounces."

Note: mintage figures for this silver coin are very low, with averages about 30,000 per year, so it may increase in value as a collectible and as a silver investment. A good way to check potential investment for any bullion coin is to look at production figures. This link allows you to do that:

http://www.usmint.gov/about_the_mint/index.cfm?action=PreciousMetals&type=bullion

Some bullion coins, as mentioned, are only sold through authorized distribution and other bullion coins (very special types) are only sold by the U.S. Mint. According to the U.S. Mint, its (non-special) bullion coins are not sold directly to the public, instead: "We distribute the coins in bulk, through a network of official distributors called "Authorized Purchasers" who, in turn, sell them to secondary retailers".

Let's take a look at these authorized distributors. They can be found on this link:

https://www.usmint.gov/mint_programs/american_eagles/index.cfm?action=lookup

There are 27 names on this list:

A-Mark Precious Metals
429 Santa Monica Blvd, Suite 230
Santa Monica, CA 90401
310-319-0200

American Bullion
12301 Wilshire Blvd, Suite 650
Los Angeles, CA 90025
800-326-9598

American Precious Metals Exchange (APMEX)
226 Dean A. McGee Ave, Suite 100
Oklahoma City, OK 73013
405-595-2100

Assets Strategies Int'l (ASI)
1700 Rockville Pike, Suite 400
Rockville, MD 20852
800-831-0007

Blanchard & Company
909 Poydras Street, Suite 1900
New Orleans, LA 70161
800-880-4653

California Numismatic Investments, Inc
525 West Manchester Blvd
Inglewood, CA 90301
800-225-7531

Chicago Precious Metals Exchange
30 S Wacker Drive, 22nd Floor
Chicago, IL 60606-7542   312-854-7084

CMI Gold and Silver Inc.
3800 N. Central Avenue, 11th Floor
Phoenix, AZ 85012 800-528-1380

CNT
350 Bedford Street
Bridgewater, MA 02324
508-697-9600

Dillon Gage, Inc.
15301 Dallas Pkwy, Suite 200
Addison, TX 75001
800-375-4653

Fidelitrade
3601 North Market Street
Wilmington, DE 19802
800-223-1080

Fisher Precious Metals
2151 W Hillsboro Blvd, Suite 210
Deerfield Beach, FL 33442
800-390-8576

Gaithersburg Coin Exchange
16 East Diamond Avenue
Gaithersburg, MD 20877 800-638-4104

Guilford Coin Exchange LLC
69 Whitfield Street
Guilford, CT 06437
203-453-9363

Investment Rarities Inc.
7850 Metro Parkway, Suite 121
Minneapolis, MN 55425
800-328-1860

Jack Hunt Coin Broker
2746 Delaware Avenue
Kenmore, NY 14217
716-874-7777

JMRC, Inc/dba ModernCoinMart
5565 Broadcast Court
Sarasota, FL 34240
800-362-9004

Liberty Coin Galleries
2201 E. Willow Street, Suite Aa
Signal Hill, CA 90755-2149
800-400-0824

Miles Franklin LTD
801 Twelve Oaks Center Dr, Suite 834
Wayzata, MN 55391
800-822-8080

Northwest Territorial Mint
2505 S 320th St, Suite 110
Federal Way, WA 98003
800-344-6468

Rocky Mountain Coin Exchg
538 South Broadway
Denver, CO 80209
800-781-4653

Rust Rare Coin Company
252 East 300 South
Salt Lake City, UT 84111
800-343-7878

Sam Sloat Coins, Inc.
606 Post Road East
Westport, CT 06880
800-243-5670

Texas Precious Metals
959 Hwy 95N
Shiner, TX 77984   361-594-3624

The Gold Center
3000 West Iles Ave
Springfield, IL 62704
217-793-8000

Upstate Coin & Gold
511 E Genesee St
Fayetteville, NY 13066
800-588-2646

Water Tower Precious Metals
141 West Jackson Blvd, Suite 130-A
Chicago, IL 60604-2901
312-435-1620

 It is important to list them because they have been screened by the U.S. Mint. So when you deal with them, you can feel comfortable that you will be dealing with reputable companies. It is not easy to qualify to become an authorized distributor. Remember, as stated before, the best way to prevent yourself from being cheated is to buy from reputable dealers.

 Three dealers in particular have a very good reputation, track record and good prices, and I want to look at them in more detail.

American Precious Metals Exchange (APMEX)
226 Dean A. Mc Gee Ave, Suite 100
Oklahoma City, OK 73013
405-595-2100

JMRC, Inc/dba ModernCoinMart

5565 Broadcast Court

Sarasota, FL 34240

800-362-9004

Texas Precious Metals

959 Hwy 95N

Shiner, TX 77984

361-594-3624

 Here is a snapshot from eBay showing the listings (and there are over 1800 of them) for APMEX. Dealers that sell on eBay have to compete with other dealers, so the prices are usually low. You also have the backing of eBay if something goes wrong.

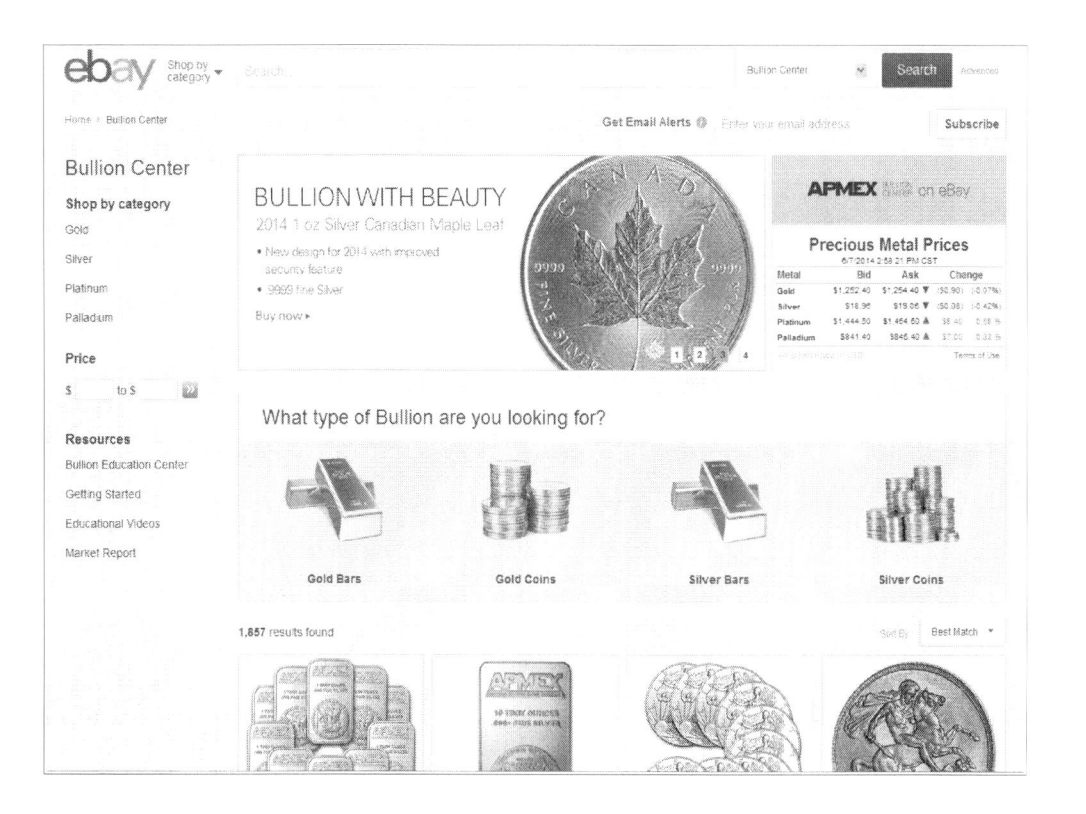

This listing on eBay from APMEX for five 1oz Silver Eagle coins appeared in July 2014. Notice the price of $123.32 with free shipping. Over 10,000 of these have been sold.

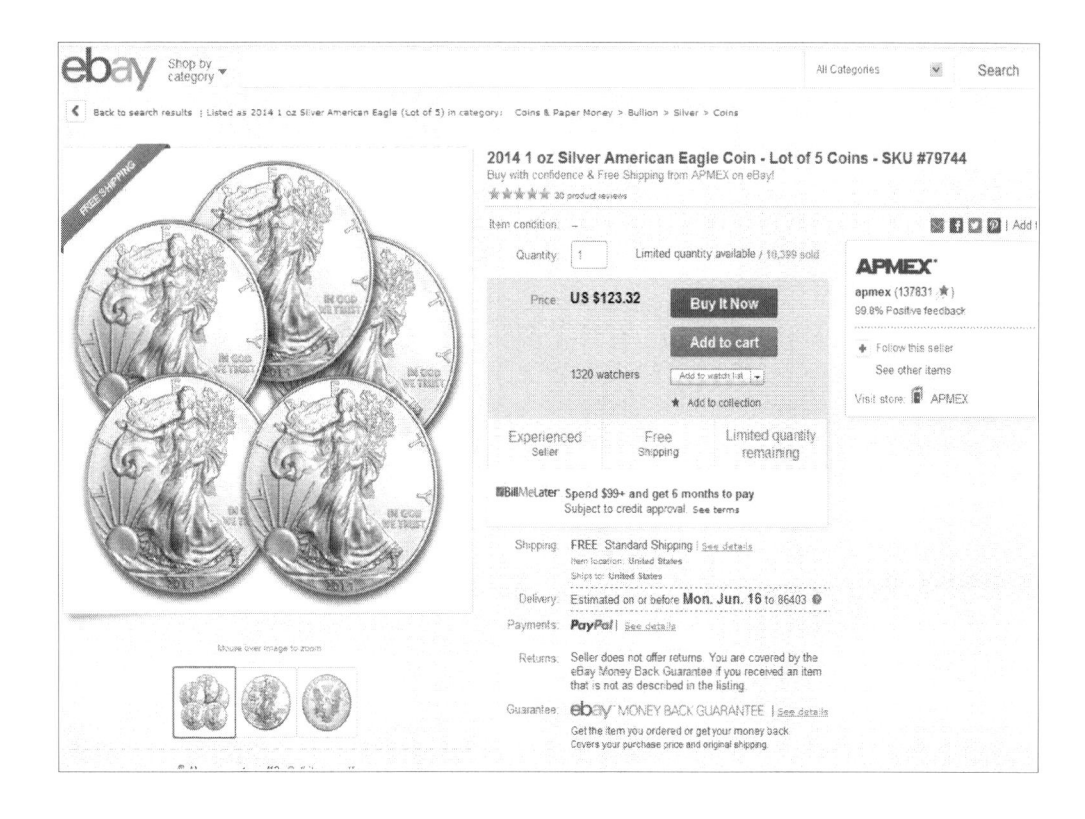

The exact same item was listed at the same time on eBay from another authorized company mentioned, MCM. Their price was $118.88, about $5 less than APMEX, and it included free shipping.

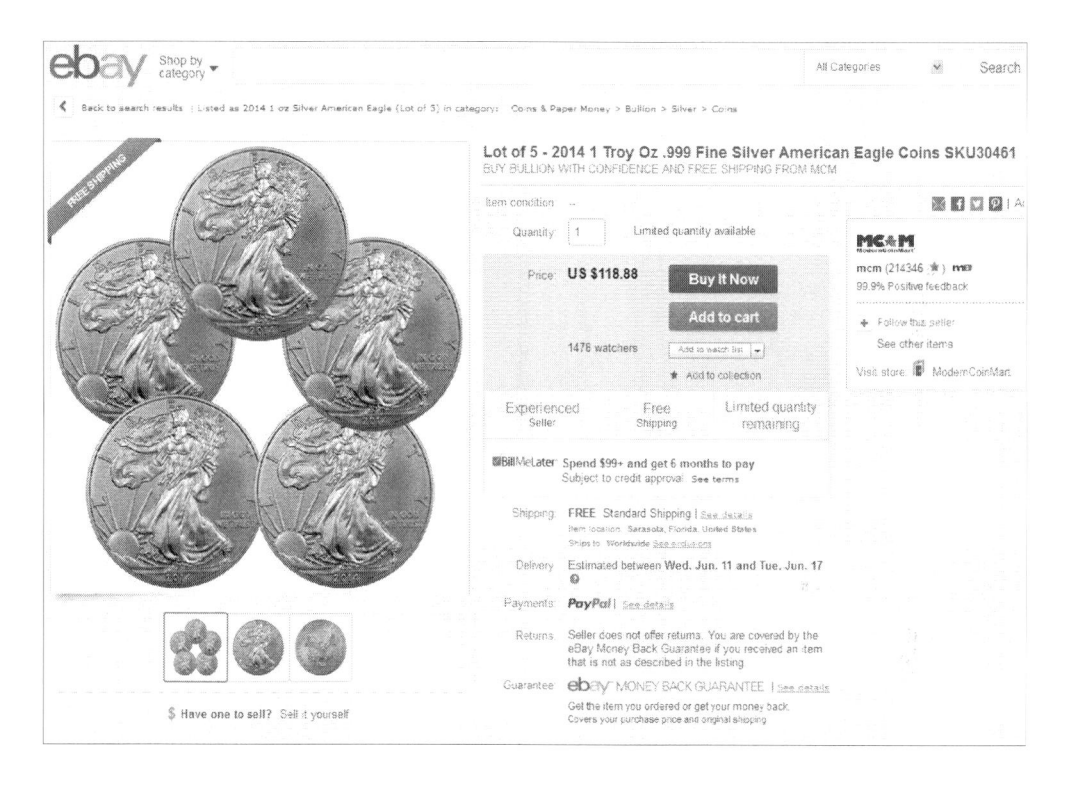

An even better deal from MCM was on eBay at the same time, but as an auction style listing. The winning bid was $116.80, which was even less than the $118.88.

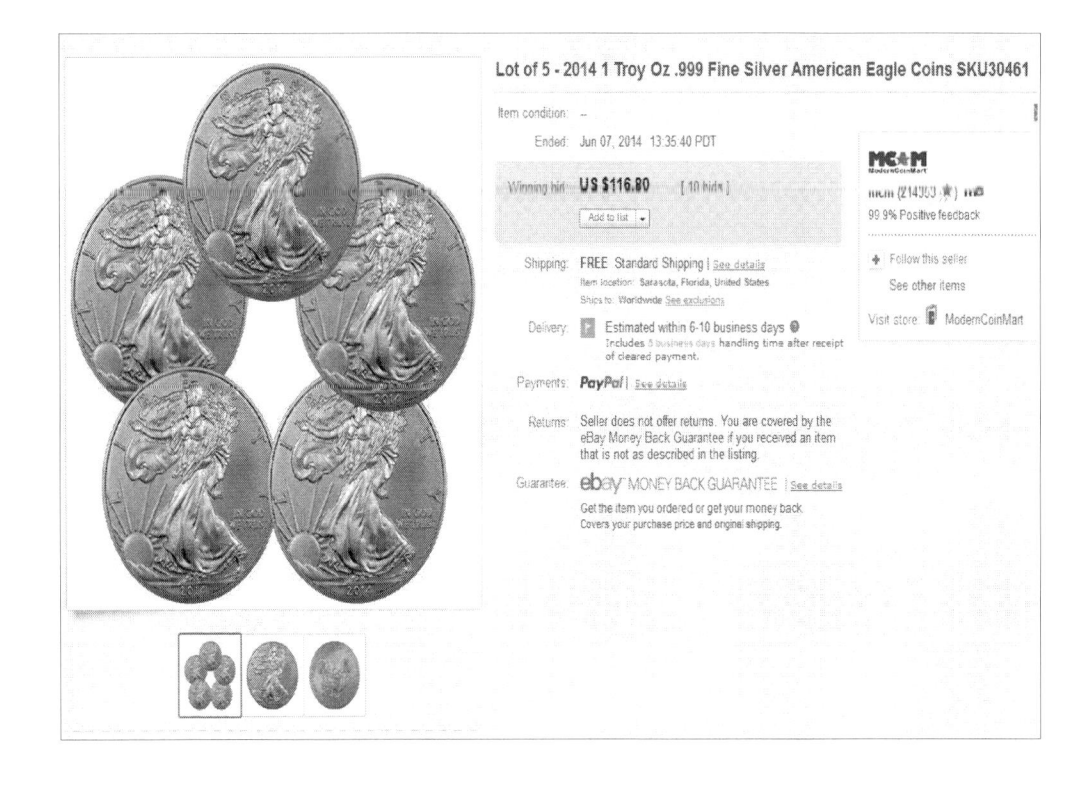

In case you are wondering about this price of $116.80, it comes out to $23.36 an ounce. The day this auction ended silver was trading at $18.98 an ounce, so the winner paid $4.38 over spot. When you consider that the coin dealer has to pay for shipping, eBay fees, PayPal fees and do all the work, and the fact that eBay stands behind the sale, this is not a bad way to get your hands on silver and gold coins or bullion.

Is it the cheapest deal in town? I know you can find these coins for less money at other sites. However, most require a shipping fee and many have a minimum purchase, so keep that in mind.

These U.S. Mint distributors sell gold coins as well (we focused on silver so far) and many sell gold and silver bars and rounds through eBay and other websites (including their own). Let's look at the third U.S. Mint distributor: Texas Precious Metals. They have a great reputation and 5 star reviews.

Let's look at their prices:

They have a $1000 minimum purchase price. To meet the minimum purchase, you would have to order 50 coins at $21.92 per coin. When the $25 shipping and insurance fee is added, it comes out to $22.42 per coin (vs $23.36 an ounce or per coin for MCM).

I am sure there are many other good companies to buy from, but I would never buy from any source outside the U.S. other than Canada. Many eBay dealers sell fake silver and gold bars and fake coins, so stick with "Authorized Purchasers" like the three we just examined. Two of them had eBay stores. Remember they also have their own websites where the price might be less.

They also sell Canadian coins. The Canadian Maple Leaf 1oz silver coin is in high demand, is .9999 pure silver and has a face value of $5. It is purer than the American Eagle .999. Canada also has gold coins. Most of the dealers (27) I listed sell these coins as well, and the three dealers we looked at, sell Canadian Maple Leaf 1oz silver coins and Canadian gold coins.

An organization that provides up to date information on the Silver Industry and one that can be of great help in furnishing information to you is the Silver Institute. They are nonprofit and have been around since 1971.

Here is a link to their web site:
https://www.silverinstitute.org/site/

They have a free newsletter that you can sign up for, and they have a list of approved retailers. The chart that follows shows some of the same names listed by the U.S. Mint. Link to these names:

https://www.silverinstitute.org/site/silver-investment/

Sources of Investor Products (Silver)

Retail Outlets	Bullion	Official Coins	Medallions (Rounds)	Certificates or Storage Accounts	Accumulation Plans	Futures and/or Forwards Contracts	Options	Exchange Traded Fund*	Mutual Funds
A-Mark Precious Metals, Inc. www.amark.com	✓	✓	✓	✓					
American Precious Metals Exchange 800-375-9006 www.apmex.com	✓	✓	✓						
The Bank of Nova Scotia 212-912-8500 www.scotiabank.com	✓	✓	✓	✓		✓			✓
BlackRock 800-iShares (800-474-2737) www.ishares.com								✓	
CMI Gold & Silver Inc. 800-528-1380 www.cmi-gold-silver.com	✓								
Commerzbank, NY 212-336-1000 www.commerzbank.com		✓				✓	✓		
Dillon Gage 800-375-4653 www.dillongage.com	✓	✓	✓	✓					
Fidelitrade 800-223-1080 www.fidelitrade.com	✓	✓	✓	✓	✓	✓	✓		
Gainesville Coins 813-482-9300 www.gainesvillecoins.com	✓	✓	✓						
Johnson Matthey 610-971-3064 www.matthey.com	✓								
Kitco 877-775-4826 www.kitco.com	✓	✓							

What's so nice about this list is that it shows all the types of silver sold by these companies. Some of these companies are the same ones mentioned earlier as authorized U.S. Mint distributors. This overlap is a good sign.

Company						
Midwest Bullion Exchange, Inc. 888-928-3390 www.privatebullion.com	✓	✓	✓			
Mitsui & Co. (USA) 212-878-4127 www.mitsui.com					✓	✓
Monex Deposit Company 800-949-4653 www.monex.com	✓	✓		✓	✓	
MTB Bank 800-535-7481 www.mtbcoins.com	✓	✓	✓	✓		
Royal Canadian Mint 613-993-3500 www.rcmint.ca	✓	✓	✓			
SilverSaver 800-701-3546 www.silversaver.com	✓	✓	✓	✓	✓	
United States Mint 800-USA-GOLD www.usmint.gov	✓	✓				

The only way to guarantee that your buying experience will be a good one is to buy from a reputable company like those listed here and on the U.S. Mint list. Remember, price is not the only factor to consider.

Now, let's take a look at coins sold through the U.S. Mint directly to the public. Some of these coins are sometimes sold via these authorized distributors, so do your homework and compare prices.

Keep in mind the fact that U.S. Mint prices tend to be on the high side, and the investment potential of the coins you buy from them depends upon future improvement in the gold and silver markets and the demand for the coin(s) as collectibles. Many of these coins never increase in value. We will address this issue in more detail, but for now let's look at some of these special coins sold directly from the Mint to the public.

Coins that are sold directly from the U.S. Mint are similar to the coins sold through the authorized distribution network. The main difference is that the U.S. Mint coins are in a higher grade or have a better finish to them. Let's look at some and you will get a sense of what I am speaking about.

This picture shown below is of a 1oz Silver Eagle in a "proof" state. If you read the description below, next to the coin, you see the fancy language the Mint uses: "frosted", "sharp relief", "brilliant", "mirror like", "cameo". It almost sounds like a movie star. It boils down to one thing: they are selling an American Eagle 1oz silver coin for $52.95 or about $32 above the spot silver price. So the question is: "Is it worth the price?" The answer is yes, if the price of silver goes way up, but no, if it does not. In other words this coin will never be in high demand because too many have been made, and the sale price is too high.

2014 American Eagle One Ounce Silver Proof Coin (ES1)

Mintage Limit: None
Product Limit: None
Household Order Limit: None
Available by Subscription: Yes

$52.95

Qty: 1   Add to Wish List   Add to Cart

Description | Program | Specifications | Purchasing & Shipping

The American Eagle Silver Proof Coin is a **collector version** of the official United States Mint American Eagle Silver Bullion Coin. Each coin contains one ounce of .999 fine silver. United States Mint proof coins are extraordinarily brilliant, with sharp relief and a mirror-like background. Their frosted, sculpted foregrounds give them a special cameo effect. Proof blanks are specially treated, polished and cleaned to ensure high-quality strikes. Each coin also bears the "W" mint mark reflecting its striking at the United States Mint facility at West Point. Each coin is packaged in a blue velvet, satin-lined presentation case

Like 105   Tweet 4   Pin it   Email   Print

Let's look at another example. Here is a proof set containing a fancy holder and some 90% silver coins. The price of $53.95 for 14 coins seems very high, and the fact that so many are available, leads me to believe that you will have a really hard time making your investment back (assuming you purchase for investment purposes). If you are a collector, then price is not an issue.

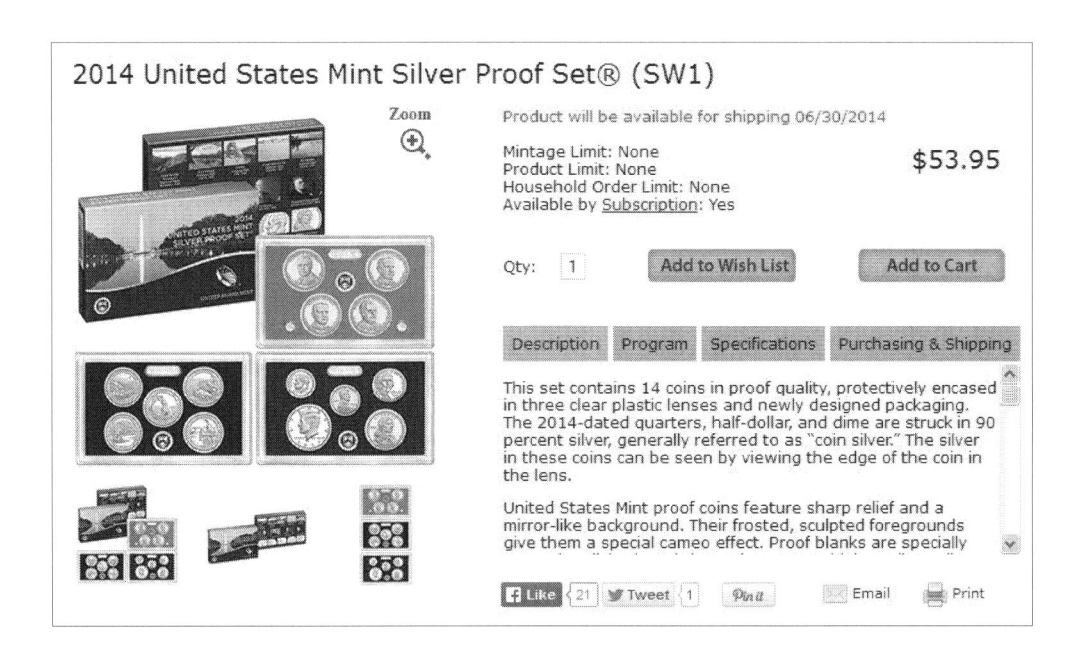

2014 United States Mint Silver Proof Set® (SW1)

Zoom

Product will be available for shipping 06/30/2014

Mintage Limit: None
Product Limit: None
Household Order Limit: None
Available by Subscription: Yes

$53.95

Qty: 1   Add to Wish List   Add to Cart

Description | Program | Specifications | Purchasing & Shipping

This set contains 14 coins in proof quality, protectively encased in three clear plastic lenses and newly designed packaging. The 2014-dated quarters, half-dollar, and dime are struck in 90 percent silver, generally referred to as "coin silver." The silver in these coins can be seen by viewing the edge of the coin in the lens.

United States Mint proof coins feature sharp relief and a mirror-like background. Their frosted, sculpted foregrounds give them a special cameo effect. Proof blanks are specially

Like 21   Tweet 1   Pin it   Email   Print

Another example is of interest. First, the price of $154.95 for 5 ounces of silver is not bad. Suppose the price of silver goes up to $30 per ounce, then you at least break even. But what I want to point out to you, and this example is dramatically different from the coins we looked at before, is the low mintage figure of 30,000. This means that only 30,000 of these 5 ounce uncirculated coins were made. In the grand scheme of things this is a very low figure. Again, the future value of this coin is hard to predict, but the 5 ounces of silver and low mintage adds to the possibility that it may increase in value.

High grade versions of this coin have sold for as much as $350 each. If people are paying these prices as part of an investment strategy, they may be kidding themselves.

Another coin, and one similar to what we saw before, is a one ounce gold proof American Buffalo selling for $1,590 (about $400 over the spot price of gold). The special finish on the coin and attractive holder is what the Mint wants you to believe justifies the added dollar value. Is it hype? Or is it a great investment? You decide.

2014 American Buffalo One Ounce Gold Proof Coin (BP5)

Zoom

Mintage Limit: None
Product Limit: None
Household Order Limit: None
Available by Subscription: No

$1,590.00

Qty: 1   Add to Wish List   Add to Cart

Description | Program | Specifications | Purchasing & Shipping

The American Buffalo One Ounce Gold Proof Coin is the first 24-karat gold proof coin ever struck by the United States Mint and is the collector version of the official United States Mint American Buffalo Gold Bullion Coin. Containing one ounce of .9999 fine 24-karat gold, these lustrous coins are among the world's purest gold coins. Each coin is presented in an elegant hardwood box with a matte finish and a leather-like inset. It is accompanied by a certificate of authenticity.

Like 43 | Tweet 0 | Pin It | Email | Print

Let's look at another coin type that many of the authorized distributors that we mentioned sell, and one that is not available from the Mint because it is so old: the pre-1933 gold coins that the U.S. Mint once made for circulation. These coins are usually sold in a certified version but non certified ones are available. The reason I mention these coins is because many investors buy them as part of their investment portfolios or investment strategies. It is generally believed that the higher the grade or condition of the coin the more money it is worth. This topic will be examined in detail as the book unfolds but for now I want to review some very basic facts as they relate to these coins. Many investors buy these coins and are convinced that they have made a wise decision. This is not the case. Here are some examples of these coins as they appear on the APMEX web site:

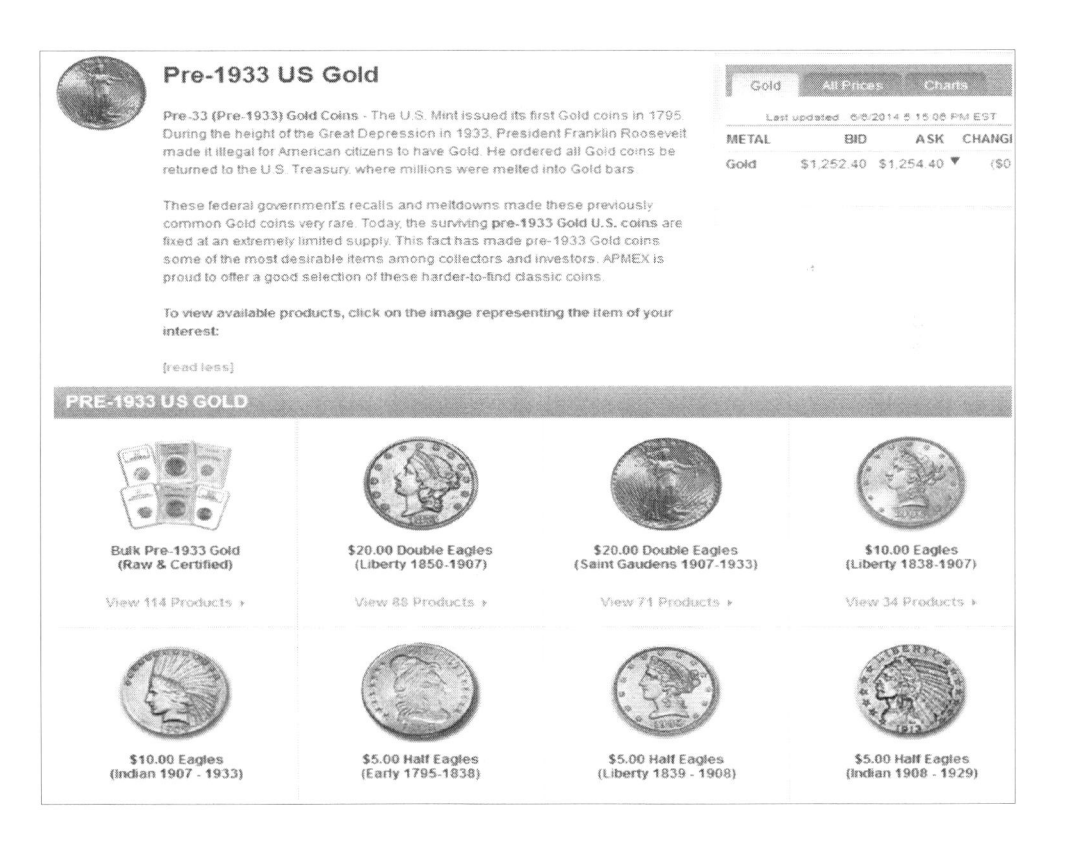

Pre-1933 US Gold

Pre-33 (Pre-1933) Gold Coins - The U.S. Mint issued its first Gold coins in 1795. During the height of the Great Depression in 1933, President Franklin Roosevelt made it illegal for American citizens to have Gold. He ordered all Gold coins be returned to the U.S. Treasury, where millions were melted into Gold bars.

These federal government's recalls and meltdowns made these previously common Gold coins very rare. Today, the surviving **pre-1933 Gold U.S. coins** are fixed at an extremely limited supply. This fact has made pre-1933 Gold coins some of the most desirable items among collectors and investors. APMEX is proud to offer a good selection of these harder-to-find classic coins.

To view available products, click on the image representing the item of your interest.

[read less]

METAL	BID	ASK	CHANGE
Gold	$1,252.40	$1,254.40 ▼	($0

Last updated 6/6/2014 5:15:05 PM EST

PRE-1933 US GOLD

Bulk Pre-1933 Gold (Raw & Certified)	$20.00 Double Eagles (Liberty 1850-1907)	$20.00 Double Eagles (Saint Gaudens 1907-1933)	$10.00 Eagles (Liberty 1838-1907)
View 114 Products ▶	View 88 Products ▶	View 71 Products ▶	View 34 Products ▶
$10.00 Eagles (Indian 1907 - 1933)	$5.00 Half Eagles (Early 1795-1838)	$5.00 Half Eagles (Liberty 1839 - 1908)	$5.00 Half Eagles (Indian 1908 - 1929)

Here is a listing from their web site showing a 1927, $20 Saint-Gaudens Gold Double Eagle that has been graded (certified) by PCGS. The asking price of $2,545 is over $1000 more than the actual gold value of the coin. Again, the high condition (MS66) seems to provide the seller with justification for the high price. This would be a good price if very few of these coins existed, unfortunately, this is not the case.

The same coin in a lesser grade and no encapsulation or grading is worth over $1000 less, according to APMEX.

Note the price of $1423 for a coin that is described as almost uncirculated:

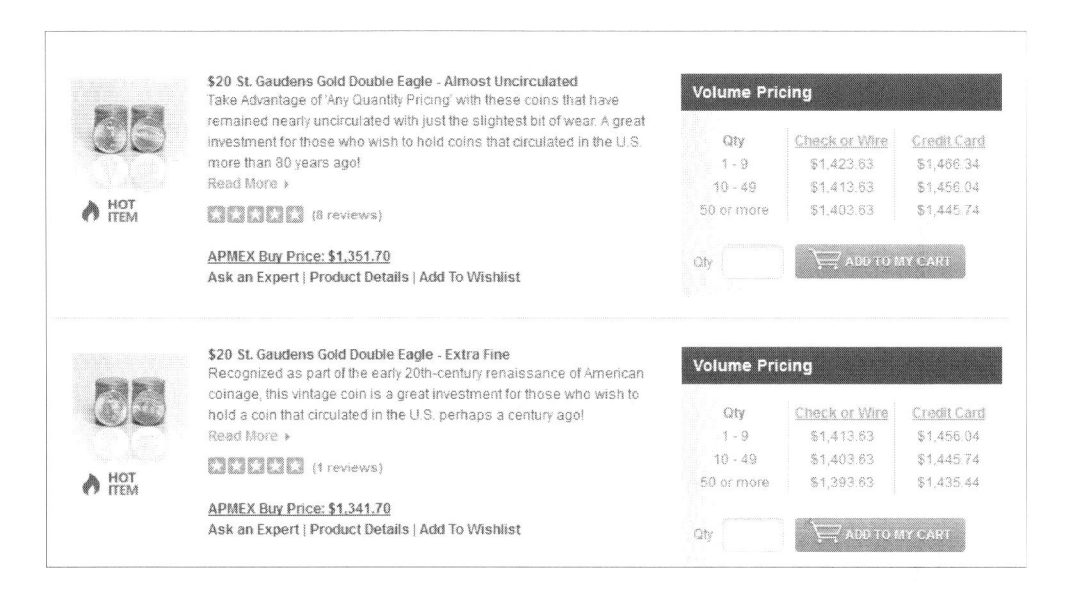

	$20 St. Gaudens Gold Double Eagle - Almost Uncirculated Take Advantage of 'Any Quantity Pricing' with these coins that have remained nearly uncirculated with just the slightest bit of wear. A great investment for those who wish to hold coins that circulated in the U.S. more than 80 years ago! Read More ▶ ★★★★★ (8 reviews) APMEX Buy Price: $1,351.70 Ask an Expert	Product Details	Add To Wishlist	**Volume Pricing**		
		Qty	Check or Wire	Credit Card
		1 - 9	$1,423.63	$1,466.34
		10 - 49	$1,413.63	$1,456.04
		50 or more	$1,403.63	$1,445.74
		Qty [ ]	ADD TO MY CART	
	$20 St. Gaudens Gold Double Eagle - Extra Fine Recognized as part of the early 20th-century renaissance of American coinage, this vintage coin is a great investment for those who wish to hold a coin that circulated in the U.S. perhaps a century ago! Read More ▶ ★★★★★ (1 reviews) APMEX Buy Price: $1,341.70 Ask an Expert	Product Details	Add To Wishlist	**Volume Pricing**		
		Qty	Check or Wire	Credit Card
		1 - 9	$1,413.63	$1,456.04
		10 - 49	$1,403.63	$1,445.74
		50 or more	$1,393.63	$1,435.44
		Qty [ ]	ADD TO MY CART	

In future chapters we will examine coin grading. You will become an expert on it, and now you can see how important it is as we mentioned in previous lectures. The higher the condition, the more valuable the coin can be. However, these pre-1933 gold coins are graded for the express purpose of driving the price up. Their actual value is not increased by grading them, but for uneducated buyers this technique works. (Pre-1933 Gold Double Eagles that we just looked at have been priced up because they have been certified and done so for questionable reasons.)

Please keep in mind that some coins that are in a high grade are very valuable because they are scarce, unlike these pre-1933 gold coins. So a high graded coin that is scarce is very valuable, if it is not scarce it is not valuable, no matter what the grade. Please note that there are a few exceptions to this statement, but for almost every situation you will come across this statement holds true.

Buying: Bars and Rounds

I want to examine a topic that often is ignored by gold and silver bullion investors. How is the price of gold and silver determined? It is strange that investors don't understand how the price of gold and silver is computed or ever ask about it! Let's look at this topic in depth, and let's look at where gold and silver bars come from and how they are made, as this will help you in the buying process.

A common misconception is that gold and silver pricing relates to supply and demand. The demand for gold and silver is greater than the supply each year. This is especially true for silver, and even though gold charts do not indicate that the supply is less than the demand, many experts argue to the contrary. This lack of supply does not push the price up higher and higher as you might expect it to. In fact, consider what happened in 2008:

"A common misconception amongst investors is that when the silver and gold price falls there is a larger amount of physical metal on the market, but this simply isn't true. It is extremely likely in the current environment to see the price of silver and gold fall and not be able to get a hold of physical silver. A great example of this was back in 2008. During this time silver fell to $9 an ounce and so many investors wanted to get in, but very few investors could buy the physical metal. Why? Because while paper silver was being sold investors holding physical metal were hoarding and were only buying more." (Lone Star Bullion)

The dynamics of the marketplace do not follow a logical theme at times, so keep this in mind. So how does the price get determined?

"Spot prices are determined by futures contracts. Futures contracts are traded in much the same way as stocks and other commodities. A future contract exchanges delivery of an item (gold and silver in this case) for a set price, with quantity and exact order details being specified from contract to contract.

When considering gold and silver, the most well-recognized platform is COMEX, which stands for commodities exchange. COMEX is based in New York, much like the majority of financial trading companies. COMEX is part of the NYMEX, the New York Mercantile Exchange. Gold and silver both find the bulk of their pricing determined by the trades that happen here. When futures contract trades take place in New York (and around the world), the prices of gold and silver adjust accordingly.

The reason futures contracts are used to set the spot prices is because the majority of the daily traded volume of gold and silver is done electronically as opposed to physically. Since more gold and silver are traded electronically via futures than physically delivered, the futures markets provide the most accurate, up to date prices for both gold and silver." This is the best description I have seen. Thanks to JM Bullion for this information.

Did you ever wonder where gold and silver bars or rounds come from? Well it may surprise you that anyone can produce gold and silver bars, and some sellers on eBay even produce their own. Their product is genuine. They get scrap gold and silver, melt it down and put their stamp on it. But if you are going to invest, you should be made aware of how the industry is set up.

Fortunately there is a system in place that helps protect buyers from fraud and guarantees high quality product. Please note: I am not saying that producers who are independent are in any way fraudulent, but there are better ways to buy product and be certain of what you are getting.

Accredited Gold and Silver Bar Manufacturers:

There are approximately 110 active gold refiners around the world whose relevant gold bars are accepted as "good delivery" by one or more of the major associations and exchanges involved in worldwide gold and silver trade. They also produce silver bars.

The **Good Delivery** specification is a set of rules issued by the London Bullion Market Association (LBMA) describing the physical characteristics of gold and silver bars used in settlement in the wholesale London bullion market. It also puts forth requirements for listing on the LBMA Good Delivery List of approved refineries.

These are the four major market associations that help determine gold and silver pricing and gold and silver accredited refiners:

- London Bullion Market Association (LBMA)
- CME Group – Market Contract (COMEX)
- Tokyo Commodity Exchange (TOCOM)
- Dubai Multi Commodities Centre (DMCC)

Here is a list of the newly accredited refiners – four are in the U.S.:

NEWLY-ACCREDITED GOLD REFINERS AND BRANDS

Association or Exchange	Refiner	Country	Refinery Location	Accreditation Date
LBMA	Heimerle + Meule GmbH	Germany	Pforzheim	3 – 6 – 2014
LBMA	MMTC-PAMP India Pvt Ltd	India	Mewat, Haryana	16 – 5 – 2014
LBMA	Kennecott Utah Copper LLC	USA	Magna, Utah	22 – 4 – 2014
LBMA	Republic Metals Corporation	USA	Miami, Florida	17 – 2 – 2014
LBMA	Nihon Material Co Ltd	Japan	Noda-City, Chiba Prefecture	19 – 12 – 2013
LBMA	Ohio Precious Metals LLC	USA	Jackson, Ohio	19 – 12 – 2013
LBMA	Sichuan Tianze Precious Metals Co Ltd	China	Chengdu	26 – 3 – 2013
LBMA	C. Hafner GmbH + Co. Ltd	Germany	Pforzheim	8 – 3 – 2013
DMCC	Al Etihad Gold LLC	UAE	Dubai	16 – 12 – 2012
COMEX	Ohio Precious Metals LLC	USA	Jackson, Ohio	4 – 9 – 2012
LBMA	PX Précinox SA	Switzerland	La Chaux-de-Fonds	24 – 1 – 2012
LBMA	Nadir Metal Rafineri A.S.	Turkey	Istanbul	8 – 12 – 2011
LBMA	Istanbul Gold Refinery	Turkey	Istanbul	8 – 9 – 2011
DMCC	L'azurde Company for Jewelry	Saudi Arabia	Riyadh	25 – 2 – 2011

Source: Associations and Exchanges

These refiners are very important. If you see product with their stamp on it you can be secure in knowing that the product is genuine (assuming you are buying from a reputable dealer). Reputable dealers carry product from these accredited refiners.

Here is a list of accredited refiners from the U.S.:

NORTH AMERICA					
Canada	CCR Refinery - Glencore Canada Corporation	Montreal East, Quebec	1955#	1974	-
Canada	Johnson Matthey Limited	Brampton, Ontario	1961	1974	1988
Canada	Royal Canadian Mint	Ottawa, Ontario	1934	1974	1988
USA	ASARCO Incorporated	Amarillo, Texas	-	1976	-
USA	Heraeus Incorporated	Newark, New Jersey	-	1989	-
USA	Johnson Matthey Gold & Silver Refining Inc	Salt Lake City, Utah	1989	1983	1994
USA	Kennecott Utah Copper Corporation	Magna, Utah	2014	2000	-
USA	Metalor Technologies USA Corporation	North Attleboro, Massachusetts	1991	1989	1992
USA	Ohio Precious Metals LLC	Jackson, Ohio	2013	2012	-
USA	Republic Metals Corporation	Miami, Florida	2014	-	-
USA	Sabin Metal Corporation	Scottsville, New York	-	1989	-

The sixth name on the list above "Johnson Matthey" is one of the better known refiners.

So what does all this mean? It is very simple. Buy a product that comes from an accredited refiner, and you know that you have purchased the genuine article. The chances of getting a fake are almost zero, the resale value will remain high and it will be easier to sell when the time comes because of brand recognition.

The image below shows a listing on the APMEX website picturing a Johnson Matthey product. Notice the Johnson Matthey logo, the serial number (A219232) and the buy back price of $19.78 on the bottom left. The selling price is $22.77 if you pay by check or wire and $23.45 via credit card. The spread is: $22.77 - $19.78 or $2.99. In percentage terms, this is 13%. So, the buy back means a 13% loss. Please keep this figure in mind. This is an important concept that will be examined when looking at ways to sell your products.

1 oz Johnson Matthey Silver Bar (New-JM Logo Reverse) .999 Fine

✓ IRA APPROVED
🔥 HOT ITEM

Silver Bid: $19.48 Ask: $19.58

VOLUME PRICING

Qty	Check or Wire	Credit Card
1 - 19	$22.77	$23.45
20 - 99	$22.27	$22.94
100 - 499	$21.77	$22.42
500 or more	$21.27	$21.91

Qty [   ] ADD TO MY CART

Add this product to your Wishlist

MARKET ALERT   PRICE ALERT

Mouse over image to zoom

Credit Card & Bank Wire orders ship NEXT business day with QuickShip™.

Share 25   Tweet 3

SATISFACTION guaranteed

We provide all our customers with a refund, return and/or exchange policy on everything we sell including all bullion and certified coins. If for any reason you have a problem, please feel free to call our offices. We will always do our best to accommodate you.

Average Customer Rating
★★★★★ 5.0

Buy Price: $19.78

Read 104 Reviews · Write a Review

Highly respected and recognized stamps and marks from refiners who are accredited from around the world are displayed below. Fake bars can have fake stamps and marks, please keep this in mind. But you can prevent this from happening when you deal with reputable companies like APMEX. Notice the Johnson Matthey stamp.

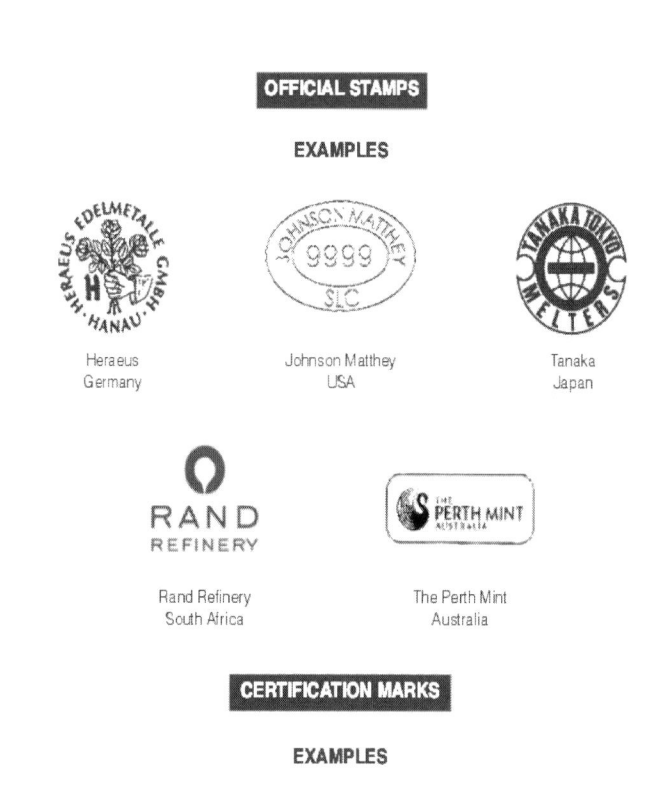

OFFICIAL STAMPS

EXAMPLES

Heraeus
Germany

Johnson Matthey
USA

Tanaka
Japan

Rand Refinery
South Africa

The Perth Mint
Australia

CERTIFICATION MARKS

EXAMPLES

Argor-Heraeus
Switzerland

Metalor
Switzerland

PAMP
Switzerland

Valcambi
Switzerland

Apart from standard bars, accredited refiners in Switzerland manufacture customized bars for many banks around the world.

Some important points to consider when buying gold and silver bars are displayed below. Reference is made to allocated and unallocated bars. What does this mean?

Allocated gold bars are held in your name. The weight and purity and serial number are recorded. Storage charges may apply.

Unallocated gold is an investment. The actual gold is held along with other people's gold. Storage charges may apply. Another form of unallocated gold is when the actual gold is used for other purposes but is guaranteed. When used for other purposes, the dealer can generate more income and wave storage charges. Your product is not kept in the form of a bar, but in name only.

PACKAGING AND CERTIFICATES

Some brands are sold by dealers in open or sealed packaging, and some with certificates issued by the refiner.

Where this is the case, you should retain the certificates and store the bars in their packaging – to facilitate their sale back to a dealer at some stage in the future.

BUYING AND HOLDING BARS IN OTHER COUNTRIES

If you intend to do this, it would be prudent to buy brands that are traded in both the foreign country and your own, in the event that you should wish to transfer them to your own country.

When transferring bars between countries, it can be borne in mind that restrictions, duties and taxes may apply.

BASIC CHECKLIST FOR NEW INVESTORS

Dealer	Does the dealer have a good reputation?
Brand	Is the bar manufactured by an accredited refiner?
	Is the bar well known in your country?
Pricing	What is the current gold price?
	What is the quoted price to buy the bar?
	Calculate the % premium (mark-up) of the bar above the current value of its fine gold content. What is the quoted price if you were to sell back the bar?
	Calculate the "spread" – the difference between the purchase and sell-back price of the bar.
Storage – if applicable	Are the bars allocated or unallocated?
	What are the storage costs?
Delivery – if applicable	What is the delivery and insurance cost?
Other Costs	Are there any other transaction-related costs? For example, taxes.

Did you ever wonder where gold is held when you buy it, and it is stored for you? There are many places where gold is stored. It can be held by the company that sells it or by the bank that sells it, but usually it is sent to a storage facility. Two of the biggest need mentioning, one is not open to the public:

The Federal Reserve Bank of New York holds the prize as the world's biggest known stockpile of gold. Some 550,000 glistening bars are buried deep into the bedrock of lower Manhattan. That's $203.3 billion worth of gold in a single place. Just 2% to 5% of it is owned by the U.S. government, though. The rest is owned by foreign countries.

Many gold sellers and dealers store their customers' gold in Delaware. All bullion stored with the Delaware Depository is fully allocated and held off-balance sheet, subject only to customers' instructions. This means that, at all times, customers are recognized as the sole owners and title holders of the bullion. Delaware Depository never lends, pledges or encumbers any bullion in its care. Delaware Depository is America's largest precious metals depository located outside New York City.

Selling: Gold, Silver, Coins

When it comes time to sell your precious metals, including gold and silver coins, there are many possibilities that can be imagined: the local pawn shop, local jewelry stores, ads online and in papers, local coin and gold shops, friends, dealers and others. So the 64 dollar question is: How do you get the best price for your product? It certainly does not hurt to price your product with local sellers, such as a jeweler. While local stores seldom pay much, if nothing else you will know that you have compared options, and you will not have to think about what might have been.

The rule of thumb is that online auctions, like eBay, and selling back to the dealer you purchased from, are probably going to be your best bet. Before you sell, it is advisable to ask yourself why you are selling now? This may seem like a strange question, but if you are selling just to raise some cash, but are not hard pressed for money, then it is wise to consider these factors:

Is the price of gold and or silver on the rise or decline? If it is on the decline then selling is not a good option, so you might want to wait. Buyers pay less when the price is going down.

If it is on the rise, then you can get a premium price. This is especially true with respect to coins. Buyers pay more during the upward swing. If it is on the rise and you do not need the money now, why not wait and see when it starts to plateau, then sell.

Another factor to consider is the amount of gold, silver or coins you have. I have noticed that you can get more money when you have a larger lot to sell, such as 50 silver coins vs 5 silver coins or 5oz of silver vs 20oz of silver. So you might want to wait until you buy more before you sell.

When it comes time to sell you may be surprised to learn that odd ball products are very hard to unload. Gold and silver bars and rounds from foreign countries and gold and silver coins from foreign countries are sometimes difficult to sell. (This does not apply to Canadian coins). Gold or silver from China or South Africa, even though it may be genuine, does not draw as much attention as American and Canadian sourced product and may get a lower price. Products without stamps and serial numbers on them can be problematic. Certification is an issue at times, especially with bigger bars.

With this in mind, you can see the benefit of buying from a reputable source. When purchasing from a reputable source do not buy odd ball products, stay with the name brands. Also keep in mind that gold and silver coins are easier to sell than gold and silver bars and rounds. Silver coins are easier to sell than gold coins. Do not sell your products to TV advertised companies that buy gold and silver. They pay on average 11% – 29% of the melt down value. The road shows that travel from town to town typically pays 40 cents on the dollar.

Coin shops and jewelers typically pay 50 - 70% of the actual value. In a previous chapter we mentioned that they sometimes buy close to spot to be competitive, but this is usually not the case. Again, it does not hurt to shop around. Remember price varies from store to store and town to town. The companies (authorized distributors) that I suggested earlier that you buy from, tell you their buy back price on their web site, so it is only logical to buy products that have high buy back prices. Typically they will pay very close to what you actually paid for the item, assuming that the price of gold or silver has not changed.

If in a big hurry and in need of immediate money, local shops will be your best bet. Compare prices and don't be influenced by their pressure tactics. If you walk into a store and they offer you what seems to be a good price, and exclaim that if you walk out the door the price walks with you, then run out of there as fast as you can and never go back. You do not need to be treated that way.

A gimmick that you need to be aware of occurs when some unethical local shops test your product using acid. They will tell you that even though it is stamped 14kt gold, for example, it is really 10kt. Unless you know what you have, and used the test we mentioned earlier, you will get cheated.

Another way to sell is through gold parties. This method yields poor results. A final way to sell that you might consider is auctioning. This method is usually the best way to sell, assuming you are not in a hurry.

There are many auctions sites online: eBay, Amazon, Etsy and coin sites. Over the past 15 years I have found that eBay is the easiest and most cost effective way to sell any form of gold or silver, especially gold and silver coins and rare coins and eBay yields the best results. If you do not have an eBay account, register for one, it is free. You will also need a PayPal account. You can register on eBay for a PayPal account, it is free (you will need a credit or debit card to put on file so you can set up your PayPal account). Use a debit or credit account that has little money in it. For example, I use my Wells Fargo debit card because I rarely have more than $100 in it. I do this to be on the safe side, but during the last 15 years I have never had a problem with eBay or PayPal.

If interested in learning more about eBay please visit my online course at this web site: www.udemy.com It is called: "Learn How Power Sellers Make Millions On eBay".

Listing an item on eBay is easy. Take some clear pictures and set a low starting price, say 99 cents, and watch as your item price goes up through biding. Silver and gold in any form usually always sells for at least spot, so don't worry about a low starting price. The low price attracts more bidders. Make sure you set your shipping fees high enough to cover your costs. Weigh your item and compute the charges and include insurance costs as well.

Using eBay is a very good option when:

- You cannot get a good price locally.
- Your supplier will not buy the item back, for whatever reason, or their price seems low.
- Your item has special appeal. For example, coins in very good condition that may sell for more than spot value.
- You have a rare jewelry item that you bought using our system to find gold and

silver.

- You have an object that has wide appeal, such as a silver pendant.
- You have junk silver coins (The term used to describe 90% silver coins and 40% silver coins). These do well on eBay and can often sell for more than spot.

A common question often asked with respect to eBay is: "What does it cost to sell on their site?" Remember a few chapters back when I said pay close attention to the 13% buy back loss with respect to your purchase from a dealer. Well it is strange, but eBay costs are roughly 13% also. The flat eBay fee is 10% of the total sale including shipping, plus 30 cents for PayPal and 2.9% of the entire sale, also for PayPal. Add it up and it comes out to roughly 13%. Please note that volume sellers and sellers with special status pay lower fees, and there is a per item fee cap of $250.

Remember: You will always get at least spot price for any form of gold or silver that you sell on eBay. I want to mention again that junk silver (90% silver coins and 40% silver coins) sometimes sells for more than spot, especially if the coins you are selling are in a high grade. I find my junk silver by coin roll hunting, but you can actually buy it. With regard to junk silver, you can purchase it from many vendors that I listed and some not listed. It usually sells for $3 over spot and although it is not a good silver investment if you have to pay too much for it, it can serve a useful purpose if you are collecting coins and are looking for pre-1965 dates: dimes, quarters or halves.

If you decide to buy some, make sure you get a variety of denominations. Some vendors only send a bunch of dimes even though they advertise a variety of coins, so ask them what you will be getting!

In the coin collecting chapters to follow these topics will be addressed again. Bottom line, eBay is probably the fastest and easiest way to sell you silver and gold coins, silver and gold bars and rounds, and you will always get spot value and maybe more. I have sold silver coins for more than spot value on many occasions. You can sometimes make up for the eBay and PayPal fees by charging extra for shipping, but be careful, neither eBay nor the buyers like this tactic.

For purposes of review and to make a key point, I want to mention that we took a look at bullion and bullion coins and jewelry, how to find them, sell them, and ways to buy them safely. We mentioned that pre-1933 gold coins are not a good investment and we will examine this in more detail again. Other types of gold and silver that can be purchased, or what I like to call, paper versions of precious metals need to be looked at. As this book unfolds we will come back to coins again and cover topics not mentioned earlier. A key point I want to make: We have intentionally not spoken about "rare coins" because this information is better explained when we cover the topic of coin collecting. Investing in "rare coins" is one of the most important subjects we will discuss, and even though these coins are typically not made of gold or silver, they yield very high returns. In fact, when it comes to investing, some believe, and the data backs this, that "rare coins" as an asset class, have no equal.

ETFs, Mutual Funds, Gold Accounts & More

Investing in precious metals and coins (gold and silver and rare coins) represents an enormous set of topics. The objective here is to shed light on these topics to help you make better financial decisions. We want you to get good results. The only way this can be done is by comparing all the options, looking at the pros and cons, and examining the dollar results or return on investment. For some, one type of investment may make sense, and for others, this same strategy might not be practical, so in this sense there is no right or wrong. The potential for a favorable outcome in increased when given good information.

I have noticed over the years that precious metal and coin investors are highly motivated and will buy with fervor. Yet, very few of them have any practical sense with respect to why they are making certain decisions. And it gets worse, they often do not compare the different options. In other words, they are investing with blinders on and buying based upon habit and convenience.

The classic argument often used as a basis for precious metal investing is as follows:

Concerns over the growing U.S. deficit, the devaluation of the U.S. dollar, giant amounts of money being poured into the economy, inflation (just check your food purchases lately) and troubling world events encourage gold and silver investing (including coins), which is perceived to be a hedge against inflation and provide a safe alternative to other investment options and a blanket of protection if the economy fails. In recent years the dramatic rise in the price of gold has helped fuel this fire and of course investors hope to make money as the price of coins and precious metals goes up over time.

With this in mind, let's take a look at the many different investment opportunities relating to the precious metal marketplace. For now just a brief review. By doing so it will establish a baseline or foundation, so you can get a feel for the many choices. We will look at the pros and cons of each as we delve into this subject in more detail.

Most investors have never considered the rate of return as it pertains to assorted investment types, particularly their own. Buyers of gold and silver bullion seem to think that as long as the price goes up over time, they come out ahead. This logic is very flawed, and I will show you why.

But first let's explain what "rate of return" is and how it is computed: The rate of return is the increase or decrease percentage in value of an investment over time, usually a year.

The **return** over a single period is:

$$r = \frac{V_f - V_i}{V_i}$$

Where:

V_f = Final value, including dividends and interest

V_i = Initial value

For example, if you hold 100 shares, with starting price of $10, then the starting value is 100 x $10 = $1,000. If you then collect 0.50 per share in cash dividends, and the ending share price is $9.80, then at the end you have 100 x 0.50 = $50 in cash, plus 100 x $9.80 = $980 in shares, totaling a final value of $1,030. The change in value is $1,030 - $1,000 = $30, so the return is 30 / 1,000 = 3%.

Another topic that should be considered is taxation as it relates to precious metal gains. I want to mention it because there is a big misconception that floats around the precious metal marketplace: **Precious metal gains are taxed at 28%!**

I am not sure why everyone thinks this is true. The reality is that precious metal gains can be taxed at 28%. It depends upon your tax rate. The tax rate is determined by your annual income.

Long term gains, bought one year, sold another year, are taxed at 28% if you are in the 28% tax bracket (figures shown apply to 2013). If your income falls within these ranges, then your precious metal gains are taxed at 28%. Otherwise your rate can be much lower than 28%, if you make less than these amounts.

You are in the 28% tax bracket if you earn:

- $146,400 – $223,050 (Married filing jointly)
- $87,860 – $183,250 (Single)

Okay, now that we have covered some basic concepts, namely "rate of return" and "28% taxation", let's take a brief look at advantageous precious metal investments. After a brief overview, we will go into depth and discover their potential by evaluating the pros and cons of each.

ETFs are one way to invest in gold and silver and are very popular these days. What is an ETF? It is an exchange-traded fund. It is an investment fund traded on stock exchanges, much like stocks. An ETF holds assets such as stocks, commodities, or bonds, and trades close to its net asset value over the course of the trading day. Most ETFs track an index, such as a stock index or bond index. ETFs may be attractive as investments because of their low costs, tax efficiency, and stock-like features. ETFs are the most popular type of exchange traded product.

Only authorized participants, which are large broker dealers that have entered into agreements with the ETF's distributor, actually buy or sell shares of an ETF directly from or to the ETF, and then only in creation units, which are large blocks of tens of thousands of ETF shares, usually exchanged in-kind with baskets of the underlying securities.

There are precious metal ETFs. For example, there are many gold ETFs. Remember gold ETFs allow you to own an interest in physical gold or some part of the gold industry. You never actually own the physical gold. Some ETFs have as their only asset gold bullion. One of them that is widely known is SPDR gold shares (GLD). The image below looks at it in closer detail. A gold exchange traded fund then consists of only one principle asset, gold. However, the fund itself may consist of gold derivative contracts that are backed by gold. You do not actually own any gold. Even when you redeem a gold ETF, you do not receive the precious metal in any form. Instead, an investor receives the cash equivalent. Notice the dollar figure in the lower right corner showing that this fund has over 32 billion dollars invested in it.

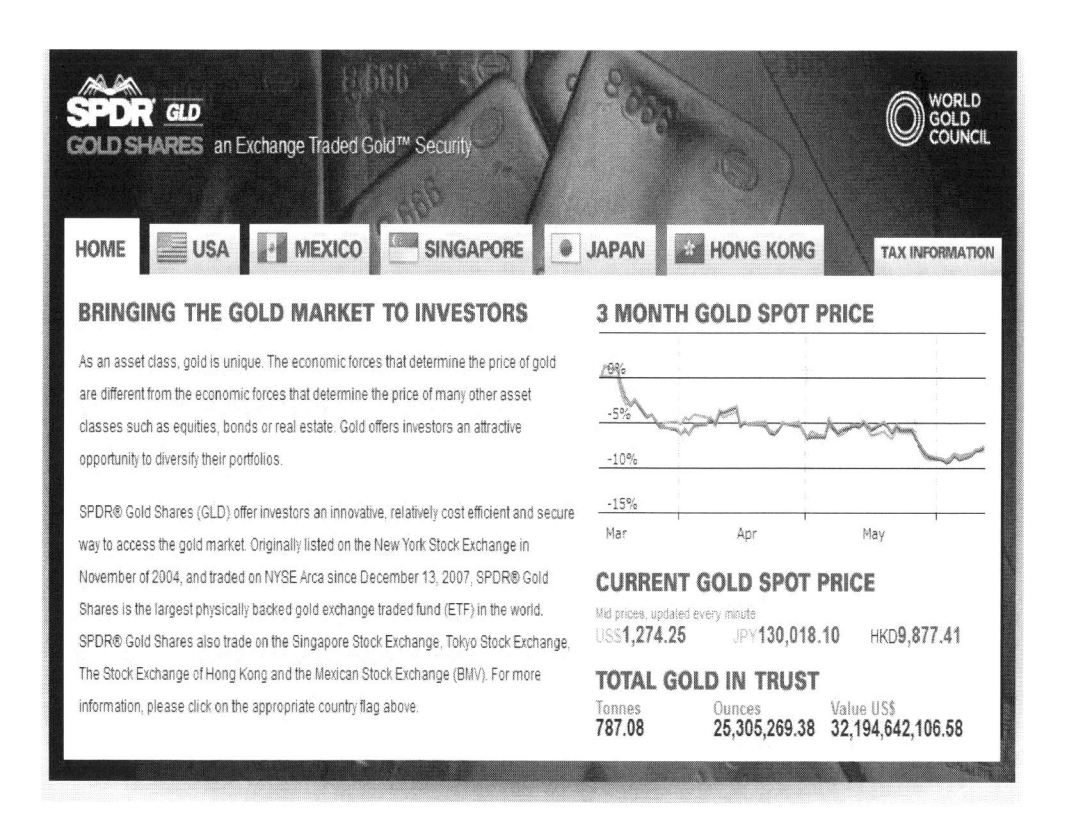

SPDR GLD GOLD SHARES an Exchange Traded Gold™ Security

WORLD GOLD COUNCIL

HOME | USA | MEXICO | SINGAPORE | JAPAN | HONG KONG | TAX INFORMATION

BRINGING THE GOLD MARKET TO INVESTORS

As an asset class, gold is unique. The economic forces that determine the price of gold are different from the economic forces that determine the price of many other asset classes such as equities, bonds or real estate. Gold offers investors an attractive opportunity to diversify their portfolios.

SPDR® Gold Shares (GLD) offer investors an innovative, relatively cost efficient and secure way to access the gold market. Originally listed on the New York Stock Exchange in November of 2004, and traded on NYSE Arca since December 13, 2007, SPDR® Gold Shares is the largest physically backed gold exchange traded fund (ETF) in the world. SPDR® Gold Shares also trade on the Singapore Stock Exchange, Tokyo Stock Exchange, The Stock Exchange of Hong Kong and the Mexican Stock Exchange (BMV). For more information, please click on the appropriate country flag above.

3 MONTH GOLD SPOT PRICE

CURRENT GOLD SPOT PRICE
Mid prices, updated every minute
US$1,274.25   JPY130,018.10   HKD9,877.41

TOTAL GOLD IN TRUST
Tonnes	Ounces	Value US$
787.08	25,305,269.38	32,194,642,106.58

The performance of ETFs and many other investment types can be tracked using a great on line tool. It is provided by U.S. News and World Report in the form of a real time interactive listing and chart display. Here is the link to gold related ETFs:

http://money.usnews.com/funds/etfs/rankings/gold-oriented-funds

When you click on this link, up pops a ranked list (displayed on the next page). Notice that the SPDR fund we mentioned is ranked #3. These rankings change all the time. What is so nice about this web site is that it provides detailed information about each fund and allows you to compare each fund to many other funds in other categories. Notice how the SPDR fund is up 4.56 % year to date. We can go in and look at any time period and go back many years to see how it has performed. You can even compare any fund, such as this ETF, to the S& P 500 and Dow Jones Industrial Average on the same chart. This way you can see how your ETF compares to a broad index. You can also compare the ETF to a mutual fund and other asset types using the same chart.

Best Fit Gold Oriented Funds

These ETFs invest in either physical gold or futures contracts to track the spot price of the precious yellow metal.

All ranked ETFs meet our Best Fit criteria.

BEST ETFS U.S. News RANKINGS

#1 iShares COMEX Gold Trust (IAU)

Asset Class: Commodity

$12.35 (0.04%)   Previous Close: $12.22
Performance (YTD): 4.54%   Avg. Volume: 3,093,518
Fees: 0.25%   Market Cap: $6.59B

Benchmark: Gold Trust

See all details for IAU »

#2 PowerShares DB Gold Fund (DGL)

Asset Class: Commodity

$42.57 (0.02%)   Previous Close: $42.15
Performance (YTD): 4.41%   Avg. Volume: 13,893
Fees: 0.50%   Market Cap: $136.29M

Benchmark: Deutsche Bank Liquid Commodity Index-Optimum Yield Gold Excess Return Index

See all details for DGL »

#3 SPDR Gold Shares (GLD)

Asset Class: Commodity

$122.56 (0.07%)   Previous Close: $121.39
Performance (YTD): 4.56%   Avg. Volume: 8,329,403
Fees: 0.40%   Market Cap: $31.92B

Benchmark: Gold bullion

The # 1 rated Gold ETF Fund on the image above is iShares (IAU). So in order to find out why, let's look at the criteria used to evaluate and rank these funds. The graph below shows the five year performance and it is up from 2010. The price per share is $12.23. It is rated on the best fit scoreboard below. The fund description is also listed below. The criteria used to identify best fit funds is shown after this image below.

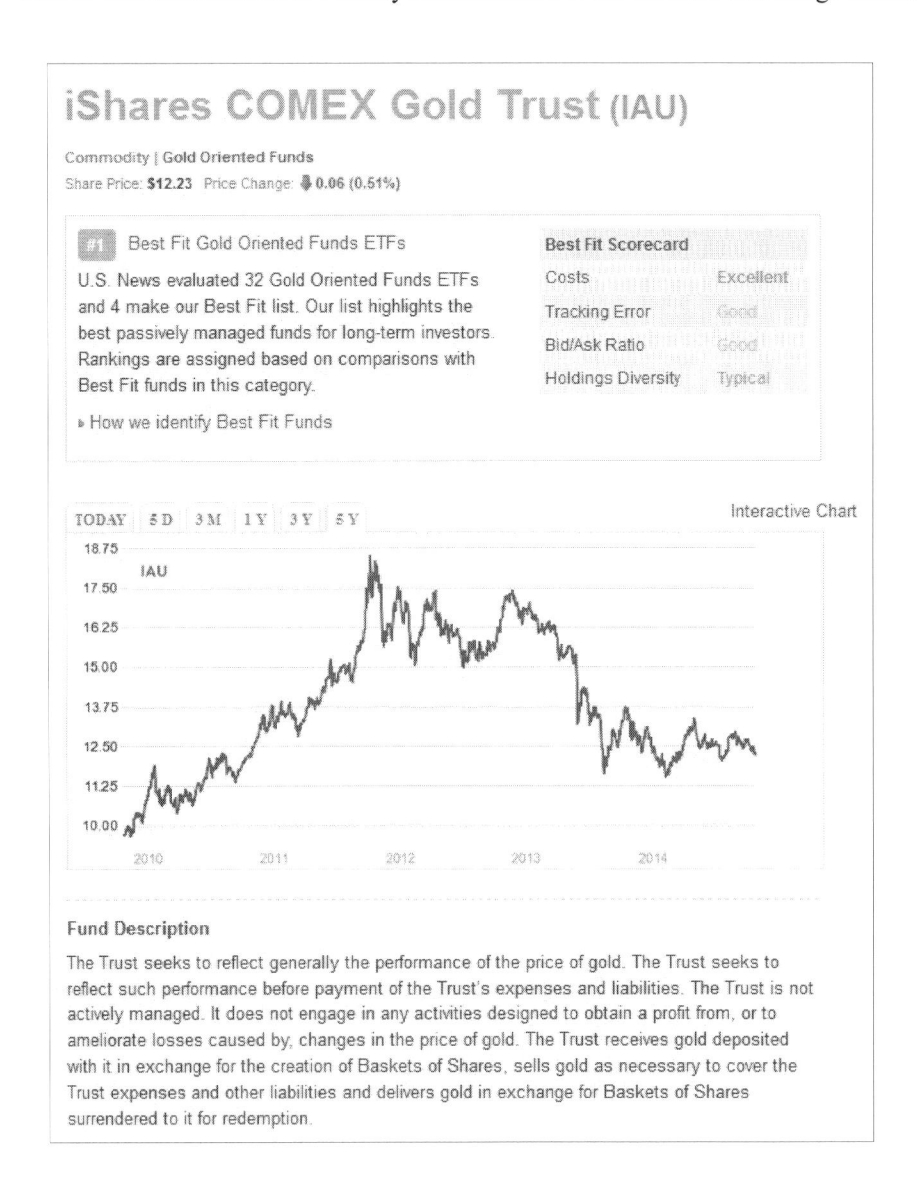

iShares COMEX Gold Trust (IAU)

Commodity | Gold Oriented Funds
Share Price: **$12.23**   Price Change: ↓ 0.06 (0.51%)

#1 Best Fit Gold Oriented Funds ETFs

U.S. News evaluated 32 Gold Oriented Funds ETFs and 4 make our Best Fit list. Our list highlights the best passively managed funds for long-term investors. Rankings are assigned based on comparisons with Best Fit funds in this category.

▸ How we identify Best Fit Funds

Best Fit Scorecard

Costs	Excellent
Tracking Error	Good
Bid/Ask Ratio	Good
Holdings Diversity	Typical

Interactive Chart

Fund Description

The Trust seeks to reflect generally the performance of the price of gold. The Trust seeks to reflect such performance before payment of the Trust's expenses and liabilities. The Trust is not actively managed. It does not engage in any activities designed to obtain a profit from, or to ameliorate losses caused by, changes in the price of gold. The Trust receives gold deposited with it in exchange for the creation of Baskets of Shares, sells gold as necessary to cover the Trust expenses and other liabilities and delivers gold in exchange for Baskets of Shares surrendered to it for redemption.

Fund Snapshot UPDATED 09.05.2014			
Previous Close	$12.29	Expense Ratio	0.25%
YTD Return	⬆ 5.22%	Avg. 30-Day Volume	1,913,384
1-Year Return	⬇ 8.7%	Market Cap	$6.73B
Bid	$12.28	Shares Outstanding	548,500,000
Ask	$12.29	Dividends	$0.00

"Best Fit funds are ranked by an overall score calculated from four component measures: a fund's expense ratio, tracking error, bid/ask ratio, and diversification. For each component measure, funds receive a score between 0 and 100, based on their performance on that measure in comparison to other funds. The top-scoring fund within a given measure (lowest expense ratio, for example) receives a score of 100 for that measure. The four component scores are then weighted (see below) to create an overall score. The overall score defines a fund's rank within its category.

Components measures and their weightings:

- Expense Ratio (30%)
- Tracking Error (30%)
- Bid/Ask Ratio (20%)
- Diversification (20%)

Funds without data for the components outlined above are excluded from ranking.

About the Component Measures

1. Expense Ratio

What is it? Expense ratio is the percentage of fund assets a fund manager may withdraw each year to pay for operating expenses.

Why is it important? Lower expense ratios mean better returns for comparable ETFs.

How is it measured? Data is for a fund's total annual expense ratio.

2. Tracking Error

What is it? Tracking error is a measure of the volatility of excess returns relative to a benchmark. Excess returns are the investment's return in excess of its primary benchmark, which is based on a broad asset class. The tracking error is calculated for the past six-month period. Benchmark indices are provided by Morningstar.

Why is it important? Tracking error tells investors whether the ETF they've purchased is actually following the performance of its underlying index.

How is it measured? Tracking error is calculated by a linear regression of the ETF's daily net asset value returns on the underlying index's daily total returns for the past six months.

3. Bid/Ask Ratio

What is it? The bid/ask ratio measures the spreads between bid and ask prices among various ETFs. It is calculated by dividing the bid price minus the ask price (the "spread") for a fund by the mid price between the bid and ask prices.

Why is it important? Bid/ask spreads can measure "hidden" transaction costs for an ETF, as well as liquidity (higher bid-ask spreads imply lower liquidity).

How is it measured? The bid/ask measure is calculated daily and based on a 30-day average of closing bid/ask spreads. Narrower spreads receive higher scores.

4. Diversification

What is it? Diversification in a fund is determined by two variables: the relative weight of the 10 largest holdings in a fund and the fund's turnover ratio, which is the rate at which a fund replaces its holdings on an annual basis.

Why is it important? A greater diversity of weightings of a fund's constituents provides better diversification when comparing funds, and reduces the likelihood of a few large holdings dragging down a fund's overall performance. At the same time, higher fund turnover can lead to higher costs for owning a fund, and turnover in index funds should generally be low, which is why we've included turnover in our fund rankings. While this measure gives a slight edge to equity funds, its lower weighting in the overall rank means low costs and great index tracking ability will be the largest determinants of fund rank.

How is it measured? There are two components used to measure diversification: the overall weight of the fund's 10 largest holdings and the published annual turnover ratio for each fund. Each component receives a 10 percent weighting to determine the total 20 percent weighting for diversification in the overall rank."

Let's look at some silver ETFs: This link to a silver ETF database has a multitude of useful information:

http://etfdb.com/type/commodity/precious-metals/silver-etfs/#overview

The next image shows an overview of some of them, and the following image shows their performance over time:

ETF Overview

This is a list of all of the Silver ETFs traded in the USA which are currently tagged by ETF Database. Please note that the list may not contain newly issued ETFs. If you're looking for a more simplified way to browse and compare ETFs, you may want to visit our ETFdb Categories, which categorize every ETF in a single "best fit" category.

* Assets in thousands of U.S. Dollars. Assets and Average Volume as of 06/12/2014

Symbol	Name	Price	Change	Assets *	Avg Vol	YTD
SLV	iShares Silver Trust	$18.90	+0.75%	$6,367,565	5,843,065	+0.96%
AGQ	ProShares Ultra Silver	$62.59	+1.49%	$449,470	258,688	-0.94%
SIVR	ETFS Silver Trust	$19.39	+0.52%	$361,372	84,734	+0.99%
USLV	VelocityShares 3x Long Silver ETN linked to the S&P GSCI Silver Index	$43.60	+1.99%	$162,221	244,043	-3.56%
ZSL	ProShares UltraShort Silver	$83.49	-0.98%	$53,351	69,987	-7.43%
DBS	PowerShares DB Silver Fund	$32.54	+0.87%	$31,670	4,389	+0.62%
DSLV	VelocityShares 3x Inverse Silver ETN linked to S&P GSCI Silver Inverse Index	$46.36	-1.90%	$15,764	63,320	-13.39%
USV	UBS E-TRACS CMCI Silver Total Return ETN	$26.87	+1.55%	$10,716	15,763	+0.37%
SLVO	Credit Suisse Silver Shares Covered Call ETN	$15.16	+0.73%	$N/A	38,833	-1.81%

This image shows rate of return over time. Notice the 23.99% gain for the Silver Trust over 5 years and the negative return of -94.37 % for the UltraShort Silver ETF over the same time period:

As of 06/12/2014.

ETF Returns

This page includes historical return information for all Silver ETFs listed on U.S. exchanges that are currently tracked by ETF Database.

Symbol	Name	1 Week	4 Week	YTD	1 Year	3 Year	5 Year
SLV	Silver Trust	+2.74%	+0.11%	+0.27%	-10.75%	-46.78%	+23.99%
AGQ	Ultra Silver	+5.53%	+0.19%	-2.17%	-27.21%	-82.90%	-40.95%
SIVR	Physical Silver Shares	+2.88%	+0.26%	+0.47%	-10.36%	-46.36%	n/a
USLV	3x Long Silver ETN	+8.42%	+0.28%	-5.44%	-47.29%	n/a	n/a
ZSL	UltraShort Silver	-4.92%	-1.35%	-6.51%	-0.90%	-5.36%	-94.37%
DBS	DB Silver Fund	+2.71%	+0.31%	-0.09%	-12.17%	-49.03%	+16.97%
DSLV	3x Inverse Silver ETN	-8.38%	-1.71%	-11.86%	-20.09%	n/a	n/a
USV	E-TRACS UBS Bloomberg CMCI Silver ETN	+1.97%	-0.41%	-1.16%	-12.70%	-48.92%	+23.13%
SLVO	Silver Shares Covered Call ETN	+2.31%	+0.54%	+4.21%	-5.16%	n/a	n/a

As you can see there is high risk here, and like gold ETFs some have done very well and others very poorly. You can see the value of these web sites, but it clearly opens the door for sound investment advice.

Another investment that is often compared to ETFs are mutual funds. There are hundreds of mutual funds in many investment categories. Many of these funds are focused upon precious metals, just as some ETFs are. I want to take a minute and point out a web site that is indispensable. It has many useful features, including an extensive investment dictionary and many fine articles:

www.investopedia.com

This site provides a good definition and explanation of what a mutual fund is:

Definition of 'Mutual Fund'

An investment vehicle that is made up of a pool of funds collected from many investors for the purpose of investing in securities such as stocks, bonds, money market instruments and similar assets. Mutual funds are operated by money managers, who invest the fund's capital and attempt to produce capital gains and income for the fund's investors. A mutual fund's portfolio is structured and maintained to match the investment objectives stated in its prospectus.

Investopedia explains 'Mutual Fund'

One of the main advantages of mutual funds is that they give small investors access to professionally managed, diversified portfolios of equities, bonds and other securities, which would be quite difficult (if not impossible) to create with a small amount of capital. Each shareholder participates proportionally in the gain or loss of the fund. Mutual fund units, or shares, are issued and can typically be purchased or redeemed as needed at the fund's current net asset value (NAV) per share, which is sometimes expressed as NAVPS.

Net asset value (NAV) is significant only for open-end mutual funds. It is a simple calculation. Just take the current market value of the fund's net assets (securities held by the fund minus any liabilities) and divide by the number of shares outstanding. Thus, if a fund has total net assets of $50 million and there are one million shares of the fund, then the NAV is $50 per share (fund liabilities include items such as fees owed to investment managers).

For open-end mutual funds, NAV is a useful determinant for tracing share price movements. However, it is not useful for evaluating overall fund performance. This is because mutual funds are required by law to distribute at least 90% of their realized capital gains and dividend income to investors each year. When a fund pays investors the required distribution, its NAV is reduced by the amount of the distribution. Investors tracking only NAV may become concerned about the drop, but in fact, the net value of their investment is unchanged; the reduction in NAV is offset by the amount of distribution they have been paid.

The most important thing to keep in mind is that NAVs change daily and are not a good indicator of actual performance because of the impact yearly distributions have on NAV (it also makes mutual funds hard to track).

U.S. News and World Report lists its 18 best Precious Metal Mutual Funds. Here is the link:

http://money.usnews.com/funds/mutual-funds/rankings/equity-precious-metals

The next image shows some of this information. Notice how the performance for the past year for the top four rated precious metal mutual funds is in negative territory. But this is misleading. You have to look closer to see the actual performance over a bigger time span.

Equity Precious Metals

Precious metals portfolios focus on mining stocks, though some do own small amounts of gold bullion. Most portfolios concentrate on gold-mining stocks, but some have significant exposure to silver-, platinum-, and base-metal-mining stocks as well. Precious-metals companies are typically based in North America, Australia, or South Africa. Morningstar®

BEST MUTUAL FUNDS U.S.News RATINGS

#1 Vanguard Precious Metals and Mining Fund (VGPMX)

Performance (1-yr.): ▼ 10.18%
Performance (1-mo.): ▼ 0.45%

Expenses: 0.26%
Total Assets: $2.54B

See all details for VGPMX »

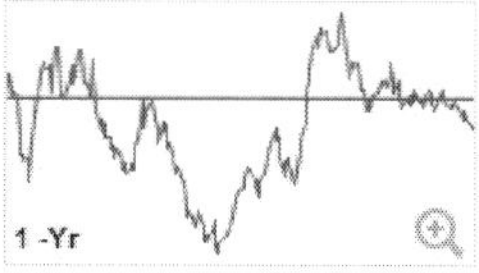

#2 Tocqueville Gold Fund (TGLDX)

Performance (1-yr.): ▼ 9.95%
Performance (1-mo.): ▲ 3.28%

Expenses: 1.35%
Total Assets: $1.37B

See all details for TGLDX »

#3 First Eagle Gold Fund (SGGDX)

Performance (1-yr.): ▼ 14.14%
Performance (1-mo.): ▲ 2.85%

Expenses: 1.25%
Total Assets: $1.35B

See all details for SGGDX »

#4 OCM Gold Fund (OCMGX)

Performance (1-yr.): ▼ 9.24%
Performance (1-mo.): ▲ 2.90%

Expenses: 2.22%
Total Assets: $74.83M

See all details for OCMGX »

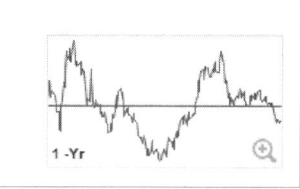

What is so nice about this link to the U.S. New and World Report web site are the real time charts that show daily performance and also cover many time periods. The #1 rated mutual precious metal fund shown below, reveals an upward trend (year to date it's up 6.7%). **The 10 year return is 5.9%.** The ranking is the result of extensive analysis from the investment industry's best firms.

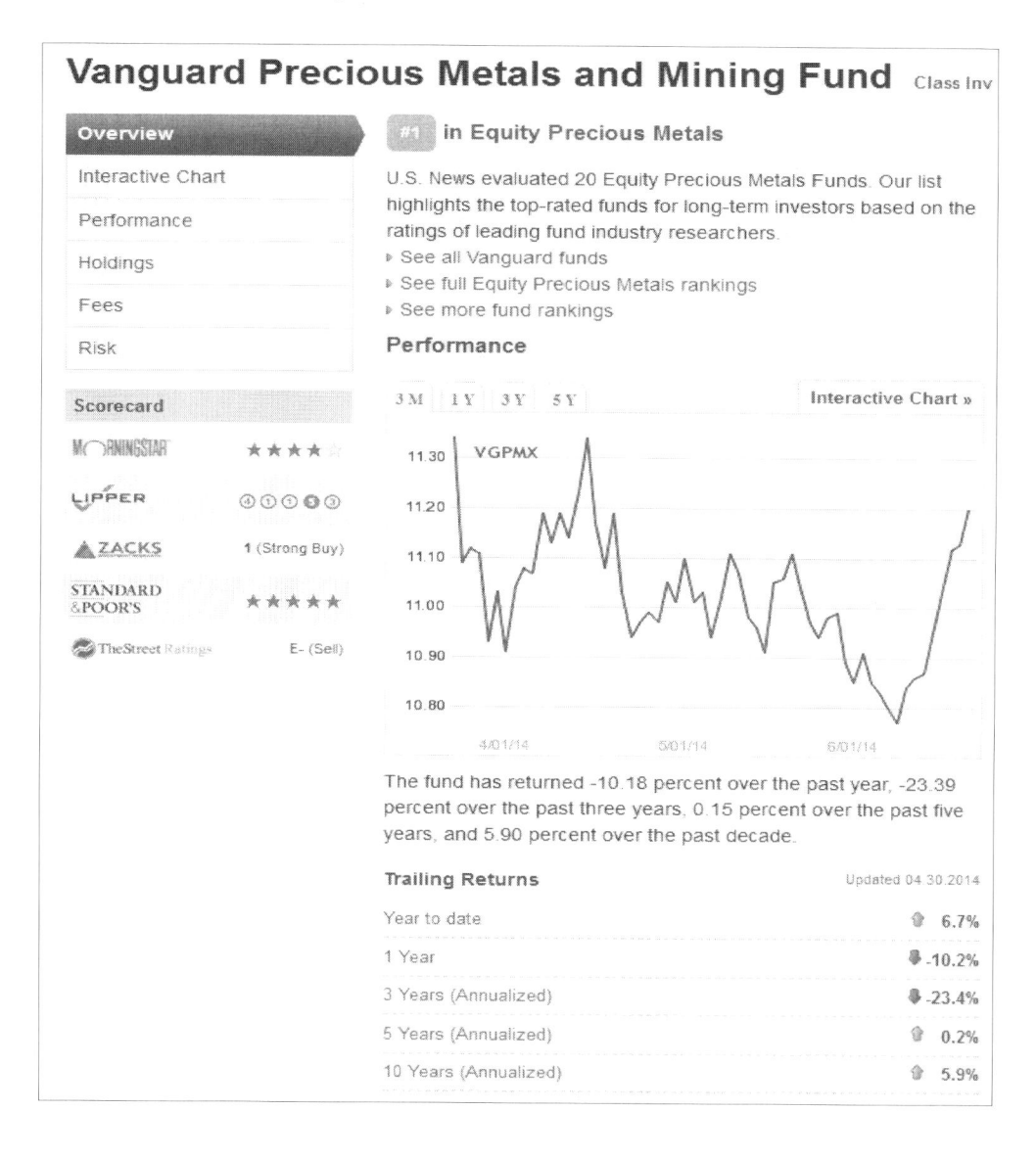

Vanguard Precious Metals and Mining Fund — Class Inv

#1 in Equity Precious Metals

U.S. News evaluated 20 Equity Precious Metals Funds. Our list highlights the top-rated funds for long-term investors based on the ratings of leading fund industry researchers.
- See all Vanguard funds
- See full Equity Precious Metals rankings
- See more fund rankings

Overview
- Interactive Chart
- Performance
- Holdings
- Fees
- Risk

Scorecard

MORNINGSTAR	★★★★
LIPPER	④①①❸③
ZACKS	1 (Strong Buy)
STANDARD & POOR'S	★★★★★
TheStreet Ratings	E- (Sell)

Performance

3M 1Y 3Y 5Y   Interactive Chart »

VGPMX chart (approx. range 10.80 – 11.30, dates 4/01/14 – 6/01/14)

The fund has returned -10.18 percent over the past year, -23.39 percent over the past three years, 0.15 percent over the past five years, and 5.90 percent over the past decade.

Trailing Returns
Updated 04.30.2014

Year to date	⇧ 6.7%
1 Year	⇩ -10.2%
3 Years (Annualized)	⇩ -23.4%
5 Years (Annualized)	⇧ 0.2%
10 Years (Annualized)	⇧ 5.9%

Investors and potential investors often ask what the basic difference is between these two investment types, mutual fund vs ETF. Here is a very brief comparison for now. If you're trying to track the performance of a large index, your results will be similar whether you choose a mutual fund or an ETF. But which is right for you will come down to whether you want to invest a big chunk of money all at once or smaller chunks of money over time.

If you want to invest a big chunk at once, for example, you're doing a rollover of a 401(k) or an IRA, you're better off with an ETF. By contrast, if you want to invest $100 a month (or you tend to invest sporadically with modest amounts of money), you're probably better off with a mutual fund because the fees will be lower.

ETFs offer tax advantages to investors. As passively managed portfolios, ETFs (and index funds) tend to realize fewer capital gains than actively managed mutual funds. ETFs are more tax efficient than mutual funds because of the way they are created and redeemed. We will revisit this topic later.

Let's take a brief look at futures and options, another investment type:

Definition of 'Futures'

A financial contract obligating the buyer to purchase an asset (or the seller to sell an asset), such as a physical commodity or a financial instrument, at a predetermined future date and price. Futures contracts detail the quality and quantity of the underlying asset; they are standardized to facilitate trading on a futures exchange. Some futures contracts may call for physical delivery of the asset, while others are settled in cash. The futures markets are characterized by the ability to use very high leverage relative to stock markets.

Futures can be used either to hedge or to speculate on the price movement of the underlying asset. For example, a producer of corn could use futures to lock in a certain price and reduce risk (hedge). On the other hand, anybody could speculate on the price movement of corn by going long or short using futures.

Okay, what is an option:

Definition of 'Option'

A financial derivative that represents a contract sold by one party (option writer) to another party (option holder). The contract offers the buyer the right, but not the obligation, to buy (call) or sell (put) a security or other financial asset at an agreed-upon price (the strike price) during a certain period of time or on a specific date (exercise date).

Call options give the option to buy at certain price, so the buyer would want the stock to go up.

Put options give the option to sell at a certain price, so the buyer would want the stock to go down.

Investopedia explains 'Option'

Options are extremely versatile securities that can be used in many different ways. Traders use options to speculate, which is a relatively risky practice, while hedgers use options to reduce the risk of holding an asset.

In terms of speculation, option buyers and writers have conflicting views regarding the outlook on the performance of an underlying security.

For example, because the option writer will need to provide the underlying shares in the event that the stock's market price will exceed the strike, an option writer that sells a call option believes that the underlying stock's price will drop relative to the option's strike price during the life of the option, as that is how he or she will reap maximum profit.

This is exactly the opposite outlook of the option buyer. The buyer believes that the underlying stock will rise, because if this happens, the buyer will be able to acquire the stock for a lower price and then sell it for a profit.

According to Investopedia the difference between an option and future is:

Investopedia explains 'Futures'

The primary difference between options and futures is that options give the holder the *right* to buy or sell the underlying asset at expiration, while the holder of a futures contract is *obligated* to fulfill the terms of his/her contract.

In real life, the actual delivery rate of the underlying goods specified in futures contracts is very low. This is a result of the fact that the hedging or speculating benefits of the contracts can be had largely without actually holding the contract until expiry and delivering the good(s). For example, if you were long in a futures contract, you could go short in the same type of contract to offset your position. This serves to exit your position, much like selling a stock in the equity markets would close a trade.

Please keep in mind that only very skilled investors should ever get involved with futures and options. I have many good friends that have lost their shirts pretending to know what they were doing. Here are a few pros and cons to consider.

Pros:
+Potential for exponential gains.
+Can speculate future prices at fraction of cost of underlying asset.

Cons:
-Highly risky.
-Physical gold often isn't in the equation and paper gold contracts don't guarantee gold ownership.

Gold Forwards are another type of investment. Gold forward contracts are similar to gold future contracts except that each contract is custom negotiated specifically by the two parties in question, and it is done in the over-the-counter market (OTC) (which is off the exchange markets). Gold warrants are another form of options but are issued by private organizations and not necessarily exchange traded. Options, futures and forwards are extremely risky and should only be considered by advanced investors.

Digital Gold Currency, E-Gold is another type of precious metal investment. This is a relatively new way of owning gold and is similar in principle to Paypal. Gold is stored in an online account (and backed by gold) and can be used as a form of payment or can be transferred to make payments. E-gold also has the benefit of being redeemable into physical gold. Criticisms have engulfed this type of online gold currency due to cases involving fraud, hacking risks and little protection in case of anything going wrong. (Source: Goldresource.net)

Another investing type, **Gold Accumulation Plans (GAP)** are a type of saving plan which allows individuals access to incremental saving in the form of gold. This allows individuals access to small sized gold investing without the associated premiums. Each month a specific amount of money is deposited by the investor, which in turn is used to buy gold in the account. Over time this amount builds up and can be cashed out for physical coin/bar delivery, jewelry, or even money if one wishes. Another advantage of gold accumulation plans is the diversification benefits it offers that most traditional savings plans are left without. (Source: Goldresource.net)

Gold Bullion Pensions are becoming more popular and widespread. Citizens in the UK can invest in gold through Sipps (Self-Invested Personal Pensions), and Americans can do the same through Gold IRA investment opportunities (Individual Retirement Account). These types of gold pension investments have the advantage of tax relief, but certain rules do apply, such as the gold generally not being allowed to be in your possession. Therefore ETFs, allocated accounts and e-gold would all qualify.

ETNs are another investment type. If you want more risk, try exchange-traded notes, debt instruments that track an index. You give a bank money for an allotted amount of time and, upon maturity, the bank pays you a return based on the performance of what the ETN is based on, in this case the gold futures market. Some of the more popular ones are UBS Bloomberg CMCI Gold ETN (UBG), DB Gold Double Short ETN (DZZ), DB Gold Short ETN (DGZ) and DB Gold Double Long ETN (DGP). ETNs are like playing the futures market without buying contracts on the Comex. ETNs are flexible, and an investor can trade them long or short, but there is no principal protection. You can lose all your money.

Gold Accounts or buying gold "on account" means purchasing gold that is held in a depository or similar facility. A gold account, also known as a bullion account or metal account, is a way to own physical gold without having to store it. We mentioned these earlier, as well as allocated and unallocated accounts. Let's review them again.

Allocated vs. Unallocated

There are two types of gold accounts. In an allocated account, each investor owns a specified selection of gold bullion. The gold that you own is kept separate from the gold owned by other investors. On the other hand, with an unallocated account, you still own the same amount of gold, but it is not differentiated from other investors' gold held in similar accounts. For example, you may own a 100 ounce gold bar on account, but you do not own a specific gold bar if your gold is unallocated. This is the more common form of owning gold on account. (Source: JM Bullion)

There are important differences between allocated and unallocated gold. With unallocated gold, your gold may be considered a deposit, appearing on the balance sheet of a bank or depository, and you are considered a creditor. With allocated gold, you are the outright owner of a specific portion of physical gold. It cannot be used as a bank's reserve or given to another investor who wishes to take physical possession of their gold. In the event of a financial crisis in which the bank or depository has the potential for failure, allocated gold accounts are safer than unallocated accounts because of this key difference.

Depository Storage

One of the advantages of owning gold on account is that you don't need to store it. Many investors rest easier knowing that their gold is safe in a bank or depository vault, rather than in a safe hidden in their closet. On the other hand, many other investors prefer to take physical possession, knowing that if an emergency arose, they would have their gold in-hand rather than stored in an account that may be many states away.

Liquidity

Another major advantage of owning gold on account is that it is easy to quickly buy and sell gold. Unlike when taking physical possession of your gold bullion, most of the transaction is completed on paper, making it possible to buy or sell anytime you desire, from anywhere in the world. This enables you to act quickly when needed, such as when the spot price of gold is changing dramatically.

Gold accounts also present an option for international diversification. A single investor can have multiple gold accounts located around the world. During times of crisis, such a strategy may ensure that at least a portion of the investment remains intact.

With both allocated and unallocated gold accounts, it is usually possible to actually take delivery of the gold you own on account. If you are interested in opening a gold account and wish to take possession of your metal at some point in the future, be sure that you understand whether the account allows transfer to physical possession.

What To Expect From Your Investment

As you can see there are so many types of precious metal investment opportunities in today's marketplace. That being said, I want to repeat the fact that what works for one person may not be suitable for another person. There is no right or wrong investment. But knowing all the options and comparing them to your situation certainly helps in this process of achieving the best possible result.

Many people have exposure to the stock market and the investment types that we spoke about, through their work plans, and they do not want to independently go this route. Others do not have any money for this type of investing (institutional and paper investing), and for some, they have no faith in the stock market or any paper investments we mentioned. Just buying some gold or silver bars or coins will satisfy their precious metal investment yearning.

Since exposure to precious metals and rare coins can take on so many forms, it is challenging to know what the best strategy is. In order to gain a handle on this subject, let's pick at all of the options and compare them so you can find a slot that seems to be best suited for your financial interests and financial capabilities. Let's face it, some types of precious metal investing and rare coin investing involve sums of money that you might not have.

I want to start this discussion with pre-1933 gold coins. I clearly stated that I did not believe that they were a good investment, and I want to drive this point home by revisiting this topic and providing more food for thought. The reason for this is very simple. Literally tens of thousands of people are investing in these coins and are making very poor choices in so doing. Why?

Gold coins were minted by the U.S. Mint in many denominations from 1795 – 1932. These were and are to this day the only gold coins minted for general circulation, readily available money. There come in many forms: Gold Dollars, Gold Quarter Eagles, Three Dollar Gold Pieces, Gold Half Eagles, Gold Eagles and Gold Double Eagles (see the Red Book for details). Over 100 million of these gold coins were minted.

The coins commonly sold as pre-1933 gold investment coins are the Double Eagles or $20 denomination gold coins. These are typically the coins referred to as pre-1933 gold coins. Liberty Double Eagles pictured below were minted from 1849 – 1907.

Saint Gaudens Double Eagles pictured below on the left side of the image were minted from 1907 – 1933. Most of the 1933 coins were destroyed. On the right side is the front and back of the current Gold Eagle made by the U.S. Mint and sold only through authorized distributors, it is not part of the circulated money supply as the pre-1933 gold coins were:

Obverse of St. Gaudens

Obverse of Gold Eagle

Reverse of St. Gaudens

Reverse of Gold Eagle

A coin is only worth what someone is willing to pay for it. I, as a 50 year veteran of coin collecting, do not consider pre-1933 gold U.S. minted coins rare. Yes, some years are in great demand because few were minted, but there is a major problem with respect to most of these coins. There appears to be a great discrepancy between what some of these coins sell for and what the Red Book says they are worth. The best way to illustrate this point is to look at selling prices from APMEX, compare them to Red Book prices and then compare these prices to sales on eBay. The following image captures a listing from the APMEX web site for $20 Saint-Gaudens Gold Double Eagles, which were minted from 1907 – 1933. Pay close attention to several things. First, look at the sale price of $1536.47 and notice that this coin is graded as MS-63, which is a high grade.

What is so interesting about this sales ad is that it says you will receive a coin from the series, but it does not guarantee a particular date. It does, however, guarantee the MS63 grade. The gold value at the time of this listing for this coin is $1234. The coin is priced at $1536.47 plus shipping (more than $300 over the gold value of the coin). The reasoning for the higher than gold price is apparently due to the rare nature of the coin and the high grade, MS63. (This is the logic used by APMEX to justify the price)

The Red Book, for a coin in this condition, regardless of the year 1907 -1933, states that the least expensive coin in the series is worth at least $2000, according to 2013 prices. So you might reason, why is APMEX selling the coin for almost $500 less than the Red Book says it is worth? Note: The buy back price is almost $100 less than the selling price. Either the grading is off (we will assume that this is not the case), they are giving you a great deal, or some other issue is at play here.

So the magic question is, what is this coin really worth? Let's answer this question. First of all, the rule of thumb is never purchase a coin unless you know the date and can see good pictures of the coin. Even though the coin may have a high grade, in this case MS63, it would be nice to see close up pictures. Why? Because if you try to sell it on eBay or to a coin auction company and then they see the pictures but are dissatisfied due to the coins flaws then you are in trouble. So buying a coin without seeing the actual coin you are buying is out of the question.

This type of coin will always maintain some value because it has gold in it, but as a numismatic or so called rare coin it has no extra value. The reason the demand has been high for these coins is due to the rising price of gold and sales pressure from companies toward buyers, which in many cases distorts the facts. These coins are in great supply, despite the fact that many were melted down when President Roosevelt issued act 1602. At least 75% of the pre-1933 gold coins survived, and many were sent to Europe. Millions were sent before and after WWII.

There were over 100 million pre-1933 gold coins minted (they date back to 1849).

No one knows for sure, but there are probably millions of the more recent coins still around, many are in Europe. Another point that is really important to make: these coins were not circulated in pocket change. Because they were made of gold and quite expensive back in the early 1900's, people saved them in cans, boxes, safes, etc…

This means that most of them are in really good condition. Coin collectors pay high prices for coins graded up, like MS63, but not when there are so many of them. Did you ever wonder why these coin dealers seem to have thousands of them to sell? It is uniqueness that drives the price up along with the grade, but these coins are not unique. There are too many of them around. If you can buy these coins at or close to the price of gold at the time of purchase then you are getting a good deal. To further prove my point, let's look at the PCGS coin index.

Before we look at the index chart, let me make a statement about the grading company PCGS. We mentioned their name several times before. When it comes to coin evaluation and coin information, PCGS is the Gold Standard in the industry. They have certified close to 29 million coins to date and see more coins' prices and sales figures than anyone else. When they speak everyone listens. They are the best.

Their rare gold coin index reflects the average value of thousands of coins over time. The chart below clearly shows that in the past year value has dropped and is heading straight down. The actual percent change is not much, but for an investment class, this clearly is not a good sign. The heading on the chart is "Mint State Rare Gold Coin Index".

Mint State Rare Gold Coin Index

DAILY DATA as of Friday, June 13, 2014 10:14 PM

	Most Recent	12Mo High	12Mo Low	All-Time High
Index	$103,708.70	$105,750.05	$103,525.86	$265,653.85
Change	0.00-	-2041.35 ▼	+182.84 ▲	-161945.15 ▼
Pct Chg	0.00%-	-1.93% ▼	+0.18% ▲	-60.96% ▼
Date	6/13/2014	6/14/2013	4/22/2014	5/31/1989

MONTHLY DATA

DATE	VALUE	CHANGE
5/13/2014	$104,061.21	-0.34% ▼
4/11/2014	$103,873.23	-0.16% ▼
3/13/2014	$104,081.39	-0.36% ▼
6/13/2013	$105,748.45	-1.93% ▼
6/10/2011	$109,640.67	-5.41% ▼
Dec 1994	$68,008.72	+52.49% ▲
May 1989	$265,653.84	-60.96% ▼
Jan 1970	$1,000.00	+10270.87% ▲

ONE YEAR GRAPH

Mint State Rare Gold Coin Index (1 year)
Six Month Moving Average

LARGE GRAPHS

[1 year] | [3 years] | [10 years] | [1970 to Date]

PCGS3000® Index

The three year chart displayed below is even more alarming. In fact, for the past nine years the value of so called mint state (MS) rare gold coins has been heading down.

Mint State Rare Gold Coin Index (3 years)

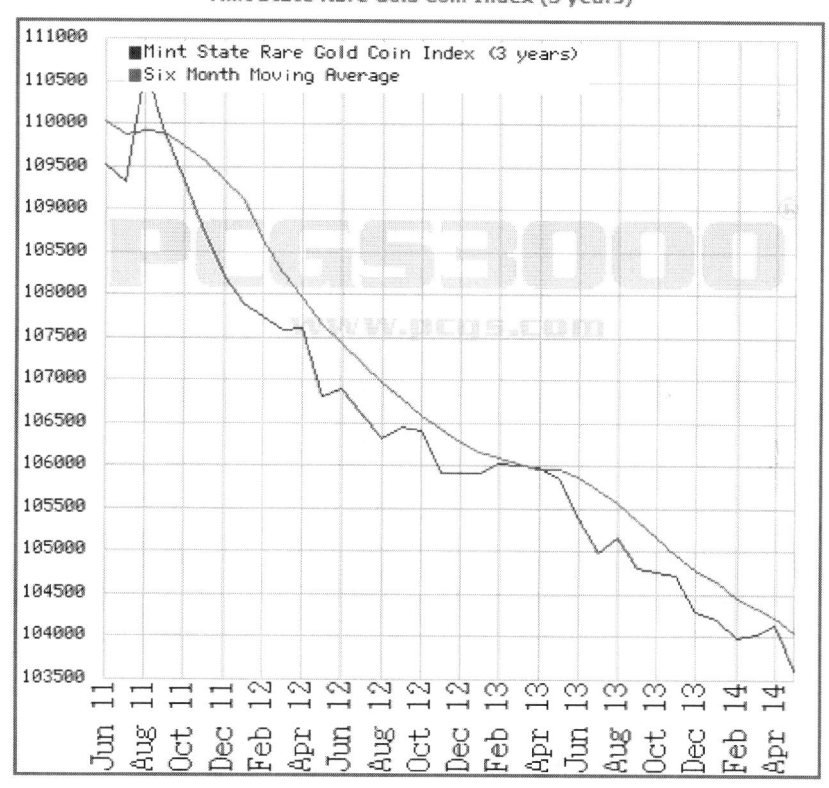

Remember the image showing the Double Eagle for sale on the APMEX site for $1536. In a retail site like eBay these coins are selling for about the same amount of money. Where's the value here? Even after 59 bids, the final price was equal to what APMEX is selling them for. Yet, the Red Book prices them at $2000.

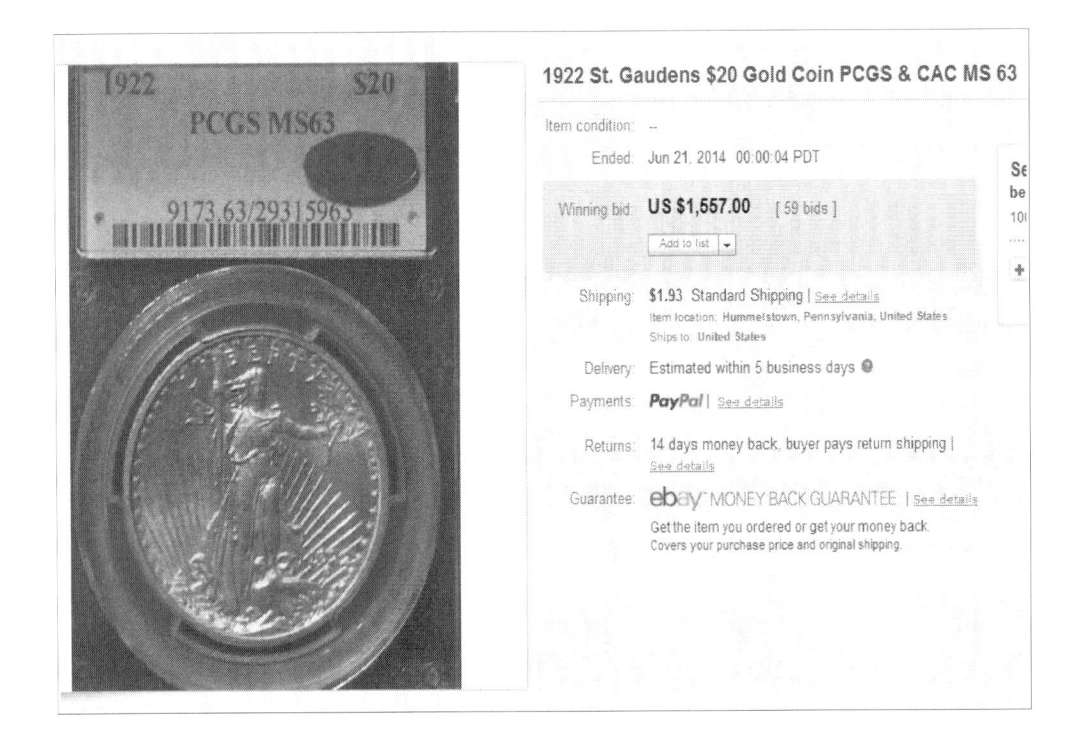

To conclude, if you can purchase Gold Double Eagles or other pre-1933 gold coins, at or near spot, especially very high graded coins for a very small markup over spot, you will come out ahead long term. But as you will learn, there are much better ways to spend your hard earned money. **These coins are over pitched and over sold. They are not rare.** A sales pitch that includes reference to gold confiscation in 1933, and implies that if you buy these so called "rare coins" they will never be taken because they have numismatic value, is a complete exaggeration. When we look at coins that I do consider rare, a whole new picture will be painted, and a new world will be discovered.

Let's look at some other coins mentioned earlier. Namely platinum, gold and silver coins recently made available through the U.S. Mint (since 1986). Here are the coins commonly purchased:

U.S. MINT BULLION COINS

Coins sold through "Authorized Distribution"

American Eagle Gold Bullion Coin Obverse (4 Sizes) 1/10oz 1/4oz 1/2oz 1oz $5-$10-$25-$50

.9167 or 22 Karat

American Eagle Gold Bullion Coin Reverse

American Eagle Silver Bullion Coin Obverse

American Eagle Silver Bullion Coin Reverse

99.9 Pure

American Eagle Platinum Bullion Coin Obverse

American Eagle Platinum Bullion Coin Reverse

Typical prices paid for these coins, based upon current spot prices at the time of this writing:

- 1oz American Eagle Silver Coin - $ 23 ($3 - $4 over spot)
- 1oz American Eagle Platinum Coin - $1522 ($95 over spot)
- American Eagle Gold Coins – 1/10 oz = $145 ($18 over spot)
  - 1/4 oz = $355 ($37 over spot)
  - 1/2 oz = $688 ($50 over spot)
  - 1 oz = $1330 ($50 over spot)
- American Buffalo $50 Gold Coin - $1335 ($60 over spot)
- 5oz Silver America the Beautiful Series - $140 ($35 over spot)

As you can see the one ounce silver version sells at close to spot, while the platinum and gold versions do not. In general all three types, silver-gold-platinum coins, should only be thought of as precious metal investments. What this means is simple, their value will always be determined by the spot price of the metal they contain. Their value as a coin, or shall we say a numismatic or collectible coin, is very minimal. (The 5oz silver may be a slight exception to the rule because of the low mintage figure of 30,000.)

Buying high grade versions of these coins (such as proof coins, highly graded slabbed coins and brilliant uncirculated coins) are more marketing hype than a reflection of any future value. The reason for this is very simple. There are hundreds of millions of these coins, so a high grade version is just one of many millions of high grade versions already available.

What some dealers are doing and some grading services are doing is slabbing or grading coins in an attempt to justify higher prices. Here are two slabbed (graded) coins on eBay being sold by APMEX. The first coin is about $18 over spot or almost twice the current price of silver, while the second is $85 over spot. An investment strategy that includes these types of coins is questionable and may never pay off.

	2003 1 oz Silver American Eagle Coin - MS-69 PCGS - SKU #9270 Buy with confidence & Free Shipping from APMEX on eBay! **APMEX**	$37.15 Buy It Now Free shipping
	1997 1 oz Silver American Eagle Coin - MS-69 PCGS - SKU #9264 Buy with confidence & Free Shipping from APMEX on eBay! **APMEX**	$103.78 Buy It Now Free shipping

Let's look at the pros and cons of these coins with respect to their investment potential. They are traded based on the market rate of their metal, plus a small premium. Their actual metal market value is much higher than their face value.

American Eagle Bullion coins are considered investment grade bullion coins, and are the only official investment-grade coins in the United States. As such, these coins can be used to fund Individual Retirement Accounts (IRAs). Major investment markets around the globe also accept them. Additionally, the Internal Revenue Service (IRS) exempts the American Eagle Bullion coins from IRS 1099 reporting, which provides the investors with an added level of privacy. So these two benefits are a big plus.

Another plus is liquidity. One measure of a good investment is its liquidity. American Eagle Bullion coins are easily bought and sold through any Authorized Purchaser. Their distinct design and brilliant luster, along with their U.S. Government backing and clear mark of fineness, makes them easily identifiable and highly tradable.

One difference between investments, such as stocks and mutual funds, and coin investments is the need for storage space. Once purchased, these silver bullion coins are delivered to the buyer's address. Depending upon the number ordered, the buyer may need to secure a safety deposit box or other secure storage facility. Buyers should be wary of sellers who, rather than delivering the coins, offer to store them in a secure facility for the buyer.

American Eagle Bullion coins are priced slightly higher than standard bullion rounds or bars. Therefore, it is necessary that buyers perform some research and carefully consider which type of coin best suits their investment goals before purchasing one or the other. Buyers should also keep in mind that American Eagle Bullion coins are also sold in rolls of 20 or boxes of 500 rolls.

Bullion coins differ from collectible coins in a few ways. The resale value of collectible coins is determined in large part by the numismatic value of the particular coin as opposed to the actual value of the silver or gold content in the coin. The value is dependent upon what someone is willing to pay for it, and therefore, is subject to wide fluctuations. Bullion coins have a resale value based on the actual precious metal content in the coin. The physical price of the metal, plus a small premium, determines the value of a bullion coin. Therefore, they should only be looked at in terms of their precious metal content but balance this with their wide recognition, easy to sell trait, IRA and IRS advantages. For someone having very small amounts of money to invest, these coins are worth considering.

When it comes time to resell bullion coins, keep in mind that because there are so many out there you may have a hard time getting your money back, unless the price of the metal goes way up. What it boils down to is this: you are investing in a form of a precious metal that can go up or down and may require time before any real gains are made. But on the flip side, everyone knows what these coins are, so in rough times they can sell quickly. And as stated, for many investors it is the only way they can afford exposure to precious metals, especially gold (a good way for some people to save).

Let's spend a few minutes talking about gold and silver bars and rounds. Buying them represents the best way to get the most bang for your buck. You come closer to actual spot value this way. You can buy this asset type from companies (such as the authorized distributors mentioned earlier), that will store the product for you. Some charge for this, some don't. The problem with large amounts of gold and silver relate to safety and storage and the associated costs.

In times of need selling large amounts and large bars can be problematic. We spoke about certified vs non certified product and the advantages of certification. So many investors prefer the actual physical product to be in their possession rather than take advantage of the many investment types that store the gold for you, such as allocated and unallocated accounts and GAP or gold accumulation plans. This may relate to mistrust or habit or lack of knowledge when it comes to the many precious metal opportunities out there, so the purpose of this book, is in part, to make you aware of these many options.

Remember we noted that many investors do not pay close attention to their investments with respect to their return over time. They buy with blinders on. In order to help you understand this topic better or see it from a different angle let's look at the return over time for stocks vs bonds vs gold.

Let me bring in two of the greatest investing experts in the world today so we can see what they say about these three classes of investments. Dr. Jeremy Siegal and John Bogle, the founder of Vanguard, have provided insight into ROI for different asset classes, in this case the inflation adjusted returns of stocks, bonds, and gold. Going back nearly two hundred years, they state:

"If you had invested $10,000, reinvested any dividends, interest, or other gains, and left the money alone, how much wealth would have today in real, inflation-adjusted terms based upon the asset class you selected? The stock investor would have turned his $10,000 into $5.6 billion. The bond investor would have turned his $10,000 into $8 million, and the gold investor would have turned his $10,000 into $26,000. That is statistically significant."

Asset Class	Real Return on $10,000 Investment in 196 Years
Stocks	$5,600,000,000
Bonds	$8,000,000
Gold	$26,000

A final word from John Bogle on gold investing as an asset class, and this applies to silver as well:

"Why has gold generated such pathetic inflation-adjusted returns over the long-run? Because gold has no intrinsic value. It isn't a productive asset. When you own a share of stock, you own a piece of a business that produces goods and / or services to consumers. A good business generates a profit. Every year that passes, gold remains sitting in the vault, but the owner of a company such as Proctor & Gamble or Golgate-Palmolive might have a giant pile of cash from the profit generated over that same year by selling dish washing soap, laundry detergent, and toothpaste.

From a financial standpoint, gold has one purpose: Rank speculation. It can fluctuate wildly and generate huge opportunities for those who are paying attention to gamble – and that is what it is. It can serve as a flight mechanism during times of total catastrophic national collapse, such as a Jewish family fleeing Germany during the second world war who wanted to be able to start over with some capital in a new country. But in terms of productive growth, gold is a dead asset that will eventually return to its baseline. It produces nothing. It creates nothing. The inflation-adjusted returns of the past 200 years reflect this reality."

The intent is not to discourage you or suggest that gold and silver in any form are not good investments, but to make you aware of what history demonstrates so you can act accordingly.

Let's look at some more pros and cons for precious metal investments mentioned:

ETFs (There are many types of precious metal ETFs.)

Advantages:

For investors who seek exposure to the physical market, but have no desire to possess the metal or pay direct insurance, assay, and storage costs, ETFs offer an alternative. They have major exchange listings and trade like equities. Investors can buy shares in a trust that owns the bullion. A very convenient and hassle free way to get gold exposure.

Disadvantages:

Because the ETFs are created to reflect the price of the metal, the market price can be as unpredictable as the price is on any given trading day. Some funds may not have the amount of gold they claim and certain taxes and fees may apply.

Key Points:

- Every time you buy or sell an ETF there may be a fee.
- An ETF that has global exposure may be influenced by the events in the country or countries involved.
- If it consists of one or just a few products or companies it may fluctuate widely in price.

Some more points to consider from the work of John Devcic, as found in Investopedia:

"The biggest factor in any ETF or stock or anything that is traded publicly is liquidity. Liquidity means that when you buy something, there is enough trading interest that you will be able to get out of it relatively quickly without moving the price.

If an ETF is thinly traded, there can be problems getting out of the investment, depending on the size of your position in relation to the average trading volume. The biggest sign of an illiquid investment is large spreads between the bid and ask. With so many new ETFs coming to market, you need to make sure that the ETF is liquid. The best way to do this is to study the spreads and the market movements over a week or month.

The rule here is to make sure that the ETF you are interested in does not have large spreads between bid and ask prices.

In some cases, an ETF will distribute capital gains to shareholders. This is not always desirable for ETF holders, as shareholders are responsible to pay the capital gains tax. It is usually better that the fund retains the capital gains and invests them, rather than distributing them and creating a tax liability for the investor. Investors will usually want to re-invest those capital gains distributions and, in order to do this, they will need to go back to their brokers to buy more shares, which creates new fees.

Buying an ETF with a lump sum is simple. Say $10,000 is what you want to invest in a particular ETF. You calculate how many shares you can buy and what the cost of the commission will be and you get a certain number of shares for your money.

However, there is also the tried-and-true small investor's way of building a position. This way is called dollar cost averaging. With this method, you take the same $10,000 and invest it in monthly increments of, say, $1,000. This is called dollar cost averaging because some months you will buy fewer shares with that $1,000 because the price is higher. In other months, the share prices will be lower and you will be able to buy more shares.

Of course, the big problem with this strategy is that ETFs are traded like stocks; therefore, every time you want to purchase $1,000 worth of that particular ETF, you have to pay your broker a commission to do so. As a result, it can become more costly to build a position in an ETF with monthly investments. For this reason, trading an ETF favors the lump sum approach. The rule here is to try to invest a lump sum at one time to cut down on brokerage fees."

Gold ETF funds are said to be backed by gold, but the legitimacy of these physical gold holdings has been a source of controversy among gold investors. Regardless, for speculative or short term investors, it's hard to beat the convenience of ETFs which have gained huge popularity over the last several years. The most famous among them, as mentioned before, is the U.S. based ETF with the ticker "GLD" and also "IAU" (iShares COMEX Gold Trust).

There is a small administration/handling fee associated with these two funds of around 0.4% per year and also commission fees might apply in some countries of up to 0.4%. The tax implications might also vary depending on your country compared to investing in physical bullion.

Large Gold Bars

Gold bullion bars are the preferred form of investing for financial institutions, governments, and anyone with a lot of money. The reason is that the amount of gold in gold bullion bars must be above 99.5% in purity to qualify as investment grade and sizes are generally quite large (1 KG or 400 ounces are common). Therefore, gold can be acquired with little to no premium over the spot price.

Pros:
+Lowest price for acquiring physical gold
+Bars usually come from large and trustworthy mints and refineries

Cons:
-Liquidating might be more difficult due to sheer value
-Risky to carry around or keep in the house
-Not convenient for using in small to mid-size transactions

Small Metal Bars

Advantages:

- Usually the least expensive
- Convertible into cash
- Internationally negotiable
- Price is widely quoted

Disadvantages:

- Must be stored securely
- Possible need for assay at time of sale
- Yields no interest

Mining Stocks

Advantages:

- Offers capital appreciation opportunities
- Dependent on the company's management and operating strength
- May yield a dividend

Disadvantages:

- May require greater investment than small physical bullion purchases
- Requires knowledge of equity market

Mutual Funds

Advantages:

- Many mutual funds offer investment programs in precious metals
- Diversified holdings among dozens of companies – so if one company has trouble you are not too heavily exposed to it

Disadvantages:
- May require greater investment than small physical bullion purchases
- Requires knowledge of equity market

Bullion Coins

Advantages:
- Relatively inexpensive, some less than $25.00
- Small and easy to store
- Instant convertibility into cash
- Easy to transport
- Internationally negotiable
- Prices quoted widely
- Usable as money
- Easy to buy

Disadvantages:
- Must be stored securely
- Yields no interest
- Premium over bullion bar prices
- Many coin types exist which can lead to confusion
- The buy sell spread does not favor the retail investor

Certificates or Storage Accounts (General overview, more on next page)

Advantages:
- High liquidity but at competitive prices
- No storage risk
- No sales tax

- Prices widely quoted
- Invest by dollar amount

Disadvantages:
- Several days' delay in delivery
- Not in physical possession of owner

Accumulation Plans

Advantages:
- Invest as little as $100
- Discounted commission rates
- Highly liquid
- No sales tax
- Offers dollar cost averaging
- No storage fees

Disadvantages:
- Metal not in physical possession of owner although some firms will deliver the metal if requested

Allocated Gold Account (Storage Account)

If you'd like to own physical gold (bars or coins) but would rather not deal with headaches associated with storing the precious metal yourself, then you can choose to invest in gold through allocated accounts. Theoretically this assures that the bank in question would keep your portion of gold in their vault somewhere attributable directly to you. You do have to pay extra for this, but don't expect to have a private storage box just for you as not all bullion banks or financial institutions have such private vaults. However, hallmark, weight and fineness are all recorded, and your gold stays in the vault and may not be used by the banks for other purposes. You actually own this physical gold and the banks job is to keep it safe.

Pros:
- No need to worry about gold delivery transportation or storage

Cons:
- May require yearly handling/storage/insurance costs

Unallocated Gold Accounts (Storage account)

For investment in gold without the storage costs, unallocated gold accounts are usually shown as a preferred choice and represent over 90% of accounts at banks. This doesn't mean that unallocated accounts are in fact better. To the contrary, they invite a lot of risk which allocated accounts do not face. In an unallocated account, the bank may do with your gold as they please, and the bank in this case is in a position of debt to you. So if the bank faces problems, they will likely sell the gold invested by its customers to meet its reserve requirements. If something were to happen to the bank, unallocated gold accounts are usually not covered by governments who only provide a guarantee for its sovereign currency.

Unallocated accounts can come in many forms and sizes and are offered through a variety of institutions through different names like gold pool accounts. Both allocated and unallocated gold accounts involve gold certificates that you hold that symbolizes your ownership position.

Pros:
- Cheap and easy way to invest in gold

Cons:
- The safety of 'your gold' is at the fate of the bank that holds it with no mechanisms in place for protection   (Source: Gold Resource)

Futures Contracts

Advantages:
- Speculative appeal
- Leverage reduces capital tie-up
- Liquidity
- Contracts widely quoted
- No storage risk

Disadvantages:
- Many trading limitations
- High risk factors
- Unlimited loss potential
- Requires market expertise

Options

Advantages:
- Speculative appeal
- Leverage reduces capital tie-up
- No storage risk
- Clearly defined risk

Disadvantages:
- Trading limitations
- Highest risk
- Less negotiable and less liquid
- Investor must be willing to sustain the loss of their entire investment in a commodity option
- High degree of knowledge required

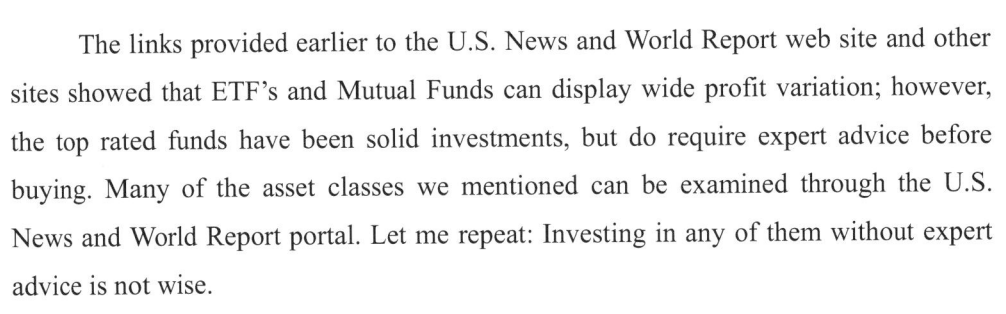

The links provided earlier to the U.S. News and World Report web site and other sites showed that ETF's and Mutual Funds can display wide profit variation; however, the top rated funds have been solid investments, but do require expert advice before buying. Many of the asset classes we mentioned can be examined through the U.S. News and World Report portal. Let me repeat: Investing in any of them without expert advice is not wise.

An unusual study covering a 30 year period compares some of the asset types we looked at. It is one of the most significant studies of its kind, and needs to be reviewed.

Year	Gold Return Jan-Dec (London Gold Price from IMF)	Stock Market Return (Compilation of NYSE, AMEX and NASDAQ)	3 month T-Bill return, 1st week Jan, from Federal Reserve	Rare coin returns-All coin types: grades XF to MS65-Weighted per Penn State Study	Rare coin returns-All coin types: MS65	Rare coin returns-All coin types, MS 63, 64, 65.
1979	100.2376	22.4060	9.3400	185.7389	198.8228	198.8228
1980	-11.9029	30.0370	12.1000	40.5420	43.8156	43.8156
1981	-26.4254	-3.3180	14.3100	-24.5094	-22.0423	-42.7251
1982	15.5887	20.0400	11.3500	-25.9318	-20.9615	-24.0826
1983	-19.1008	21.1920	7.9200	40.0571	42.6923	39.2666
1984	-13.6856	3.7260	8.9500	6.3572	6.1008	6.2785
1985	5.9688	27.7440	7.8300	12.5282	18.6483	16.9934
1986	13.2752	15.3810	7.0400	-32.6972	-1.4913	-7.6643
1987	19.1177	5.7920	5.6500	-1.2276	7.9549	2.1522
1988	-12.1889	17.2660	5.7300	24.8685	43.8001	35.2282
1989	1.3317	25.7260	8.2400	48.0588	79.5269	61.1580
1990	-7.7906	-5.1790	7.5900	-33.1110	-40.5529	-37.2781
1991	-5.8857	29.8970	6.4700	-9.8637	-11.1114	-10.1249
1992	-5.5438	9.0450	3.8700	-1.1509	-0.1312	0.4155
1993	16.5162	11.2010	3.1500	-6.8403	-3.7460	-6.0044
1994	-1.9618	0.0190	3.0500	-0.8138	-0.4560	-0.6409
1995	2.3484	36.8000	5.6700	0.5531	-1.0308	-0.2904
1996	-7.8122	21.8200	5.0200	15.1988	-1.9279	-1.1243
1997	-26.0500	31.7800	5.0500	-15.6343	1.7852	0.0409
1998	0.0914	24.1400	5.2400	17.3834	12.2541	14.9032
1999	-1.5000	20.1900	4.4400	0.6788	-2.1341	-0.8182
2000	-3.3000	-7.4600	5.2600	-1.2789	-2.1473	-2.1295
2001	1.4000	-11.4600	5.3600	3.1180	1.3649	2.3103
2002	24.9000	-21.5000	1.7000	1.8672	-0.6557	0.8505
2003	21.4000	31.1000	1.2000	5.7664	3.6859	5.3358
2004	4.8000	11.9000	0.9000	14.1956	13.5977	14.2650
2005	17.8000	6.1000	2.2900	6.1013	3.5353	5.0379
2006	23.2000	15.7000	4.1000	4.4303	3.9276	3.7153
2007	31.9000	5.1000	4.9200	5.7656	3.9177	4.7514
2008	4.3000	-37.3000	3.1900	20.6744	24.9400	20.9676
Average Return	5.3676	11.9295	5.8977	10.0275	13.3994	11.4475

This study compares the return for gold bullion vs the stock market vs three month T-Bills vs rare coins (all grades) vs rare coins MS 65 vs rare coins MS63-MS65 for 30 years from 1979 – 2008.

(Please do not confuse rare coins with pre-1933 gold coins, which as I stated before are not rare. In the pages to follow we will define rare coins and look at coin collecting in depth.)

What is so surprising about this study are the results, showing that a wide variety of rare coins on average, out perform all the other asset classes listed. The study happened to end during the economic collapse of 2008 when the market crashed, yet even after 2008 rare coins went up and the market went down.

Notice the performance of the stock market, which is more than twice that of gold and T-Bills, yet less than that of MS65 rare coins. Don't worry, we will explore rare coins and grading (MS65) in great detail. For now I wanted to point out how significant rare coin returns are in terms of their investment potential.

This chart was compiled by Raymond E. Lombra, Ph.D., a Professor of Economics and Dean for Research, Graduate Studies and College Advancement at Penn State University. He has authored, co-authored and contributed to numerous economic and financial books, publications and periodicals. Professor Lombra is a consultant to the House Banking Committee of the U.S. Congress, the Federal Reserve System, the Congressional Budget Office, the Joint Economic Committee, Prudential Bache, Morgan-Stanley Dean Witter, the International Monetary Fund and the U.S. Treasury. His many honors and awards include election to Who's Who in Economics.

I'd like to spend a few minutes and speak about certain purchases that people make from TV ads. These ads take on many forms, from coin ads, to precious metals, to buying your gold and silver from you. I'm sure you have seen them. Do not purchase any coins or any metal from a TV ad or magazine ad.

An example is the TV shopping show Dealers and Mints. Most of the Uncirculated Morgan Dollars I've seen on TV shopping shows like this sell for $300 each, but can be purchased from a normal coin dealer or on eBay for $40.

Another TV seller is the National Collector's Mint. The U.S. Mint has issued warnings about this company's misleading advertisements in the past, particularly its Freedom Tower Coins. National Collector's Mint ads imply that Freedom Tower and other coins have meaningful amounts of precious metal in them when they do not.

Other examples include: the Franklin Mint and the Bradford Exchange. They are aggressive marketers who do sometimes sell genuine bullion coins, but their coins usually do not have any after-market value among coin collectors and investors.

Another bad investment are "sets" of coins. This is another popular TV shopping show product; plus they're often found in magazines and swap meets. "Spurious sets," are sets that are put together out of lower grade and/or common coins according to some kind of theme. The coins are usually placed in fancy plastic holders, with nice quality packaging. You then pay $38.99 for a set of five coins that are worth $2.99 just because they were all minted during World War II or the Vietnam War, or because they're from around the world and commemorate movie stars or some sort of cartoon character. Such coins are usually genuine and will probably appreciate in value, but they probably won't be worth what you paid for them anytime during the next five generations! These are a favorite of dealers like Littleton.

Other TV ads from so called "metal dealers" offer to buy your silver or gold for 1 % over cost, implying that you are getting a good deal. Let me ask you a question. If they are paying one million dollars for prime time TV ads on popular stations like FOX, can you imagine what their costs are? **Don't buy from TV shows and magazine ads!**

Gold vs Silver - Who Wins This Fight?

A question that is often asked concerns silver vs gold: which investment over time, makes the most sense? Because there are so many types of gold and silver and you have seen them reviewed earlier, it is hard to pick a winner. They all have pros and cons. But let's take a look at some of the differences, and how these relate to which asset has the most bang for the buck over time, particularly in the years ahead.

A concept that is often overlooked is the relatively low price of silver in relation to gold. Silver should be priced much higher than it is. The price relationship of these two metals is of great interest. Let's look at what happens when silver goes up 10% and gold goes up 10%. For silver to go up this much, the price has to only climb a few dollars, say $20 to $22 per spot ounce. Gold on the other hand, has to move up well over $100 for it to increase 10%. For example, $1280 per ounce to $1408 per ounce, or an increase of $128. Let's look at this concept in terms of large dollar amounts.

Let's say you buy one million dollars worth of gold and one million dollars worth of silver, and silver goes up 10%, yielding $100,000 profit. Gold on the other hand goes up $40 per ounce when silver just went up $2 or 10% per ounce, but the actual percentage change is less than 4% per ounce for gold, so the one million dollar investment went up much less than the silver one.

Let's look at this from another angle: you buy 60 ounces of silver for $1220, and you buy one ounce of gold for $1220. Since the silver ounce price moves in greater proportion than gold, a $2 increase per ounce means a 10% gain or $122 profit. Gold, let's say, moves up $60 per ounce at the same time, but this equals about a 5 % gain, which is typically how the prices for these two metals move. So buying the same dollar amount of silver as gold, suggests that your chance of a greater return is with silver. A small move in silver yields a much higher percent gain.

I will prove this to you. Here is an actual example. Look at this chart. Notice how the gold price per ounce went from $1247.25 to $1317.5 in the three week period, a climb of $70 or 5.5%. While silver went from $18.81 per ounce to $21.04, a climb of only $2, but equal to 11%, or twice the increase of gold. If you monitor these changes you can pick trends and know when to buy.

London gold and silver fixing price in previous days

	Gold Ounce	Gold Kilo	Gold Gram	Silver Ounce	Silver Kilo	Silver Gram
2014-06-27	1317.5	42358.61	42.36	21.04	676.45	0.68
2014-06-26	1311.75	42173.74	42.17	20.83	669.7	0.67
2014-06-25	1316.75	42334.5	42.33	20.78	668.09	0.67
2014-06-24	1318.5	42390.76	42.39	21.12	679.02	0.68
2014-06-23	1313.5	42230.01	42.23	20.75	667.13	0.67
2014-06-20	1312.5	42197.85	42.2	20.62	662.95	0.66
2014-06-19	1293	41570.92	41.57	19.94	641.09	0.64
2014-06-18	1269.75	40823.41	40.82	19.73	634.33	0.63
2014-06-17	1267.5	40751.07	40.75	19.55	628.55	0.63
2014-06-16	1276.25	41032.39	41.03	19.67	632.41	0.63
2014-06-13	1273	40927.9	40.93	19.58	629.51	0.63
2014-06-12	1265.75	40694.81	40.69	19.33	621.47	0.62
2014-06-11	1262	40574.24	40.57	19.2	617.29	0.62
2014-06-10	1259.5	40493.87	40.49	19	610.86	0.61
2014-06-09	1253.5	40300.96	40.3	19.11	614.4	0.61
2014-06-06	1247.5	40108.06	40.11	19.03	611.83	0.61
2014-06-05	1252.5	40268.81	40.27	18.81	604.76	0.6
2014-06-04	1245.25	40035.72	40.04	18.76	603.15	0.6
2014-06-03	1242.75	39955.34	39.96	18.87	606.68	0.61
2014-06-02	1247.25	40100.02	40.1	18.81	604.76	0.6

Another point to consider relates to the gold-silver ratio over time. Gold and silver follow the same path, one goes up, the other goes up, and they also follow each other going down. The historic silver/gold price ratio is 15 or 16:1, but in recent years, silver is relatively cheaper. Today the ratio is 66:1 which means that silver is currently undervalued, and cheaper than historic norms, and thus it is a better investment than gold if you want to "buy low and sell high".

Based upon a "normal" ratio, silver should be priced at least $90 per ounce. The supply and demand fundamentals for silver are extraordinary. There has been an ongoing supply/demand deficit in silver for 12 years. More silver is consumed by industry than is produced by mining and recycling combined. Some say this deficit reaches back 60 years, and has consumed virtually all the known silver mined since the beginning of the world. The annual deficit has recently ranged from 100 million to 200 million ounces per year.

Just look at the 2013 figures from the Silver Institute:

Total supply = 978 million ounces

Demand = 1081 million ounces

Net deficit = -113 million ounces (That's negative 113 million ounces)

Remember most silver mined has actually been used, while most gold ever mined still remains above ground and intact. There is also less silver in the ground than gold. The actual chart that shows these figures is displayed below:

World Silver Supply and Demand
(in millions of ounces)

	2004	2005	2006	2007	2008	2009	2010	2011	2012	2013
Supply										
Mine Production	613.6	639.7	642.7	666.1	683.1	713.8	750.6	754.6	792.3	819.6
Net Government Sales	61.9	65.9	78.5	42.5	30.5	15.6	44.2	12.0	7.4	7.9
Scrap	198.6	202.5	206.0	202.9	200.7	199.7	225.5	258.7	252.6	191.8
Net Hedging Supply	-2.0	45.9	-11.6	-24.1	-8.7	-17.4	50.4	12.2	-47.0	-41.3
Total Supply	872.0	954.1	915.6	887.3	905.7	911.7	1,070.7	1,037.6	1,005.3	978.1
Demand										
Jewelry	187.1	187.9	176.0	183.2	178.2	177.3	190.6	183.4	181.4	198.8
Coins & Bars	53.0	51.5	48.7	51.2	187.7	87.9	146.1	212.6	139.3	245.6
Silverware	68.1	69.4	63.2	61.3	59.5	54.2	52.6	48.1	44.6	50.0
Industrial Fabrication	608.9	637.1	645.2	656.7	651.3	540.2	643.2	624.8	589.1	586.6
...of which Electrical & Electronics	191.8	211.1	223.1	239.8	245.5	203.1	272.6	260.6	237.0	233.9
...of which Brazing Alloys & Solders	48.9	52.4	54.4	58.1	61.3	53.3	60.6	62.4	60.3	62.4
...of which Photography	178.8	160.3	142.2	117.0	100.2	78.4	68.8	61.7	54.4	50.4
...of which Other Industrial	189.4	213.2	225.4	241.9	244.4	205.4	241.2	240.0	237.4	240.0
Physical Demand	917.1	945.9	933.1	952.3	1,076.7	859.5	1,032.6	1,068.9	954.4	1,081.1
Physical Surplus/Deficit	-45.1	8.2	-17.5	-65.0	-171.0	52.2	38.1	-31.3	51.0	-103.0
ETF Inventory Build	0.0	0.0	157.8	54.8	101.3	153.8	132.6	-24.0	55.1	1.6
Exchange Inventory Build	-20.3	15.9	-9.0	21.5	-7.1	-15.3	-7.4	12.2	62.2	8.8
Net Balance	-24.8	-7.7	-166.3	-141.3	-265.2	-86.3	-87.1	-19.4	-66.3	-113.3

Another point to consider and this is according to the First Majestic Silver Corporation:

"In the gold market, there has been a large increase in paper futures contracts which are used to suppress the price. In silver, the relative amount of paper contracts is much larger. In other words, there are more paper shorts who will be caught in an impossible situation when the price of silver really begins to rise due to the fundamental supply demand gap. They will be forced to buy silver or go bankrupt. Either action will cause a dramatic rise in the silver price. If they default on the silver contracts, that will signal to the world the severe shortage of silver, and signal a great investment opportunity."

We must also consider geo-political events, particularly what has happened in China and India recently and how this affects the price of gold. On June 26, 2014 it was reported in QZ.COM that:

China's National Audit Office reported today it has discovered 94.4 billion yuan ($15.2 billion) in fraudulent loans backed by gold stocks that don't exist. Unnamed banks were using "fictional" cross-border currency-swap loans backed by gold to take advantage of interest-rate differences inside and outside China, the report says. The report marks the "first official confirmation of what many people have suspected for a long time - that gold is widely used in Chinese commodity financing deals," Liu Xu, an analyst at Capital Futures in Beijing, told Bloomberg.

China's grab for all the gold it can mine and can get its hands on is cause for concern, because of a lack of transparency. In theory, they could corner the gold market and impose a pricing structure by the leverage they have. This is not something that would happen any time soon, but they are feverishly looking for gold deposits in their vast country.

Remember, the Arab world fixes the price of oil according to their needs because they have so much of it. Events in India are even more troubling. India is one of the world's leading gold consumers along with China. India's thirst for gold has many components:

- Religious associations – temples and religious groups hoard gold
- Social prestige – gold is a sign of status
- Savings venue – Indians prefer to save gold rather than money
- Marriage traditions – families start saving for gold when their children are infants (Gold that the bride brings to the wedding symbolizes status and is a sign of good luck)
- Inheritance – gold is the preferred type of wealth transfer

An amazing 12.5% of India's imports (2012-2013) are in the form of gold. This desire for gold has actually weighed down the economy to the point where the government has taken action. It has curbed gold imports by as much as 41% and may impose measures as are needed over time. Will this result in downward price pressure on the world gold market?

Uncertainties in China and India do one thing, help make gold investing an unpredictable action. With most of the gold consumption in the form of jewelry and investments rather than actual industrial need for the precious metal, you end up having doubt as to how good an investment it is over time. Silver usage on the other hand is mostly of an industrial nature. An important point to remember, and this is often overlooked, when gold goes up silver follows and the reverse is true, so if you need an indicator to point you in the direction of a buy, look at gold, as it heads up silver will follow – time to buy. Silver will out perform gold over time, mainly because it is under priced.

Coin Collecting – What Every Investor Must Know

We are going to explore coins and coin collecting in depth. There are many reasons for this, but the principle one is to help you develop a strong knowledge of your own investments so you can make sensible decisions. As stated before, certain rare coins return a higher rate of return than any other investment class over time. Certain coins, like pre-1933 gold coins, do not make good investments. U.S. Mint bullion coins are often purchased at prices that make it hard for the investor to recoup anything, especially over short time periods.

Remember the chart we looked at for a 30 year time period showing how the stock market returned about 11% and rare coins in high grade about 13%? I want to update these figures using more current data. The long term appreciation for high quality rare coins have achieved returns exceeding those of the major equity indices. Looking back over the past 40 years, rare coins have had a compounded (IRR) rate of return greater than 11%, while the DJIA and S&P500 indices have grown at rates less than 7%. Interestingly, rare coins increased slightly in value between 2006 and 2010, while the equity markets went down. We must balance this information with events of the last few years which have seen the DJIA and S&P500 have extraordinary growth, more than the 7% just mentioned. But the facts over time are clear. Rare coins do very well.

An interesting chart reflecting a long term study shows how well rare coins do over the years. The study compares rare coins to many other asset classes. Silvano DeGenova is one of the world's greatest coin authorities, and his rare coin tracking data is based on real sales. Note how his UNC (uncirculated) returns for 35 years rank above all other investment classes on the following chart:

	Five-Year Holding Period Returns (1970-2005)			
Asset Type	Average	Standard Deviation	Sharpe Ratio	Rank
Silver	5.52%	16.83%	-0.03	14
Gold	8.81%	19.28%	0.14	8
Oil	8.70%	15.79%	0.17	6
Homes	6.12%	2.82%	0.02	11
Land	6.17%	6.35%	0.02	12
MSCI World	7.84%	10.97%	0.16	7
S&P	8.14%	9.29%	0.22	4
DJIA	8.15%	8.72%	0.24	3
T-Bill	6.07%	2.54%	0.00	13
DiGenova AU	7.96%	9.12%	0.21	5
DiGenova UNC	9.50%	10.07%	0.34	1
DiGenova Both	9.07%	9.33%	0.32	2
BU Rolls	7.45%	17.60%	0.08	10
Solomon	6.73%	6.73%	0.10	9

A description of the data is presented in the appendix.

The fourth line from the bottom (DiGenova UNC) shows a return of 9.5%. Compare this to silver, gold, oil and the others. Notice the ranking of from 1 to 14 on the right hand column. The top two rankings are for coins. Again, keep in mind the years for the study, which ended in 2005. The world is different now. The stock market is very robust but coin returns still rank high. You can see why coin information is so critical. Let's start at the beginning and we will work our way up.

What is coin collecting?

Anyone who saves one or more coins for any reason is coin collecting. Some collect coins as a hobby while others for immediate or long term financial gain. Some individuals collect to teach their children about math, coins and money. Some people collect because they want to invest now, but plan on passing the collection down to their heirs. Some save a specific coin type or date because it holds sentimental value (gold, silver, error, foreign, ancient, commemorate or proof coins for example). Some collect every major coin made. The list goes on.

Don't let the coin field box you in mentally. There isn't a single person that knows it all and every collector has a different degree of knowledge. In other words, do not let the vast amount of information overwhelm you, everyone started at ground zero, we are here on this earth to help each other.

Let's define the term "rare coin". After all we have used this term so much. What is a rare coin? Is a rare coin one that has considerable value attached to it? The word "rare" means uncommon, distinctive, extreme of its kind. So, a definition of "rare coin" can be a coin that is uncommon in some way and may or may not have value. In other words, some coins are very rare and very uncommon, yet do not have much value. Some are very valuable. I will show you why this is.

Coin collectors, on the other hand, typically think in terms of dollar value, when using the term "rare coin". For example, I have seen very uncommon coins, maybe only a few in existence, have no value and therefore coin collectors would not consider them rare. The problem with the term "rare coin" is that there is no standard definition, for example, is a coin that is worth $1000 a rare coin or not? If you are interested in buying rare coins, what should you buy? Don't worry it will all become clear to you.

Coins that continually go up in value over time and are hard to find and or buy because they are scarce and when found can only be purchased for much more than their face value, is probably a good definition for "rare coins". As far as investing and this book is concerned, this is the definition we will use. Remember a coin is only worth what somebody is willing to pay for it. I have seen a one of a kind coin worth an estimated $100,000 and other coins that have had over 50,000 of them minted, and they sell for $50,000 in very good condition. I am going to show you what coins are considered "rare" and why.

Coin Collecting - Getting Started (Tools)

It's a known fact that coin collectors have more knowledge of precious metals. The reason for this is simple. Many coins are made of silver and gold and collectors usually have handled them. This gives them an edge. They are familiar with fake coins and fake gold and fake silver and they know the value of silver and gold coins. If you want to sharpen your precious metal skills you will need to understand more about coins, especially bullion coins. Knowledge is the key. When you look at paper investments, like ETFs and mutual funds you can compare their return to coin returns, especially rare coins. If you know what a rare coin is and how to determine a coins value you will be in a much better position to make investment decisions based upon fact rather than habit or market trends or suggestions from aggressive sales people.

This is a very good time in the book to take a close look at tools you will need to be successful at coin collecting and precious metal evaluation. I am going to show you exactly what these tools are, why they are needed, what they cost, and how to get them.

The tools mentioned were:
- Nitrile gloves
- Two coin books (So far only one book was mentioned)
- A jewelry loupe
- A gram scale and a larger scale
- A magnet
- A digital microscope
- A non-glazed ceramic tile or dish
- A gold-silver testing kit

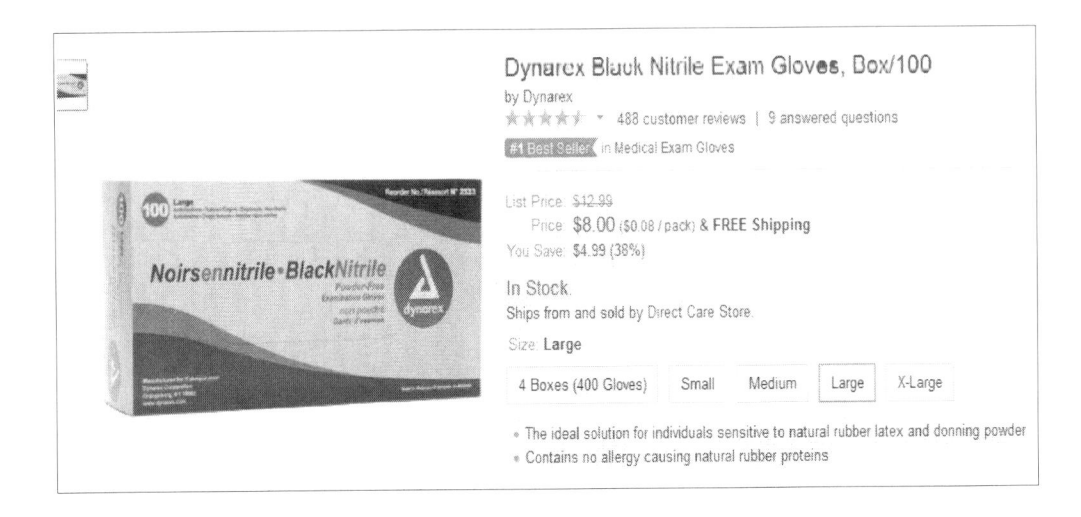

Dynarex Black Nitrile Exam Gloves, Box/100
by Dynarex
★★★★☆ ▾ 488 customer reviews | 9 answered questions
#1 Best Seller in Medical Exam Gloves

List Price: $12.99
Price: $8.00 ($0.08 / pack) & FREE Shipping
You Save: $4.99 (38%)

In Stock.
Ships from and sold by Direct Care Store.
Size: Large

| 4 Boxes (400 Gloves) | Small | Medium | Large | X-Large |

- The ideal solution for individuals sensitive to natural rubber latex and donning powder
- Contains no allergy causing natural rubber proteins

Nitrile gloves are used to handle coins because they are very dirty. They can also be used to handle nitric acid for gold testing. If you look at a lot of coins in one sitting, they come in handy. You will be amazed at how dirty they get from coins.

The above ad from Amazon shows latex free gloves. I also recommend that you get powder free gloves. They come in different sizes, so order accordingly. Always order 100, you will be glad you did. They come in black and blue colors. I like the Dynarex brand. Sometimes Walmart carries them.

Two books that I recommen are: *The Red Book – A Guide Book of United States Coins 2015* by R.S. Yeoman and *Strike It Rich With Pocket Change: Error Coins Bring Big Money* by Ken Potter. The error book is an added bonus to have, but not needed in the beginning. The next two images show them on the Amazon web site.

The spiral bound Red Book works best.

A Guide Book of United States Coins 2015: The Official Red Book Spiral Spiral-bound

by R. S. Yeoman (Author)

★★★★☆ ▾ 26 customer reviews

#1 Best Seller in Antique & Collectible Reference

▸ See all 3 formats and editions

Hardcover-spiral	Spiral-bound
$16.04	$12.71
8 Used from $11.01	14 Used from $8.66
25 New from $12.04	41 New from $8.56

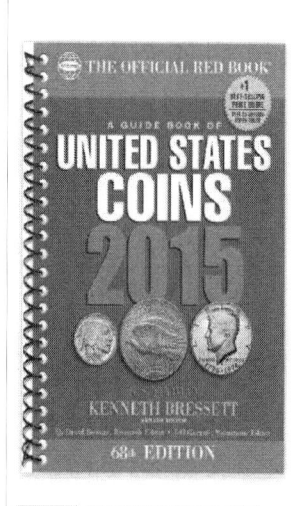

See all 11 images

The Official Red Book - A Guide Book of United States Coins - is 68 years young and going strong. Collectors around the country love the convenience of the spiralbound edition. It opens up and lies flat on a table while you study your coin collection. And of course it includes all the grade-by-grade values, auction records, historical background, detailed specifications, high-resolution photographs, and accurate mintage data that turn a new coin collector into an educated numismatist. How rare are your coins? How much are they worth? The Red Book tells you, covering everything from early colonial copper tokens to hefty Old West silver dollars and dazzling gold coins. You'll find prices for more than 6,000 coins, tokens, medals, sets, and other collectibles. You'll also round out your education in commemoratives, Proof and Mint coins, error coins, Civil War tokens, Confederate coins, private gold, and all the latest National Park quarters, Presidential and Native American dollars, Lincoln cents, and more. Articles on investing, grading coins, and detecting counterfeits will make you a savvy collector; and entertaining essays on the history of American coinage, shipwrecks and hoards, and the modern rare-coin market give you an inside look at "the hobby of kings." These are just some of the features, invaluable Red Book-the world's best-selling coin price guide.

7

Strike It Rich with Pocket Change: Error Coins Bring Big Money Paperback

by Ken Potter ▼ (Author), Brian Allen (Author)

★★★★★ ▼ 15 customer reviews

▸ See all 2 formats and editions

Kindle	Paperback
$9.99	$13.92
Read with our free app	16 Used from $11.23
	37 New from $11.03

That odd-looking coin could be worth a fortune!

Mistakes happen. Now you can cash in on them.

The U.S. Mint produces error coins every year on every denomination. From doubled die cents to rotated reverse quarters to missing letters on dollars, these coins can be worth far more than face value.

Featuring expert insight, hundreds of close-up images, concise details on what to look for and where, and up-to-date market values, you will learn how to spot and profit from even the most well disguised treasures in the new edition of *Strike It Rich with Pocket Change*.

SE - Loupe - LED and UV Illuminated, 12x, 20x, 30x
by SE

★★★★☆ ▼ 298 customer reviews

List Price: $9.36
Price: **$7.10** & **FREE Shipping** on orders over $35. Details
You Save: $2.26 (24%)

In Stock.
Sold by hobbytoolsupply and Fulfilled by Amazon. Gift-wrap available.

Want it tomorrow, June 19? Order within 21 mins and choose One-Day Shipping at checkout. Details

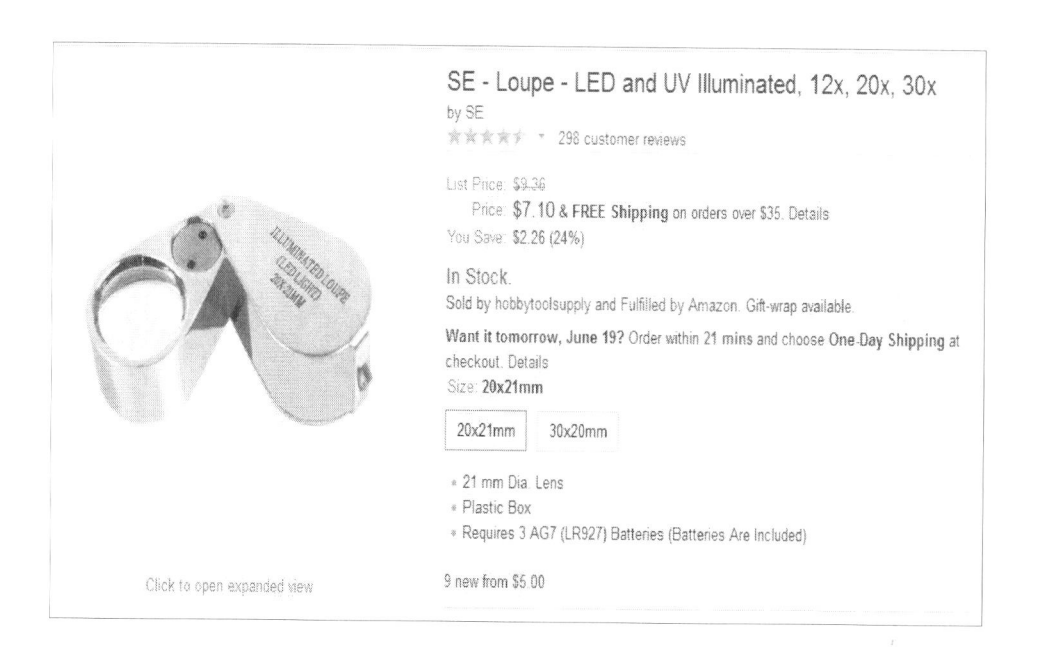

Size: **20x21mm**

| 20x21mm | 30x20mm |

- 21 mm Dia. Lens
- Plastic Box
- Requires 3 AG7 (LR927) Batteries (Batteries Are Included)

9 new from $5.00

A jewelry loupe is needed to examine coins close up and to check gold and silver for purity or maker markings. I buy them on Amazon and prefer those that have a LED light. The loupe shown above works well.

Smart Weigh SWS100 Elite Digital Pocket Scale 100 x 0.01g - Black
by Smart Weigh
★★★★☆ 27 customer reviews | 3 answered questions
#1 Best Seller in Lab Analytical Balances

List Price: $19.99
Price: $14.99
Sale: $9.99 & FREE Shipping on orders over $35. Details
You Save: $10.00 (50%)

In Stock.
Sold by MeasuRite and Fulfilled by Amazon. Gift-wrap available.

Want it tomorrow, June 19? Order within 9 mins and choose One-Day Shipping at checkout. Details

- The Elite series is designed with a stainless steel platform and a protective flip cover, this scale is a lightweight and compact size solution for all your portable weighing tasks
- The SWS 100 allows you to weigh a maximum capacity of a hundred grams and readabilities of 0.01g, to guarantee you an accurate and precise weighing session
- Its tactile easy touch buttons, large size digits and stark contrast LCD blue backlight display, makes it easy to read in all light conditions.
- Featuring 4 different weight modes: g / oz / gn / ct for easy weight translations, tare function for net determination and a 60 second auto shut off to preserve battery life
- Use the smart weigh SWS100 scale to measure a versatile range of objects. Such as: Gold, Silver, Coins, Jewelry, Gems and other small knickknacks

A gram scale is indispensable for weighing coins, jewelry, gold and silver. These small scales are limited to 8 ounces. Certain coins need to be weighed to determine metal content, authenticity and error types. Make sure the scale you buy weighs in the 100th of a gram as this one does from Amazon. I use this one, and it has worked for many years. Shop around on Amazon, prices and products change all the time.

Here's a real life example of why these small scales are so important. Notice the weight difference, 11.20 grams vs 11.45 grams.

If we did not have the Red Book handy or the internet and had these 2 Kennedy Half Dollars and we were looking at them and noticed their appearance was somewhat different, the gram scale confirms that one weighs more than the other

The 1973 Kennedy on the left has no silver in it – but the 1967 one on the right weighs a little more because it is 40% silver (Can you see the silvery appearance?)

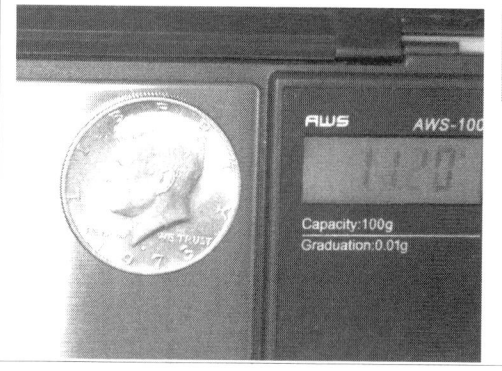

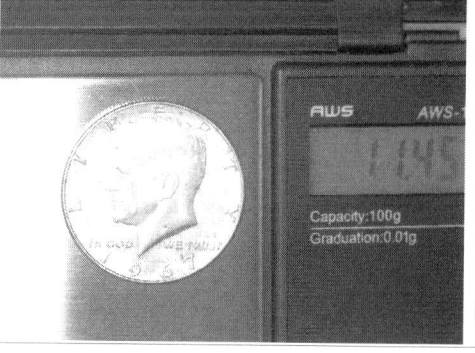

Digital Postal Shipping Postage Bench Scales 75 lbs
by LW Measurements
★★★★☆ ▾   292 customer reviews | 23 answered questions

Price: **$22.90** & **FREE Shipping** on orders over $35. Details

In Stock.
Sold by EZ SELL and Fulfilled by Amazon. Gift-wrap available.

Want it tomorrow, June 19? Order within 15 mins and choose **One-Day Shipping** at checkout. Details

- Bigger Than most Postal Bench Scale
- Large back lighted display for ease of reading
- Auto Off Selectable Auto Hold or Manual Hold
- Tare Feature Can Be Calibrated With Any Know Weight
- A/C Adapter Included

18 new from $22.90   1 used from $26.21

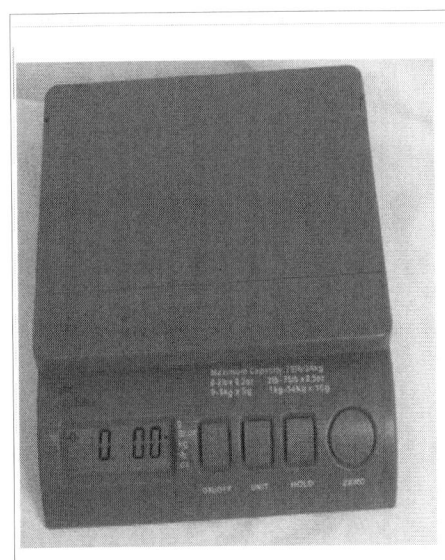

Roll over image to zoom in

This scale above is used for weighing any form of heavy gold or silver and for shipping. It is very accurate and weighs in grams, pounds, ounces and kilograms. I have used it for years and love it. The weight stays on for a few seconds after you lift the item off the scale so you can see it better. I bought this one on Amazon. The company was great to work with. It cannot be used for weighing very light objects.

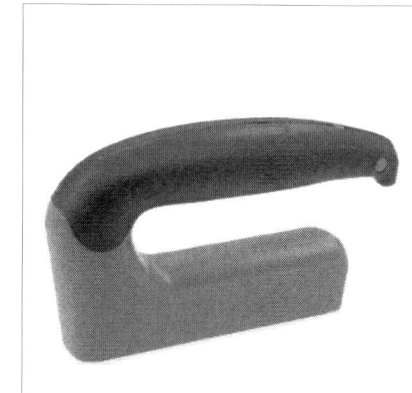

by Master Magnetics
Powerful Handle Magnet with Ergonomic Handle, 4.50" Length, 1" Width, 3.375" Height Including Handle, 100 Pounds Pull, 1 each

27 customer reviews | 3 answered questions

List Price: ~~$9.40~~
Price: **$5.25** & **FREE Shipping** on orders over $35. Details
You Save: $4.15 (44%)

In Stock.
Sold by Deerso and Fulfilled by Amazon. Gift-wrap available.

Want it tomorrow, June 19? Order within 0 mins and choose **One-Day Shipping** at checkout. Details

20 new from $4.96

A powerful magnet is used to detect fake coins, gold, silver and jewelry. This one on Amazon has a handle and is affordable. Remember, even though an item may not stick to the magnet, it can still be fake gold or fake silver or a fake coin.

Can you guess how I took this beautiful picture of an 1885 Morgan Silver Dollar? A digital microscope allows you to take great close ups of coins and jewelry. This picture shows its capability. Good quality pictures help when trying to sell an item and when trying to identify an item. Also, the magnification allows you to see the object close up.

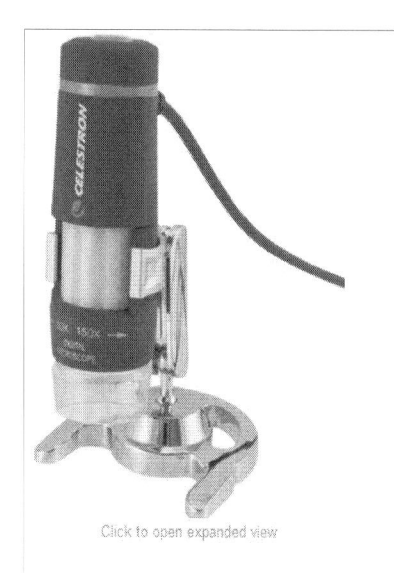

Celestron 44302 Deluxe Handheld Digital Microscope 2MP

by Celestron

★★★☆☆ ▼ 244 customer reviews | 23 answered questions

#1 Best Seller in Lab Handheld Digital Microscopes

List Price: $81.95
Price: **$46.95** & **FREE Shipping**. Details
You Save: $35.00 (43%)

In Stock.
Ships from and sold by Amazon.com. Gift-wrap available.

Want it Friday, June 20? Order within 2 hrs 51 mins and choose **Two-Day Shipping** at checkout. Details

- USB-powered handheld digital microscope with 10x to 40x magnification (up to 150x on some monitors)
- Built-in 2MP digital camera for capturing images and videos
- 6 LED ring illuminator
- Use the included Windows software to capture images and video of your discoveries. Measure your specimens with built-in measurement tool.
- Computer requirements: CD/DVD drive and USB 2.0 port. UVC plug-and-play with Windows 7, Vista, and XP. Also compatible with Mac OSX 10.4.9 and above (without measurement feature).

Click to open expanded view

I use this one and it was purchased on Amazon. It plugs into your USB port so make sure it is compatible with your computer ports (USB 2.0 vs 3.0). It comes with software that is amazing. It even takes video. For best results when trying to take pictures of objects that are reflective, move the object to the side slightly so the lights from the microscope are not shinning on the object directly.

A non-glazed ceramic tile can be purchased at any hardware supply store like Lowes or Home Depot for only a few dollars. It is used as a rubbing stone. You rub the gold item on it, and test the mark or look at the mark color. The gold and silver kit was illustrated before. Here is the link again:

http://cgi.ebay.com/ws/eBayISAPI.dll?
ViewItem&item=310825248614&ssPageName=ADME:X:RTQ:US:1123

Coin Collecting – Clubs and Terminology

Most cities and towns have a coin club. There are a number of reasons to join one, especially if you are new to coins and have children. Here are web sites that have many of the coin clubs around the country listed, along with other useful links:

http://collectingclubs.com/

http://www.coinlink.com/directory/clubs.html

Joining a local coin club is easy and very rewarding. They usually have a low yearly fee, mine is $16. They hold regular meetings, usually once a month and the benefits are enormous:

• They always make educational presentations – great learning resource.

• They are a great way to educate your children. Very few children participate and the members will try to help them – like helping the next generation.

• The members have hundreds of years of coin experience and can help you identify your coins.

• They routinely have auctions where you can buy coins and stamps well below market value.

• Members that you get to know will often have extra coins that they will sell to you at low prices so you can complete your collection.

• Members will buy coins from you.

• Members will have tons of resources – names of reliable dealers e.g. I routinely buy things at my coin club auctions and resell them on eBay.

Some terminology was listed in an earlier chapter. Let's cover some new terms and provide a link to a complete coin dictionary. This link is also a coin forum that is well worth joining, it is free:

http://www.coincommunity.com/dictionary/

Mintmark: A small letter(s) designating where the coin was produced.

    C = Charlotte, NC (gold coins only; 1838-1861)

    CC = Carson City, NV (1870-1893)

    D = Dahlonega, GA (gold coins only; 1838-1861)

    D = Denver, CO (1906 to date)

    O = New Orleans, LA (1838-1909)

    P or No Mintmark = Philadelphia, PA (1793 to date)

    S = San Francisco, CA (1854 to date)

    W = West Point, NY (1984 to date)

BU: Brilliant Uncirculated refers to the coins condition or grade – it is a coin that is in its original condition or mint state and has original mint luster.

Bullion/Bullion Coin: A coin (American Eagle) or other object (bars, ingots, etc…) consisting primarily of a precious metal, e.g. silver, gold, platinum.

Business Strike: A coin minted for general circulation.

Certified: A coin that has been authenticated and graded by one of the major grading services, like: PCGS or NGS.

Circulated: Coins with obvious signs of wear due to being "circulated" in regular commerce.

Clad: Coins made from more than one layer of metal, e.g. quarters since 1965 have a pure copper core, with the outer layers copper-nickel (.750 copper, .250 nickel).

Grade or Grading: A term used to define the coins condition.

Key/Key Date: Refers to the scarcest coins in a series and carries a higher price, e.g. 1909-S VDB Lincoln Cent which is the rarest coin in the Lincoln Penny series.

Luster: The brilliance or shine of a coin and is considered to be one of the main factors in the coins value and grade.

Mint Set: An official set containing one uncirculated coin for each denomination made that year.

MS/Mint State: A term to describe a coin in the condition as it left the mint, uncirculated coins or BU.

NGC: Numismatic Guaranty Corporation is one of the major grading companies.

Numismatics: The study, art or collection of coins, medals, tokens and similar objects.

Numismatist: A person who is knowledgeable in the collecting of coins, medals, token and similar objects.

Patina: A term used to describe the lighter shades of toning on a coin.

PCGS: Professional Coin Grading Service is one of the major grading companies.

Proof: A specially produced coin made from highly polished planchets and dies and often struck more than once to accent the design. Proof coins receive the highest quality strike possible and can be distinguished by their sharpness of detail and brilliant, mirror-like surface and sometimes cameo effect.

Proof Set: A complete set of proof coins for each denomination made that year and specially packaged.

Relief: The part of a coin's design that is raised above the surface.

Reverse: The back of the coin or tails.

Rim: The raised outer edge of the coin, that helps protect the design from wear.

Slab: A nickname referring to coins that have been graded by a third party service and placed in a plastic holder.

Strike: The act of impressing the image on to the planchet. The quality of the strike is an important part of the grading process.

Toning: Coloring on the surface of a coin caused by a chemical reaction, such as sulfur from older cardboard books, flips or envelopes. Rainbow-colored toning and original toning is often a desirable characteristic to many collectors.

Type Set: A collection of one coin for each denomination and/or a particular design.

Ask Price: The selling price a dealer offers.

Bid Price: The price a dealer pays for bullion or coins.

Bullion: Precious metals like platinum, gold or silver in the form of bars or other storage shapes. Bullion coins are made of these metals, too.

Collector Coin, Historic Coin, or Numismatic Coin: A coin whose value is based on rarity, demand, condition, and mintage; in fact, it may be worth more than its bullion value.

Melt Value: The basic intrinsic bullion value of a coin if it were melted and sold.

Premium: The amount by which the market value of a gold coin or bar exceeds the actual value of its gold content. The seller can recover part of the premium at resale.

Spot Price: The current price in the physical market for immediate delivery; sometimes called the cash price.

Spread: The difference between the buying price and the selling price.

Troy Ounce: The unit of weight for precious metals. One troy ounce equals 480 grains, 1.09711 ounces, or 31.103 grams.

One of the best ways to learn about coins is by joining a forum. We mentioned one earlier, here are some more:

CoinTalk Forums: These forums are perfect for beginning coin collectors and expert coin collectors. I really love the community here.

Coin Network: This site is more than just a coin collecting forum. It is a social network for coin collectors. The Coin Network has a forum section, a blog post section, and a section to create groups.

Susan Headley's Coin Forum: Susan Headley is one of the best coin bloggers. She writes the Susan's Coins Blog at About.com. If you have not read Susan's blog articles, head on over there right now. She is an excellent writer and very passionate about coins. In addition to being a great writer, Susan has a great coin collecting forum.

Collector's Universe Forums: Collector's Universe does not just cater to coin collectors. However, this forum does have an active coin collector community.

Another great forum: www.Coinpeople.com

How To Start Collecting

The best way to learn about coins, even if you have no intention of actually collecting, but want to increase your understanding so your investment strategies can be more fruitful, is to get your hands on some and build a small collection. One way to do this is to pick a coin denomination that is easy to work with, costs little, and can be found easily so you are able to complete a set. Several possibilities come to mind: Lincoln Pennies, Jefferson Nickels and Ancient Coins. Ancient coins are harder to find than pennies and nickels, but are so fascinating that you should consider collecting them. I will show you how.

Of the three listed I suggest Jefferson Nickels. It is very easy to complete a set and this will give you confidence and a sense of accomplishment. You will learn a lot about coins in the process. The Jefferson Nickel came into existence in 1938 to replace the Buffalo Nickel. The most valuable coins are only worth $3 - $15 in good condition, so completing a set is easy and it may require some investing, but not much. Many of the coins can be found in change. Let's look at the type of nickels you may come across:

1938 – 2003 Design (Jefferson front, Monticello back)

2004 - 2005 Design (Westward Journey Series)

2006 – Present (Monticello on reverse again)

The Red Book lists all the dates in the series including some error coins, which are hard to find, and can be expensive, but should be mentioned. We will look at the errors later. A good way to get started is to buy a coin folder that holds the nickels you will be looking for. Several companies make folders: Whitman and H E Harris make folders. Whitman is the cheapest and best for getting started.

The Whitman Folder below can be purchased online for as little as $2 used and $3-4 new from Amazon and most major retailers. Three folders are needed for the entire Jefferson Nickel Series.

The Warman folder below can be purchased for $4.99 online. It is designed for children and is loaded with educational facts. Amazon has it.

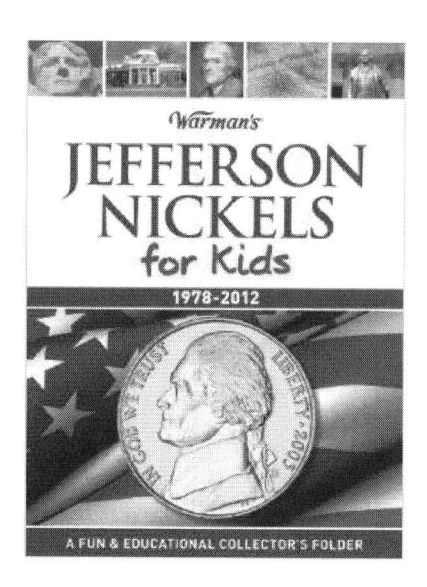

You will notice when you examine the Red Book that there are dates listed that will not be in the coin folders. These are coins that have errors on them, and some coins (not errors) are only minted in special sets and not released into circulation. They show up in change upon occasion, but are not listed in the coin folders. Don't worry about these error and special set dates. Stay focused on the coins listed in the folders. How then does one find the coins to put into the folder?

Besides looking through pocket change, the best way to get your hands on large numbers of nickels is to order a box from the bank. Some banks charge you to do this, some don't. If you have a good working relationship with your bank they will not charge you. Chase, Compass and Citibank are pretty good about this. Each branch is different, so shop around. How then does one order a box of nickels?

Tell your bank to order a box of nickels (not new coins) and they will call you when it comes in, usually three days. You only pay for it when it comes in. A box of nickels holds 50 rolls, $2 each, for a total of $100 and weighs 22 pounds (heavy). This weight is a dead weight so be careful handling them. They are much heavier than you think.

You have two options when opening these rolls. One is to reuse the roll wrappers by prying one end open carefully with a small flat screw driver. Or, ask your bank for plastic deposit bags. You can dump all the coins into them and mark it with the amount and your bank account number for redeposit (some banks charge for these – they cost the bank about 75 cents each). My bank gives them to me for free.

It is important to know about the metal composition of nickels because at times they are worth a lot more than 5 cents. A standard nickel is 25% nickel and 75% copper. "War Nickels" (mid-1942 to 1945) are 56% copper, 35% silver, and 9% manganese. Silver nickels contain 0.05626 troy ounces of silver.

When the price of copper and or nickel rises the actual value of a nickel is more than 5 cents. When this happens people hoard them for resale. All wartime nickels are worth more than 5 cents because of their silver content. The web site coinflation shows them to be worth $1.14 each (June 2014).

http://www.coinflation.com/silver_coin_values.html

Any coins found with "S" mint marks should be saved and all silver coins should be saved (the coin folder has spaces for certain coins, no spaces for newer "S" coins or error coins).

Wartime silver nickels have a mint mark above the dome, see the letter "P" below. It could be a "D" for Denver or an "S" for San Francisco or a "P" for Philadelphia, the cities that minted the coins.

In order to properly identify your Jefferson Nickels that you find it is important to know where the mint marks or letters indicating where the coins were made are located. It can be confusing.

Located from 1938 to 1964 to the right of Monticello, except for "wartime nickels" which have a large mint mark above Monticello shown above (no mint marks used from 1965 to 1967).

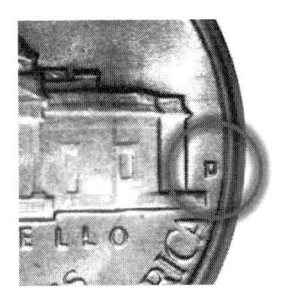

From 1968 to 2004, slightly clockwise from the last digit of the date.

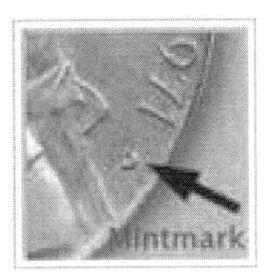

In 2005, under "Liberty".

Since 2006, under the date. Philadelphia Mint specimens before 1980 lack a mint mark, except for wartime nickels, which have a P for Philadelphia, if struck there.

When you go through the coin rolls start by looking at the dates and mint marks. As you find coins to fill the slots in the coin folder make sure you have your gloves on. Coins are very dirty. If you find a duplicate coin for a coin already placed in the folder, replace the old one with the new one, if the new one is in better condition, and keep doing this for all the coins. Yes it is a lot of work, but worth the effort.

Any coins that seem different in some way should be saved, and as stated before, all silver and newer "S" coins should be saved as they have some value. Check the Red Book for coin values and coinflation for silver and copper-nickel values. When a nickel is worth more than a nickel you should save them.

As you fill the slots you will notice that the empty spaces typically hold the harder to find coins. As you can see in the image below the 1938 D and 1938 S slots are empty. They were minted in low quantities compared to the other coins and therefore are more difficult to find. At some point you might consider purchasing some of these missing coins in order to complete your set. Ebay is a good place to buy coins. We will look at this subject in a future chapter.

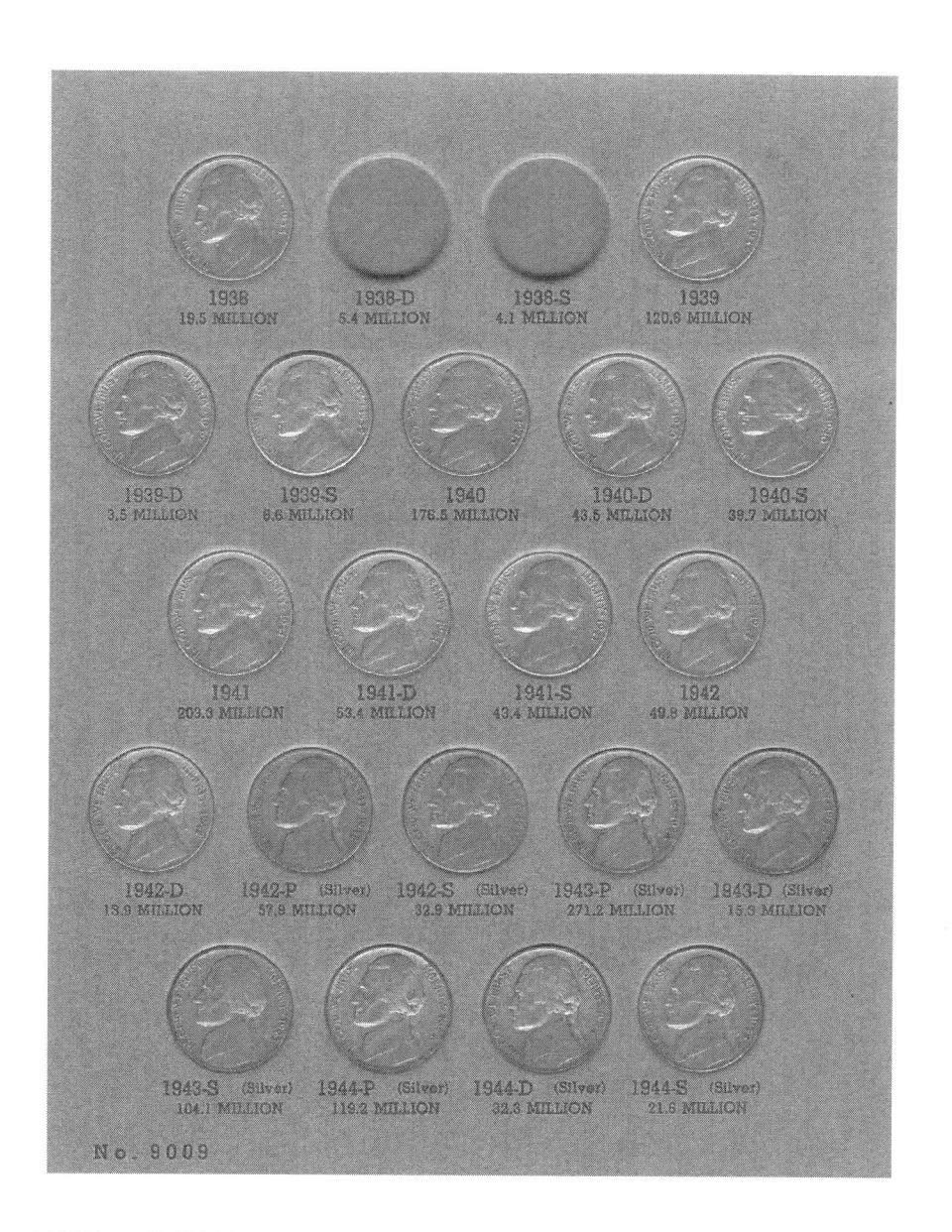

The 1938D and 1938S are missing. Notice the low mintage figures of 4.1 and 5.4 million.

Error Coins Can Be Very Valuable

When you start searching for Jefferson Nickels you will immediately notice that the Red Book lists error coins along with the coins you will search for to fill your coin folder. The coin folder has no slots for error coins. Because they have value, I suggest looking for them while searching through rolls of nickels and other coins.

The Red Book mentions eight nickel error types, but if you look at Ken Potters book *Strike It Rick With Pocket Change* he lists thirty error types worth looking for. He states that there are many more, but they are minor in nature. So where does one begin? What does an error coin look like and which ones are worth looking for without spending hours looking at each coin? There is no easy answer, but a good starting point is to look for the eight mentioned in the Red Book and one mentioned on the PCGS web site, the speared bison, for a total of nine.

Let's look at the nine error coins in some detail so you can easily spot them. The Red Book suggests a value for them. The speared bison, not mentioned in the Red Book, is worth $60+. Get out your magnifying loupe – you will need it.

The first error to look for is the 1939 Double Monticello:

You can clearly see the doubling of the letters: O – V – N – S. It is worth $75 or more – value depends upon coin condition.

The 1942D: D/D Horizontal D. The mint mark shows up twice – one over the other. The top "D" is vertical and the bottom "D" is horizontal. It is worth from $75 on up.

1943P: 3 over 2. This one is hard to spot - a faint 2 is present under the 3. It is worth $50 on up.

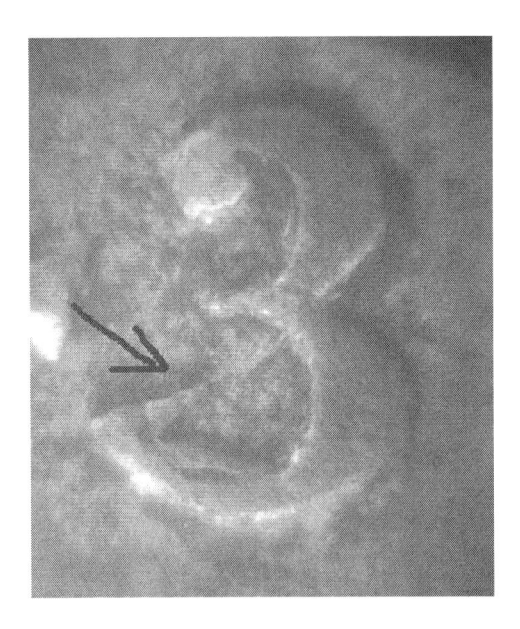

1943P: Double Eye. There is some doubling on the date and letters and the eye – hard coin to spot. It is worth $25 on up.

1945P: DDR (Double Die Reverse). You should notice doubling on letters. It is worth $20 and up.

1949D: D over S. It is hard to see this one. It is worth $150 on up.

1954S: S over D. It is worth $26 on up.

1955D: D over S. It is worth $36 on up.

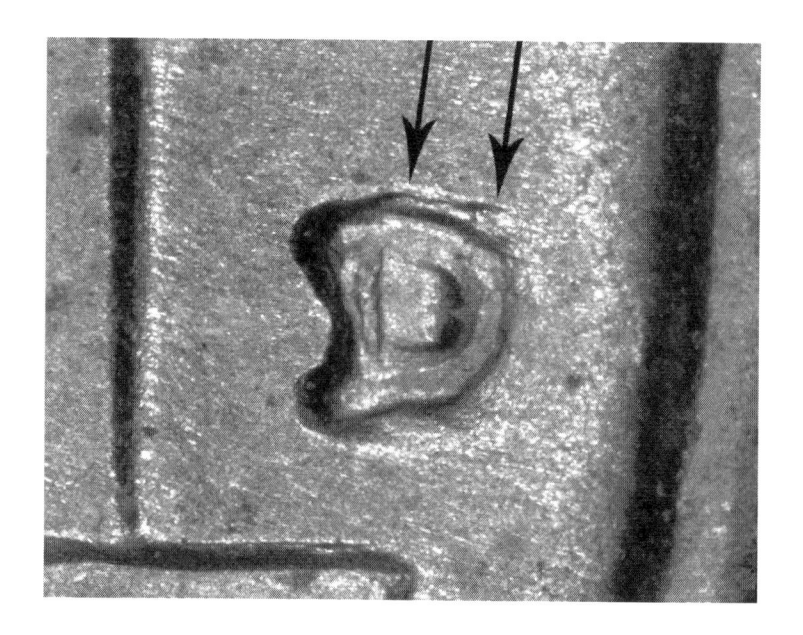

2005D: Speared Bison. It is worth $60 on up.

The easiest way to remember these errors is to make a list of them and keep it handy when looking at the nickels.

- 1939 Double Monticello
- 1942D: D over horizontal D
- 1943D: Double Obverse eye and letters doubled
- 1943: 3 over 2
- 1945D: Double Reverse
- 1949D: D over S
- 1954S: S over D
- 1955D: D over S
- 2005D: Speared Bison

Please keep in mind the fact that error coins can occur at any time on any coin. We looked at nine errors common to the Jefferson Nickel. However, there are some errors that occur when the coin is minted that affect the appearance of the coin, and therefore, can be found at any time on any coin. In other words, the same error may exist on many denominations, pennies, nickels, dimes, etc...

These errors are very noticeable. You can easily see them without any type of magnification. Let's take a few minutes and look at some of them on Jefferson Nickels. Any coin can suffer from these mishaps. The value of these error coins ranges from a few dollars to thousands, depending upon the coin and the error.

This web site gives some values for these errors, also check eBay:

http://coinsite.com/us-error-coin-values/

A rotated reverse or die rotation results in a reverse not being vertical with the front or obverse of the coin - when you flip a coin over the back should be in the same vertical position as the front

The more the coin is rotated the greater the value – just flip each coin over to check for this

A clip error occurs when a new blank coin is punched from a piece of metal that already had a hole in it from previous use.

Off center stikes – coin blank was not placed in collar properly.

Double strikes – coin imprinted more than once.

Lamination error – top layer coming off or not placed on coin properly.

Jefferson Nickel coin blank. Incomplete coin or coin missed its mark, the blank metal onto which a coin is pressed had the rim raised (now called a planchet), but the final imprinting of the coin was never done.

Broadstrike: When a perfectly centered planchet is struck out-of-collar, it expands evenly in all directions. This error can be called a "centered broadstrike". However, since the majority of broadstrikes are centered, hobbyists usually refer to it simply as a broadstrike. If the planchet is not well-centered, but the design remains complete on both faces, the error is called an "uncentered broadstrike".

Dies and Cuds: Extra metal – many variations of this error type. It occurs when the die breaks and extra metal is placed on the coin.

One of the best web sites ever developed on error coins is listed below: http://www.error-ref.com/index-of-entries.html

This site lists every possible error by name and provides detailed pictures. It is designed for the advanced collector, but worth taking a look at and having as a reference.

Once you look at this site you realize that the error topic in and of itself can become a life time pursuit.

How To Grade Coins

When you start collecting nickels you will notice some are worn out and some look new. As you can imagine, the condition of a coin affects its value. So, to determine value we need a point of reference. The Red Book tells us general values for each coin type based upon a condition that it describes for each coin series.

This image below from the Red Book shows the grades or conditions in relation to the Jefferson Nickel, making this information very valuable for the beginner. It provides a reference point to help determine the condition of the nickels you find.

JEFFERSON (1938 TO DATE)

This nickel was originally designed by Felix Schlag, who won an award of $1,000 in a competition with some 390 artists. His design established the definite public approval of portrait and pictorial themes rather than symbolic devices on our coinage.

Designer Felix Schlag; weight 5 grams; composition (1938–1942, 1946 to date), .750 copper, .250 nickel, (1942–1945), .560 copper, .350 silver, .090 manganese, with net weight .05626 oz. pure silver; diameter 21.2 mm; plain edge; mints: Philadelphia, Denver, San Francisco.

VG-8 Very Good—Second porch pillar from right nearly gone, other three still visible but weak.
F-12 Fine—Jefferson's cheekbone worn flat. Hair lines and eyebrow faint. Second pillar weak, especially at bottom.
VF-20 Very Fine—Second pillar plain and complete on both sides.
EF-40 Extremely Fine—Cheekbone, hair lines, eyebrow slightly worn but well defined. Base of triangle above pillars visible but weak.
AU-50 About Uncirculated—Traces of light wear on only high points of design. Half of mint luster present.
MS-60 Uncirculated—No trace of wear. Light blemishes.
MS-65 Gem Uncirculated—No trace of wear. Barely noticeable blemishes.

1939, Doubled MONTICELLO and FIVE CENTS

There is a standard that has been developed to help us decide what the condition or grade is. On a 70-point grading scale coins are assigned a numeric value. It is called the Sheldon Scale. The Sheldon Scale ranges from a grade of Poor (P-1) to Perfect Mint State (MS-70.) Grades are usually assigned at key points on this scale, with the most commonly used points being: (information from about.com)

(P-1) Poor - Barely identifiable; must have date and mintmark, otherwise pretty thrashed.
(FR-2) Fair - Worn almost smooth but lacking the damage Poor coins have.
(G-4) Good - Heavily worn such that inscriptions merge into the rims in places; details are mostly gone.
(VG-8) Very Good - Very worn, but all major design elements are clear, if faint. Little if any central detail.
(F-12) Fine - Very worn, but wear is even and overall design elements stand out boldly. Almost fully-separated rims.
(VF-20) Very Fine - Moderately worn, with some finer details remaining. All letters of LIBERTY, (if present,) should be readable. Full, clean rims.
(EF-40) Extremely Fine - Lightly worn; all devices are clear, major devices bold.
(AU-50) About Uncirculated - Slight traces of wear on high points; may have contact marks and little eye appeal.
(AU-58) Very Choice About Uncirculated - - Slightest hints of wear marks, no major contact marks, almost full luster, and positive eye appeal.
(MS-60) Mint State Basal - Strictly uncirculated but that's all; ugly coin with no luster, obvious contact marks, etc.
(MS-63) Mint State Acceptable - Uncirculated, but with contact marks and nicks, slightly impaired luster, overall basically appealing appearance. Strike is average to weak.

(MS-65) Mint State Choice - Uncirculated with strong luster, very few contact marks, excellent eye appeal. Strike is above average.

(MS-68) Mint State Premium Quality - Uncirculated with perfect luster, no visible contact marks to the naked eye, exceptional eye appeal. Strike is sharp and attractive.

(MS-69) Mint State All-But-Perfect - Uncirculated with perfect luster, sharp, attractive strike, and very exceptional eye appeal. A perfect coin except for microscopic flaws (under 8x magnification) in planchet, strike, or contact marks.

(MS-70) Mint State Perfect - The perfect coin. There are no microscopic flaws visible to 8x, the strike is sharp, perfectly-centered, and on a flawless planchet. Bright, full, original luster and outstanding eye appeal.

A simplified version may be more helpful:

Prefix	Numerical Grade	Description
MS	60–70	Mint State (Uncirculated)
AU	50, 53, 55, 58	About Uncirculated
XF	40, 45	Extremely Fine
VF	20, 25, 30, 35	Very Fine
F	12, 15	Fine
VG	8, 10	Very Good
G	4, 6	Good
AG	3	About Good
FA	2	Fair
PR	1	Poor

Valuable coins, worth $100 or more are often sent to grading companies for certification. Certified coins sell for much more money than the same coin that is not certified, and it lets the seller and buyer know that the coin is not a fake. Buying certified coins assures us that we are getting what we pay for. However, there are certified fakes out there, but not many.

Let's look at some nickels and try to determine their grade or condition.

The Red Book description for a VG-8 Very Good coin shows the 2nd pillar from the right nearly gone, as is the case for the coin below. The other three pillars are visible but worn, so this coin is Very Good or perhaps one grade higher, Fine.

The Red Book states a coin that is AU-50, about uncirculated has traces of light wear on only high points of the design. Half of the mint luster is present. Notice the mint luster.

How To Handle Coins

It is important to know how to handle coins. Coins are dirty, so wearing gloves helps. Handling valuable coins and special coins should be spoken about. Some coins can be damaged just by breathing on them, and some can be damaged by touching them. This results in lowering their value. Valuable coins should never be cleaned by you, only by professionals.

Proof coins, for example, if for some reason need to be taken out of their plastic covers, can be damaged by breathing on them and touching them. Years ago coin holders were not properly made and coins became damaged when stored in them. This problem has been corrected today. The chemical in the holder (usually a card board holder) reacted with the coin, producing a discoloring of the coin or a toning of the coin. Toned coins can have value. The reason I mention this subject is due to the fact that you may come across a very valuable coin and you should only handle it with cotton gloves to maintain its value, no cleaning. Please note: a valuable coin after improper cleaning can be reduced in worth by 90%.

Common coins can be cleaned with soap and water, but no abrasive material or cleanser should be used. Use your fingers to soak the coin in soap and water, do one coin at a time. Rub the coin with your fingers, then rinse the soap and water off with distilled water then place the coin on a towel to dry (don't use your nails).

Because you may come across a toned or sometimes called rainbow toned coin it is important to examine this subject in some detail. Coins react to chemicals around them, either by touch or by exposure through the air. Believe it or not some toned or rainbow toned coins actually are more valuable than plain coins. It depends on the coin and how they look. Never buy a toned coin unless it is certified. Many dishonest sellers bake coins in the oven and produce fake tones.

It is very important that you understand toning. If you clean a toned coin you can take a coin worth maybe $30 - $50 and turn it back into just a quarter, assuming it is a 25 cent piece you just cleaned. Recently PCGS, the coin grading company, tweeted this picture of a Silver Eagle featuring spectacular concentric rainbow toning.

Certified by PCGS – a red coin like this can sell for hundreds and sometimes thousands of dollars.

Another cleaning method:

Soak the coin in vinegar. If unsightly tarnish, dirt or rust deposits, or other contaminants remain on the coin after a thorough rinse, soak the coin for anywhere from a few seconds to a few minutes. For gold coins, soaking in very hot soapy water works the best. For old pennies, soak the coin in vinegar for at least 24 hours. Silver, copper, and nickel-clad coins can be soaked in distilled water or, to remove tough stains, white vinegar. A 6-minute soak in lemon juice may also be used on silver coins. This will not only protect the coin but it will help give the coin a finish at the end of the cleaning. Always rinse with distilled water and let dry on a clean towel after any cleaning method.

Fake Coins

      Unfortunately it seems that money is more important than ethics, and many places on earth produce vast numbers of fake coins. For example, Lebanon produces fake pre-1933 gold coins. In fact, it has gotten so bad that they even fake certification. They copy the PCGS plastic holder, fake the grading and claim the coin is real when it is not. Fortunately most certified coins are not fake.

    Almost every U.S. Mint gold coin has been faked. Many are made in the Middle East. What is so scary about this fake shown below is that it is made of gold and has the same weight as the real coin on the right. Let's look at the reason it is fake.

1892
$5.00

Counterfeit   Genuine

There is moderate softness on both sides but primarily at the digits and letters, which can appear almost cartoonish. There are also a number of raised lines, often seen on fakes, by the denticles, especially on the reverse. A few particularly noticeable raised lines can be seen above the D in UNITED. These are almost never seen on genuine specimens. The denticles are the many little squares around the coin next to the rim. Notice the metal above the D, the extra metal next to the denticle. (Looks like streaks)

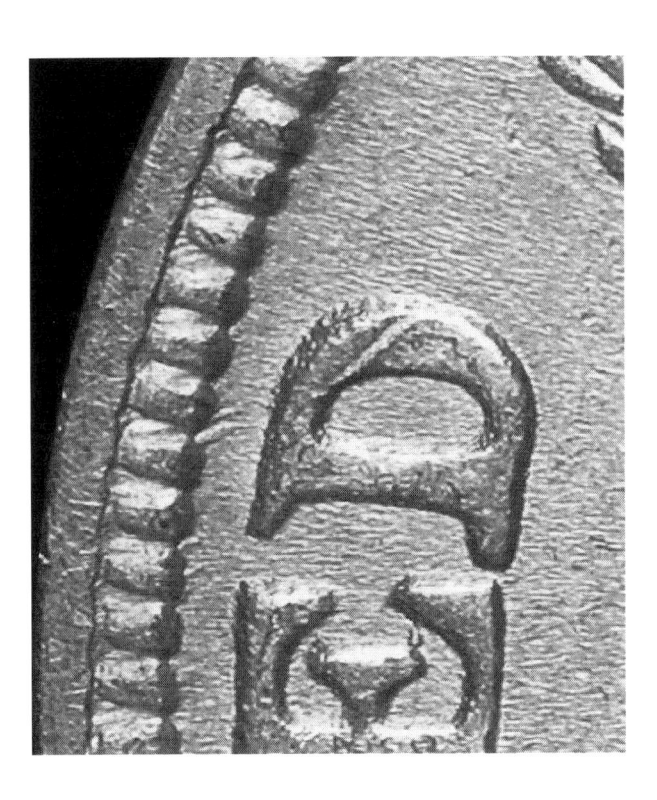

Chinese made fake silver dollars "Morgan". The easiest way to spot a fake coin is just by looking at it. Most fakes look perfect, no ware, plastic like, hot off the press.

Photos from Jinghua Shei.

Looks like fake silver coins

Chinese fake coin factory

Fake Indian Head and Large US Cents

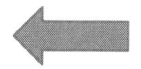

Most fake coins will not weigh true. The Red Book tells you the weight of every coin so you can use this as a guide. Many fake coins have incorrect information on them, check the date and mint mark of the coin, and look it up in the Red Book. If the coin in question has a mint mark in the wrong place, the wrong type of mint mark or a date that is not listed in the Red Book, be careful, it may be a fake.

Fake Morgan Silver Dollars and fake older large cent pennies are becoming more common due to the large scale production runs from China and other places. The acid test is fine for silver coins if you can hold them before purchasing. But buying coins online can present challenges, since you cannot test them. I will list some steps to help protect yourself. Keep in mind the fact that pictures of coins online from bad dealers may not show the actual coin being sold. Here are some web sites that you can look at to help determine the authenticity of a coin, but this information is usually useful after you buy, not before.

http://coinauctionshelp.com/Counterfeit_Silver_Dollars_Fake_Trade_Dollars_Fake_Morgan_Dollar.html#.U8PvkEDb4z4

http://www.silver-coins.org/counterfeit_dollars.html

http://meridiancoin.com/contemporary-fake-silver-dollar-guide/

http://www.ngccoin.com/news/viewarticle.aspx?IDArticle=3526&counterfeit-morgan-dollar-fake

If you Google fake coins, fake Morgans, fake silver you will discover more valuable information. You will never end up with a fake coin if you:

- Buy only from a reputable dealer – red flag are private auctions.
- Buy only slabbed or certified coins (PCGS or NGC).

If you are going to spend over $50 on a coin make sure it is certified. Never buy from a dealer that sells slabbed and unslabbed coins – this is a red flag. I see so many dealers online who have a few certified coins and a bunch of coins that have not been graded. I think they do this to convince you they are reputable. Be very careful.

- Many fake coins look like plastic – they look too perfect to be real.
- Many eBay dealers sell fake coins – just look at the pictures.

Another big red flag are dealers who sell coins every week and have large numbers of great coins for sale. It is impossible to have this many good coins unless they inherited them or got their hands on a giant batch of coins from an estate. Even then, I would be very cautious. Probably buying fakes from China.

- Any coin that is worth way more than the asking price is usually fake.

Never buy a coin that you cannot see clearly and in great detail – even a high grade coin may not look so good after you buy it. (I have seen coins on eBay selling for a fraction of their true value – just by looking at them you can tell they are fake).

Another type of fake occurs when an actual coin is altered (the coin is not fake but has been manipulated in some way). A very good article that talks about fake (changed) coins that were sold on eBay is shown below:

http://www.ebay.com/gds/Coin-Fake-Detection-1909-S-VDB-Lincoln-Cent-/10000000015293333/g.html

Let's look at an altered coin:

The highly sought after 1922 penny can be made by removing the "D" from under the date so it appears to be a 1922 coin.

The highly sought after 1922 penny can be made by removing the "D" from under the date so it appears to be a 1922 coin - This coin was done so skillfully that you cannot see any trace of the "D"

The "D" is under the date

A 1922 "D" coin is worth $20   A 1922 plain coin is worth $750 - $27,000

You can see the wisdom of buying only certified coins

When buying online from sites like eBay (this does not apply to well known coin auction sites mentioned earlier), it is advisable to make one small purchase from the dealer, and when you get the coin, pay to have it certified. This way you know they are selling genuine merchandise. It is better to pay $30 before shelling out hundreds only to find out you have fakes. You can email me at any time to look at coins in question. This topic will be addressed again in the chapter called: Buying Coins.

Children and Pennies

Penny collecting is another great way to start learning about coins, and it is a great way to introduce children to this fantastic hobby. What is so sad, is that coin collecting does not appeal to the younger generation because technology offers more pizzazz. Just go to a coin club meeting in any town. There are no young people in attendance. But the good news is if you introduce your children or a friend's or relative's child to penny collecting they will love it. The approach you take is what matters.

The best way for kids to get started is with the Warman's Lincoln Cents For Kids Folder. Amazon has it. We mentioned this before.

Lincoln Cents for Kids: 1979-2012 Collector's Lincoln Cent Folder (Warman's Kids Coin Folders) Hardcover
by Warman's (Author)
★★★★☆ 6 customer reviews

Hardcover
from $0.91

28 Used from $0.91
26 New from $0.95
1 Collectible from $15.99

Lincoln Cents for Kids: 1979-2012 collector's Lincoln cent folder

From Lincoln cents to the new National Parks quarters, Warman's coin folders for Kids offer everything the young numismatist needs to start on a hobby that could last a lifetime. As you collect, learn why Abraham Lincoln grew his beard, how Thomas Jefferson delivered his addresses to Congress, where the smallest National Park is located and which state features the roadrunner as its state bird. Featuring 75 high-quality die-cut slots and chock-full of fascinating and educational facts, *Lincoln Cents for Kids* is perfect for the young coin collector.

It is an easy book to fill because it starts in 1979, and it is loaded with fun facts. When working with children they must wear gloves, and very young children should not work with coins because they are a choking hazard. I like to order a box of pennies. It is only $25 and contains 2500 coins (caution – it weighs 14 pounds and is dead weight). Lincoln pennies were minted from 1909 – today (see the Red Book).

There is so much you can do with pennies. You can turn the hunt into a game for your kids. They can practice their math skills by calculating the age of pennies they find. See who can find the oldest coin. They will find foreign coins, dimes, shiny new pennies and copper pennies that are worth 2 cents each – see coinflation.com for current rates. You can even find Indian Head pennies, but it takes patience.

Copper pennies were minted from 1909 – 1982 (some 1982 pennies are not copper so you have to weigh them to be sure). A copper penny weighs 3.11 grams. A zinc penny (1982 – present) weighs 2.5 grams. Copper is worth about 2 cents per penny so when children find copper pennies they are doubling their money immediately. This gets them excited. You will find many copper pennies in a box of 2500 coins. This 1974 copper penny shown below weighs 3.08 grams. We know this because of its date.

- The value of a gram scale becomes very apparent now - Some coins can only be verified by weight – fake coins often do not weigh the same as real coins

This 1974 copper penny on the left weighs 3.08 grams – we knew this because of its date – the 2000 zinc penny on the right weighs 2.49 grams

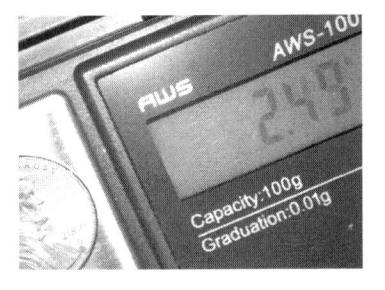

1982 pennies can only be verified by weighing them – some are copper – some are zinc

This zinc penny (2000D) above, only weighs 2.49 grams. Some pennies weigh a little more or less than others, depending upon how worn out they are.

In 1943 the U.S. Mint made pennies out of steel instead of copper. Known as steel war penny or steelie, it had the same design as the copper penny. Due to wartime needs of copper for use in ammunition and other military equipment during World War II, the U.S. Mint researched various ways to limit dependence and meet conservation goals on copper usage. After trying out several substitutes (ranging from other metals to plastics) to replace the then-standard bronze alloy (95 % copper and five % tin and zinc), the one-cent coin was minted in zinc-coated steel. This alloy caused the new coins to be magnetic and 13% lighter. They were struck at all three mints: Philadelphia, Denver, and San Francisco. As with the bronze cents, coins from the latter two sites have respectively "D" and "S" mint marks below the date.

Steel pennies are easy to find and fun to collect. In really good condition (mint) they can easily bring $20 or more. You will find them when looking at penny rolls. Many, however, were destroyed by the government after the war. Notice the gray steel color of the 1943 steel penny on the right compared to the copper penny on the left.

Once children get hooked on coins they will develop a lifelong passion for a hobby that can actually help pay for their education. The Red Book shows the value of pennies, and it shows some error coins as well. My *Penny Treasure* ebook sold on Amazon lists penny coin errors.

A complete Lincoln Penny set in a very high grade can be worth well over $100,000.

The front of the Lincoln Penny has always remained the same since its inception in 1909 – the reverse has had 7 designs listed below

Wheat (1909–1958)

Lincoln Memorial (1959–2008)

Birth and early childhood in Kentucky (Lincoln Bicentennial, 2009)

Formative Years in Indiana (Lincoln Bicentennial, 2009)

Professional life in Illinois (Lincoln Bicentennial, 2009)

Presidency in DC (Lincoln Bicentennial, 2009)

Union shield (2010–*present*)

The world's most expensive penny, a Lincoln cent struck in the wrong metal at the Denver Mint in 1943, sold for a world's record price of $1,700,000 in September 2010:

The Lincoln Penny Series has great appeal to any age group, and it is one of the most sought after coin series in the world of Numismatics. The Whitman Coin Folders can also serve as a starting point for children or for anyone that wants to learn about coins. The next image shows the Whitman Folder Series. Also consider the Harris Folders as well, also made by Whitman. Most large department stores carry these folders. Amazon, as well as other online stores, have them for less money. A good price is $2.99.

Whitman Coin Folder Lincoln Cents 1909-1940

Whitman Coin Folder Lincoln Cents 1941-1974

Whitman Coin Folder Lincoln Cents 1975 to Date

It takes multiple folders to cover the entire Lincoln Penny Series starting in 1909

Special coins, sold only in sets by the US Mint, are not listed in these folders – more expensive folders list all the coins

Penny error coins are well worthy of your time and study, and the Red Book lists some of them. Many are quite valuable, and the major ones can be found when looking through your pennies. Some examples are shown below.

This 1969-S double die penny was graded PCGS MS-64 Red, which is tied with one other specimen for the finest known - It sold at a Heritage auction for $126,500 on January 10, 2008!

Several 1983 "Copper" pennies have been found – at auction they could easily fetch $15000 or more

1983 pennies are normally made of zinc (97.5%) (2.5% copper)

"AM" Separated by Space

"AM" Touching

In 1992 the word "America" on the reverse was supposed to have the letters "AM" far apart instead of almost touching – an example of this error in mint condition sold for over $24,000

Coin Roll Hunting

We briefly mentioned coin rolls with respect to Lincoln Head Pennies and Jefferson Nickels. However, it is important to cover this topic again. I will divide this chapter into two parts, coin roll hunting and buying coin rolls. I could cover the latter, buying coin rolls, in one word: DON'T, but you will then wonder why.

Coin roll hunting refers to the act of opening up coin rolls and looking at the enclosed coins to find a particular coin(s). It could be for the purpose of finding copper pennies, buffalo nickels, silver coins and much more. There is so much mentioned about the topic, especially on YouTube. Most of what you read or see is inaccurate and misleading.

The YouTube videos often mention the frustrations associated with looking at rolled coins. They can't find any silver or they look for certain dates and have little or no success. The problem is very simple. They do not know what they are doing. The only way to be successful at finding silver is by looking through half dollar rolls for 90% and 40% silver coins. And at the same time you should look for half dollar error coins so you have the added bonus of errors along side silver. When you look at half dollars, you will find a lot of 1964 Kennedy Halves because people do not realize that they are 90% silver, and many of them are dirty and hard to spot. Looking for silver with dime and quarter rolls is a waste of time. Looking for quarter errors is not a waste of time. For detailed information on this subject please check out my course: "Learn How Power Sellers Make Millions On eBay" found on www.Udemy.com.

The other topic of interest is buying coin rolls online, especially on eBay. In one word, don't. Almost all the rolls on eBay are fake. They have been manipulated by the seller to appear in such a way that the buyer is tempted to buy or bid because of the end coins that have some value. How is this done?

It is very simple. Just buy a coin crimping machine and some old looking wrappers and put a few Indian Head Pennies at each end and you are in business. Here's a machine on Amazon that could make big money if you were unethical.

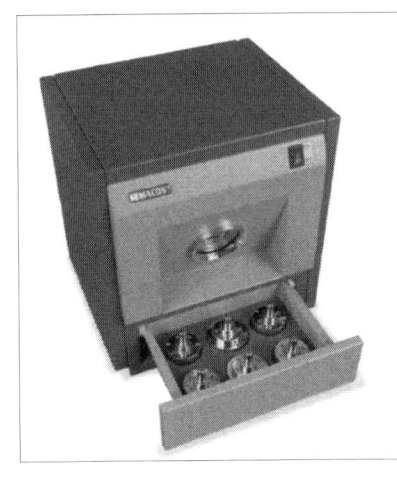

Semacon CM-75 Coin Roll Wrapper Crimping Machine (Crimper) w/ 6 Heads
by Semacon
Be the first to review this item

List Price: $775.00
Price: $706.88 + $42.75 shipping
You Save: $68.12 (9%)

In stock.
Usually ships within 2 to 3 days.
Ships from and sold by Sale Stores.

- Safe, you can touch the rotating head while it's spinning and it won't hurt you.
- Requires only a couple of seconds to proficiently seal coin wrappers.
- Includes the following crimping heads: 1¢, 5¢, 10¢, 25¢, 50¢, $1 (SBA/Golden)
- Includes a crimp head storage drawer.

2 new from $700.20

Buying unsearched rolls:

A great article from eBay illustrates my point:

At any given time, eBay has a few hundred auctions for unsearched rolls. The new fad on eBay is bank wrapped rolls showing a key or semi-key date on the end, and the old fad is pointing to their (the seller's) feedback on how many key dates that have been found in the rolls they are selling. Most coins found in bank wrapped rolls are common and well circulated coins. Shot gun wrapped rolls can be opened, searched, then re-crimped as if it came from a bank. The same rolls can be searched and a key date put on the end, then re-crimped as unsearched.

For example, let's say I have a shot gun roll of Lincoln Wheat Cents, and all are common dates. So, I buy a 1909-S key date for $125, (this is the actual book value of the coin in good condition), and I replace the end coin with the 1909-S Lincoln. Also, I know that a 1909-S with the VDB on the back is worth $900, and I also know that you can't see if the 1909-S on the end of the re-crimped roll has a VDB or not. Now I start my auction on eBay with a statement "Unsearched shotgun roll with a 1909-S showing", and a question "Is this a 1909-S VDB?".

I sit back and watch my $125 investment sell for over $255.00 because some buyers wanted to risk the chance to discover a 1909-S VDB. So, they pay $130 more than the roll is worth, and my paypal account grows over a hundred dollars more. Now I'm thinking, "What if I did this with 10 rolls? I could make well over a thousand dollars in a week!" To top it all off, other eBay sellers see my success and copy my act. Now, it's a huge problem. Don't get into "lottery" wars like this with other bidders. It's never worth it!

Let's look at one of these tempting eBay rolls: Unbelievable, a roll of pennies with an Indian Head at one end probably worth $2 is selling for $42, and the bidding hasn't ended yet.

Look at the seller's feedback, yet people are still bidding:

⊖	Worthless junk, worn out coins, rolls setup & searched. Waste of good money! unsearched penny roll very old coins lot #31 (#121262431102)	Buyer: i***s (268 ☆) US $52.01
⊖	Worthless junk, coins all worn, Flying Eagle (reverse)! Rolls set up & searched! unsearched penny roll very old coins lot #32 (#121262433791)	Buyer: i***s (268 ☆) US $71.09

Rare Coins

The subject of rare coins is of vital interest. We mentioned the term several times before and provided a definition:

Coins that continually go up in value over time and are hard to find and or buy because they are scarce, and when found can only be purchased for much more than their face value, is probably a good definition for "rare coins".

So logic tells us that coins, like most pre-1933 U.S. Mint gold coins, the Double Eagles e.g., are not rare, because they are not scarce. I can prove this to you, and it bears repeating, especially when you consider that thousands continue to buy these coins at prices beyond what they will ever be worth.

- A 1927-D Saint-Gaudens Double Eagle graded NGC MS 66 set a new record for the date when it sold for $1,997,500. With only 12 or 13 examples known, the 1927 $20 gold piece is one of the rarest regular issue United States coins struck 1793 to date.

- Here is a picture of the "Rare Coin"

> Here is a listing on eBay for a 1927 Double Eagle just like the one above – MS66 (same grade) – only difference is that this is a coin minted in Philadelphia instead of Denver – why is it worth a fraction of the value of the other coin?
>
> 1927 $20 St. Saint Gaudens Double Eagle Gold PCGS MS66 Coin Twenty Dollar (*)
>
> $2,627.00
> Buy It Now
> Free shipping
>
> FAST 'N FREE - Get it on or before Thu. Jun. 26
>
> There are only a dozen of the other coin in existence – this coin is one of thousands available

So to claim that Double Eagles in mint states are rare is a completely misleading statement. Advertising pre-1933 Gold Double Eagles as rare coins and using the rare coin index as a point of reference indicating the ROI of around 11% over time is a complete misinterpretation of the facts. Please note: reliable coin dealers and bullion dealers are going with the flow, trying to make a buck. But I think they are somewhat confused about what is rare and what is not rare.

The rare coin index as a term, has many meanings. Its interpretation is a result of what each coin dealer or coin information company or investment journal implies it to be:

For example, the *Wall Street Journal* refers to it this way:

"For the past several years, Coin World has provided a "Classic U.S. Rarities Key-Date Investment Index" for use in the Wall Street Journal's investment scoreboard.

The scoreboard tracks investment groups in the categories of stocks, bonds, mutual funds, bank instruments (bank certificates of deposit and money market accounts), money market funds, precious metals and residential real estate. Coins are listed in the category, "rare coins, top investment grade, in the year-end survey." (Steve Roach)

Here is the index they refer to: (rare coins listed on bottom at 10.30%).

SPECIAL REPORT: YEAR-END REVIEW OF MARKETS & FINANCE
2010 Investment Scoreboard

	TOTAL RETURN ON INVESTMENT		
	2008	2009	2010
STOCKS (includes price changes and dividends)			
Dow Jones Industrial Average	-31.93%	22.68%	14.06%
Standard & Poor's 500 Stock Index	-37.00	26.46	15.06
Russell 2000	-33.79	27.17	26.85
Dow Jones Wilshire 5000	-37.23	28.57	17.62
BONDS (Barclays Capital Indexes)			
Long-Term Treasury Index	24.03%	-12.92%	9.38%
U.S. Credit Index AA-rated segment	2.74	7.80	7.10
Municipal Bond Index	-2.47	12.91	2.38
Intermediate-Term Treasury Index	11.35	-1.41	5.29
Mortgage-Backed Securities Index	8.52	5.75	5.50
MUTUAL FUNDS			
Lipper Growth Fund Index	-42.24%	35.91%	16.22%
Lipper Growth and Income Fund Index	-37.54	29.10	14.22
Lipper Balanced Fund Index	-26.18	23.35	11.90
Lipper International Fund Index	-43.63	35.30	11.03
Lipper Multi-Cap Value Index	-37.65	26.59	14.54
BANK INSTRUMENTS (Bankrate.com National Index)			
One-Year Certificate of Deposit	2.39%	1.16%	0.65%
30-Month Certificate of Deposit	2.46	1.44	0.99
Money-Market Deposit Account	0.72	0.39	0.21
MONEY MARKET FUND			
iMoneyNet/12-month yield on all taxable funds	2.04%	0.18%	a0.04%
PRECIOUS METALS (S&P Goldman Sachs Commodity Index)			
Platinum	-38.75%	r54.03%	19.35%
Gold	5.83	r22.85	28.73
Silver	-23.84	47.64	81.83
RESIDENTIAL REAL ESTATE			
Office of Federal Housing Enterprise Oversight	-8.16%	-rb4.00%	-3.18%
COLLECTIBLES			
Rare Coins, top investment grade	8.80%	-7.90%	10.30%

r - Revised.
a - Estimated.
b - Through third quarter.
Sources: Thomson Reuters; WSJ Market Data Group; Russell Investments; Coin World (Classic U.S. Rarities Key-Date Investment Index Rare)

In addition to the *Wall Street Journal*, there are many world class coin companies, like PCGS that have their own coin index. PCGS has the PCGS3000. Let's look at it in some detail:

> Key Dates and Rarities Index (1970 to date)

Key Dates and Rarities Index (1970 to date)

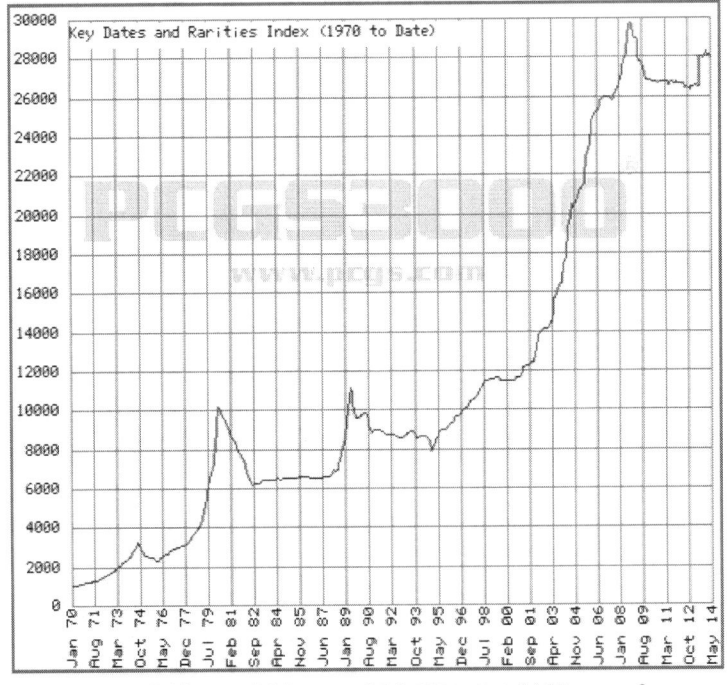

[1 year] | [3 years] | [10 years] | [1970 to Date] | [Summary]

The figures in their charts represent an average sale of 3000 rare coins over a period of time. It is based upon prices they monitor and have first hand knowledge of. As you can see in this 44 year chart, rare coin sale prices have increased dramatically. The coins on the lists can be found here: http://www.pcgs.com/prices/PCGS3000.aspx

Let's address the question again, what are rare coins? To begin with, there is no way to invest in the rare coin index because the coins listed are so rare and hard to find that you cannot get your hands on them easily or invest in them as if they are sitting somewhere like a stock or fund. You as a collector, can learn what types of coins are rare, and if money permits, begin buying them in the hopes that they will appreciate about 11% over time, which is what their track record indicates.

- So coin collecting involves learning about Rare Coins and how to acquire them if that is what your objective is

- Let's look at some **very rare** coins – pictures are worth a thousand words:

This 1913 nickel just sold for over $3,000,000

This 1933 double eagle sold for $7,000,000

A coin does not have to be old to be rare – only a few of these test aluminum coins exist

- Coins do not have to be worth millions to be considered rare – some rare coins are worth much less

- Most of the coins listed on the PCGS rare coin list are in high grades but some are not

- eBay auctions - examples of rare coins for sale:

A 1793 VF35 PCGS graded ½ cent

Price is $18,500

This coin is old, rare and in VF condition (not a high grade)

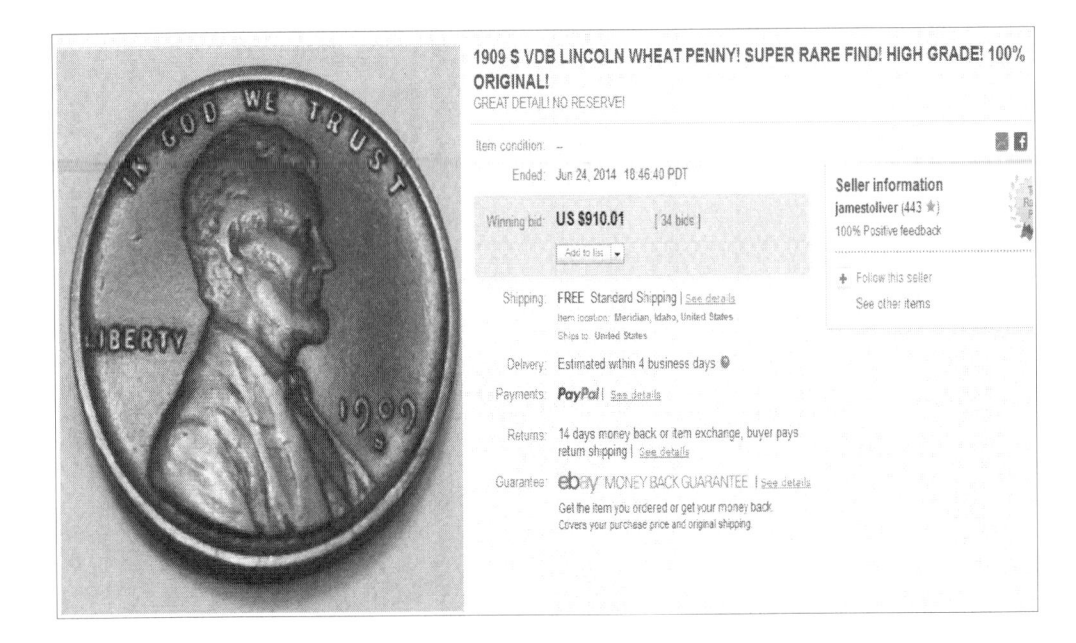

Another example of a rare coin.

The 1909S VDB Lincoln Penny is a key date in the series and one in this condition is rare. Based upon what you have learned, you should not consider a coin like this that has not been certified by one of the major coin grading companies. Why didn't the seller spend $30 - $40 for certification? I can tell by looking at the coin, based upon an earlier link in the course, that it is real, but I would not take a chance with that much money on the line. The selling price of $910, is far less than the $1500 plus it would have generated had it been graded!

Let's refine the definition of rare coins now that we have looked at some more coins that I consider rare:

Coins that continually and (dramatically) go up in value over time and are hard to find or buy because they are scarce, and when found can only be purchased for much more than their face value, and have been certified by a major grading company, and most likely are selling for a bare minimum of $300 (most rare coins sell for much more than that), and coins that typically are very old (more than 50 years). Error coins are usually not considered to be rare coins but there are some exceptions.

Major investors in rare coins, such as foreign billionaires, typically buy coins worth millions of dollars knowing that their investment will climb faster than any other asset class. You, however, can enter the rare coin arena with purchases in the $300 - $1000 range (the low end of the rare coin marketplace), and by running ads and hoping to locate a coin that way.

Let's go into the PCGS rare coin index and look at some rare coins so you can get a better feel for ones that the experts consider "rare". I will examine coins on the low dollar end of the index. The next image captures some most people are familiar with, the Lincoln Head Penny:

What I did is capture all the listings for Lincoln Pennies and as you can see there are only 3 dates on the chart: 1909S VDB, 1914D and 1955 DDO

The 1955 is an error coin – the front of the coin is doubled – one of the few error coins on the chart

These are actual coins that were sold and their prices are factored into the index

Let's look at the least expensive coins:

1909-S VDB F12 = $1050
1914-D F12 = $385
1955 F12 = $1500

Note: these dollar amounts are based upon the 2013 Red Book

242612	1909-S VDB	F12	1C	**$1050**	
242630	1909-S VDB	VF30	1C		
242640	1909-S VDB	EF40	1C		
242655	1909-S VDB	AU55	1C		
242863	1909-S VDB	MS63RD	1C		
242864	1909-S VDB	MS64RD	1C		
242865	1909-S VDB	MS65RD	1C		
242866	1909-S VDB	MS66RD	1C		
242867	1909-S VDB	MS67RD	1C		
247112	1914-D	F12	1C	**$385**	
247130	1914-D	VF30	1C		
247140	1914-D	EF40	1C		
247155	1914-D	AU55	1C		
247363	1914-D	MS63RD	1C		
247364	1914-D	MS64RD	1C		
247365	1914-D	MS65RD	1C		
282512	1955	F12	1C	**$1500**	Doubled Die Obverse
282530	1955	VF30	1C		Doubled Die Obverse
282540	1955	EF40	1C		Doubled Die Obverse
282555	1955	AU55	1C		Doubled Die Obverse
282763	1955	MS63RD	1C		Doubled Die Obverse
282764	1955	MS64RD	1C		Doubled Die Obverse
282765	1955	MS65RD	1C		Doubled Die Obverse

You can see from this chart and from these prices that you can enter the rare coin market with small investments like the ones illustrated here. ($385 - $1050 - $1500)

Special Coins

Each year the U.S. Mint makes a limited number of special coins that it sells directly to the public. Examples include: Proof Sets, Mint Sets and Commemoratives. They are usually sold for a premium price because of their unique qualities, and you can sign up to have them sent to you on a regular basis, like an auto ship program. Many who invest in them do so with the expectation of future financial gain, and some just love collecting them.

Proof Sets: Proof refers to the way a coin is made and not a coin's condition. Proof coins are usually sold in sets each year and sold in a protective casing to maintain their beautiful appearance. They are sonically sealed in their case and inspected for quality by U.S. Mint employees wearing gloves (they are not air tight). I have found numerous proof coins in change, apparently someone opened the set to cash in the coins not knowing their value while in the holder. Proofs are commonly known to have mirror like surfaces, but other surface types have been made: Frosted and Matte Proofs are examples.

- Here's a picture of a proof half dollar I found while coin roll hunting – it pays to look through rolls of coins:

Even though this coin has been worn down from handling it still has its original mirror like proof finish – the reflection of the pen on the coin surface illustrates this point

It is worth very little out of its original case and in this condition, but worth keeping

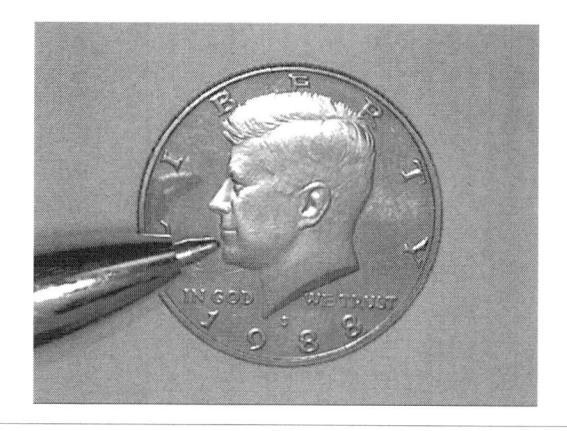

This beautiful 1979S Proof Set has a penny, nickel, dime, quarter, half dollar and dollar coin in it. What is interesting about this set, and this point illustrates how these sets, which are commonly collected for investment purposes, are mistakenly valued, is its current value of $6. But it cost $9, 35 years ago. Had you invested $9 at 1% simple interest for 35 years you would have $12.75 today.

Each year proof sets are minted, and over the years the sets have contained different coin types. The Red Book has a complete list of them. Because of their beauty, they are considered collectible, but the notion that they will increase in value of time is subject to debate. Some do, but most don't. Let's examine this issue in some detail. It has been my experience that owners of proof sets have a misguided sense of their value.

Many proof sets do not increase in value over time. In fact they decrease. Some do appreciate, but at such a slow rate, that they should not be thought of as an investment, just a collectible. The PCGS proof index for the last 10 years bears this out: it shows a minor price increase over a long period of time. There are better ways to invest your money.

Proof Type Coin Index (10 years)

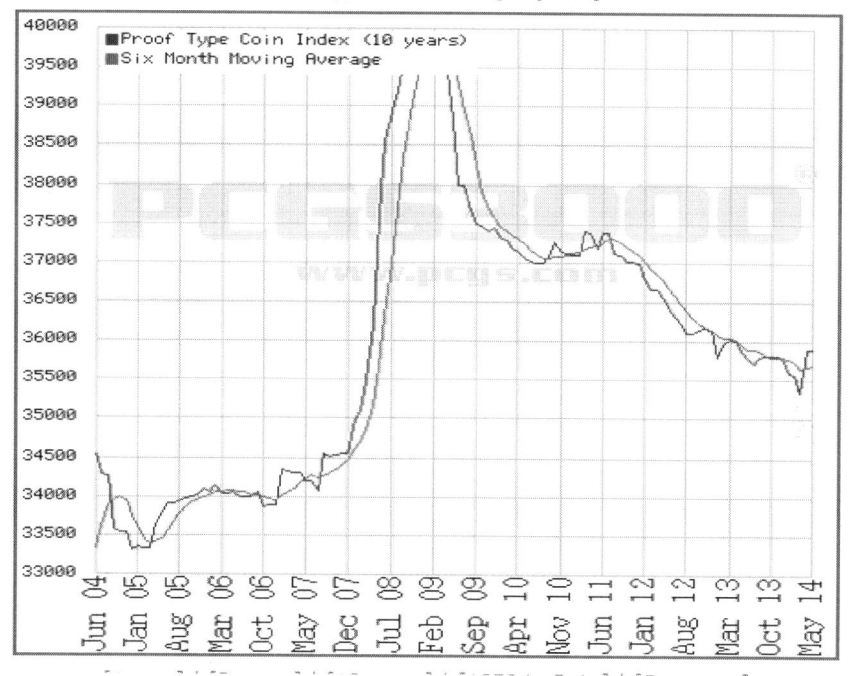

Mint Sets: Just like proof sets, mint sets are packaged in containers but not sealed like proof sets are. They contain uncirculated, not proof, coins. Most of them are worth less than their original price.

Commemorative coins are authorized by Congress to celebrate and honor historic events, individuals, and places. The coins are legal tender; however, they are not minted for general circulation. Commemorative coins are produced by the United States Mint in limited quantity and are only available for a limited time before minting ceases. Money raised by the sale of these coins helps worthy causes , museums, e.g.. Examples of some commemorative coins recently sold by the U.S. mint:

2009	Abraham Lincoln Commemorative Silver Dollar Program
	Louis Braille Bicentennial Silver Dollar Program
2010	Boy Scouts of America Centennial Silver Dollar
	American Veterans Disabled for Life Silver Dollar
2011	Medal of Honor Commemorative Coin Program
	United States Army Commemorative Coin Program
2012	Star Spangled Banner Commemorative Coin Program
	Infantry Soldier Silver Dollar

Most coins of this type have little future value unless mintage was very small or some other anomaly takes place. In the modern era, the two most valuable coins are the 1997 Jackie Robinson $5 Gold Coin and the 2000 $10 Library of Congress bi-metallic gold and platinum coin. The Jackie Robinson coin, commemorating Major League Baseball's first black player, achieved just six percent of its authorized minting. The 5,174 pieces that were issued are now worth an estimated $3,500 to $6,000. Just 7,261 of the Library of Congress coins were minted, now fetching about $3,750 to $5,200.

This 50th anniversary coin to celebrate the 1964 Civil Rights Act may not have future value because of the large quantity being minted, but for those of us who were alive then it has special meaning.

2014 Civil Rights Act of 1964 Proof Silver Dollar (CR1)

Zoom

Mintage Limit: 350,000 across all product options
Product Limit: None
Household Order Limit: None
Available by Subscription: No

$54.95

Qty: 1   Add to Wish List   Add to Cart

Description | Program | Specifications | Purchasing & Shipping

2014 marks the 50th anniversary of the enactment of the Civil Rights Act of 1964. This law greatly expanded civil rights protections, outlawed racial discrimination and segregation, and served as a model for subsequent anti-discrimination laws. Celebrate this ground-breaking law and its impact on our Nation with the 2014 Civil Rights Act of 1964 Silver Dollar.

The **obverse** (heads side) design features three people holding hands at a civil rights march. The man holds a sign that reads *WE SHALL OVERCOME*. The design is symbolic of all

Like 349 Tweet 14 Pinit   Email   Print

The U.S. Mint also makes medals that can be purchased. Some examples:

George W. Bush 3" Bronze Medal (146)
Price: $39.95   Qty. 1
Add to Wish List   Add to Cart

George W. Bush 1 5/16" Bronze Medal (846)
Price: $6.95   Qty. 1
Add to Wish List   Add to Cart

William J. Clinton (2ndTerm) Bronze Medal 3" (145)
Price: $39.95   Qty. 1
Add to Wish List   Add to Cart

William J. Clinton (2nd Term) Bronze Medal 1-5/16" (845)
Price: $6.95   Qty. 1
Add to Wish List   Add to Cart

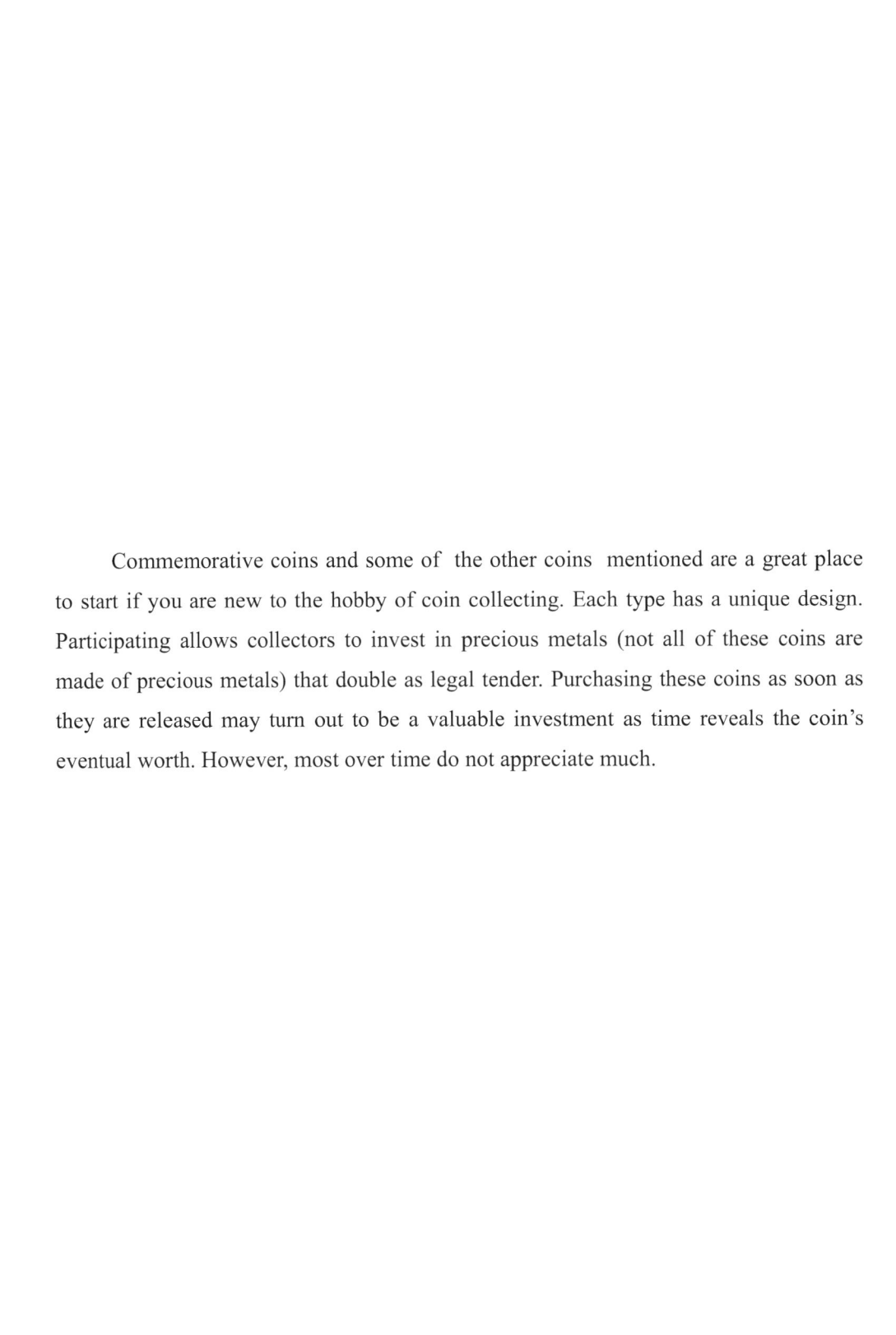

Commemorative coins and some of the other coins mentioned are a great place to start if you are new to the hobby of coin collecting. Each type has a unique design. Participating allows collectors to invest in precious metals (not all of these coins are made of precious metals) that double as legal tender. Purchasing these coins as soon as they are released may turn out to be a valuable investment as time reveals the coin's eventual worth. However, most over time do not appreciate much.

Ancient Coins

"Ancient Coins" is a topic that may be of interest to the first time collector and also to the experienced coin enthusiast who may not know much about this subject. The world of ancient coins is now open to everyone because of the internet. Simply go onto eBay, for example, and you can find hundreds of these coins for sale. What is an ancient coin?

An ancient coin is a coin minted many years before modern civilization began, usually associated with ancient Greece and Rome and believed to be first minted at least 1000 years before the birth of Christ, possibly in China. Examples of ancient coins include: Chinese coins, Roman coins, Greek coins, Islamic coins, Byzantine coins and Egyptian coins. For a brief but interesting history of very ancient coins, the first coins minted, please read this:

http://www.ancient.eu.com/coinage/

The subject of ancient coins is very complex and very controversial. It seems that one can never be sure that the coin they buy is real or fake. According to the FBI, 50% of the coinage, especially those sold online, are fake. Even the best dealers have been accused of selling fake coins and overcharging. Do not be dismayed though. If you proceed with caution and follow basic rules you will be okay.

We spoke about buying coins before and buying from reputable dealers. This concept applies to ancient coins as well. Ancient coins are fascinating and a fun way to start collecting coins and a great add on to an existing collection. Literally millions of these coins exist and are buried in the ground. There were no banks in ancient times so they were buried. I have assembled a great deal of information for you, mainly in the form of links to web sites that are packed with facts on this subject, but we will cover the basics.

A Gold Octadrachm from the reign of Ptolemy II in Alexandria from 285-246 BC. The Veiled head of Arsinoe II facing right appears on the obverse, while a double cornucopia appears on the reverse. It is very rare and in very fine or better condition, justifying its value at $11,500. *Alexandria is a port city on the Mediterranean Sea in northern Egypt founded in 331 BCE by Alexander the Great*

As you can imagine you do not go to the bank and order ancient coins or contact your favorite coin dealer and order them. They are discovered in a few parts of the world by digging and detecting, mainly in Europe and the Middle East, and then show up for sale on the internet, usually for auction.

As you can see from the history of just one gold coin shown above, this type of collectible can be more compelling and has so much more history than say a typical U.S. Mint coin, whose design may actually be based upon ancient Greek coinage. Imagine touching a coin from the time of Alexander the Great, Socrates, Plato, Aristotle, Hippocrates, Caesar and Jesus! In fact it is believed that many ancient coins depict a very accurate rendering of Christ.

Believed to be the earliest (700 A.D.) numismatic portrait of Christ

Actual pictures of gold, silver and bronze coins made to depict all the Roman Emperors. Every time a Roman Emperor came into power a new coin was made.

Despite their history and beauty, ancient coins can actually be less expensive than modern coinage. A wide range of prices, from very low (less than $1) to high exists, as it does with modern coins. I am often asked what is the most expensive ancient coin? A rare collection of ancient Greek coins, called the Prospero Collection, fetched a record price of $25 million at an auction in New York. Included in the collection is a coin which has been regarded as a rare artistic masterpiece by experts. It features the head of a satyr, a character widely used in Greek mythology, and was sold for $3.25 million, thereby breaking all previous world records for an ancient Greek coin.

As with any new endeavor it can be challenging to get started. First and foremost: read-read-read. Get involved with every forum and link I mention, and saturate yourself with information. If you start small and proceed slowly you will help protect yourself.

> **Ancient coins were made using simple tools:**
>
> The basic tools were an oven for heating blanks or "flans," tongs for handling hot flans, a table or bench on which an anvil was mounted, and a pair of dies struck with a heavy hammer to impress the design into the flan
>
> This ancient Roman coin shows how coins were made

Ancient coins were made from various metals and abbreviations are used to identify them. Sometimes it is hard to tell from photographs, but there is a series of abbreviations that let you know what metal you're dealing with – AE is Bronze; AR is Silver; AV is Gold, and there is fourth category called Billion which means either that the coin has a low silver content or that it was washed in silver. Saying a coin is washed in silver is a little like saying it is silver plated.

What are uncleaned coins? Ancient coins are found in the ground so they become encrusted with dirt and can erode, so they are referred to as uncleaned or crusty. The most common variety of uncleaned coins comes from the Balkans, also referred to as Dacia. They can come from Austria, England, Spain and the Middle East. Coins from Spain are the most desirable, because the dry climate has kept them very well preserved.

Both Spanish and Middle Eastern uncleaned coins often possess a patina highly valued by collectors that has a sandy color and texture. Austrian coins are generally very interesting as well. British coins can be the most challenging of uncleaned coins because of the soil conditions in England. The patinas tend to be more fragile because of the acidic nature of the soil, and are not recommended for newcomers to uncleaned coins. But they also yield some of the rarest coins that you will not generally find in the Balkan lots.

Holy land uncleaned coins will surprise you with the variety of different coins you can find in one lot. They could contain: Greek, Roman, Provincial, Jewish, Islamic, and Byzantine coins. It was a center for trade and many different cultures sprang from this area. Holy land uncleaned coin lots will contain a rich variety of coins! This is a nice way to start if you haven't found something you want to focus on; it's like the appetizer platter at a chain restaurant - a little bit of everything.

Greek and Byzantine coins are harder to come by, and usually more expensive than Roman coins. Greek coins, from before and during the early Roman Empire, tend to be twice as thick as regular uncleaned coins, and the legends on them are hard to decipher because the text is in Greek and not Latin. Latin is pretty easy to figure out once you get the hang of it, but Greek remains elusive because it uses a different alphabet. They are also harder to clean than Roman coins because their surfaces are often fragile and powdery.

Understanding the sizes of coins is very important, and often overlooked aspect until you get a couple of batches of very small coins because you didn't know what an AE 5 was! The following sizes are not fully agreed upon in the coin community, but generally accurate:

AE 1, larger than 25mm
AE 2, 21-25mm
AE 3, 17-21mm
AE 4, under 17mm
AE 5, around 10mm or smaller

As a point of reference a dime is 17.9 mm wide

Buying a small lot of uncleaned coins is not a bad way to get your feet wet, for under $20. If you start out with a minimum purchase and learn how to clean ancient coins, and then try to identify them you are off to a good start. Finding a reputable source for uncleaned coins is very challenging. Many good dealers seem to come and go. Lists I have of recommended dealers seem to out date themselves very quickly.

Uncleaned coins can be purchased from many sources. They can be found on eBay, Amazon, vcoins.com and just by searching Google for "uncleaned coins" or "Roman Coins" or "uncleaned Roman Coins" or "Crusty Coins" or "Crusty Romans".

The next pages provide a list of online resources that you can examine and investigate. It is very extensive, and will require some time. Please keep in mind that many of the sources they list as reputable sellers of ancient coins, particularly uncleaned coins, are outdated. They no longer exist.

Great article on cleaning ancient coins:

http://www.ebay.com/gds/Minimalist-Approach-to-Cleaning-Restoring-Uncleaned-Ancient-Coins-/10000000178368748/g.html?_trksid=p2047675.m2468

Great article on cleaning ancient coins: this person also sells them:

http://www.romancoins.net/cleaning.htm

Another article on cleaning coins:

http://www.forumancientcoins.com/numiswiki/view.asp?key=complete%20guide%20to%20uncleaned%20coins

Good article on fake coins. Also has some good resources listed:

http://www.mindspring.com/~kroh/Empirecoins/fakes.html

This eBay article provides tips for buying ancient coins on eBay:

http://www.ebay.com/gds/10-Tips-for-Buying-Uncleaned-Ancient-Coins-/10000000008769720/g.html

This eBay article helps you identify fakes before buying:

http://www.ebay.com/gds/How-to-avoid-buying-fake-ancient-coins-on-eBay-/10000000001336206/g.html

List of genuine eBay sellers, many are no longer active on eBay!

http://www.ebay.com/gds/GENUINE-SELLERS-LIST-OF-ANCIENT-COINS-ARTEFACTS-/10000000003542741/g.html

Great resources:

http://esty.ancients.info/numis/sitelinks.html   (Best link – Best resource) http://tjbuggey.ancients.info/dealers.html

Another great resource:
http://rg.ancients.info/guide/ancients.html

A link to a great coin forum that has discussions on ancient coins:
http://www.coincommunity.com/forum/topic.asp?TOPIC_ID=138699
I suggest you join this forum and get involved – it is free.

Let's make an actual purchase (which I will do on eBay) and proceed with the cleaning. But before we do, in case you are not too familiar with eBay, I want to show you how to find an eBay seller by their ID name. Many of the links I just provided list eBay sellers who they recommend by their eBay name, e.g. "ancientcaesar".

Let's find this eBay seller.

First – open eBay

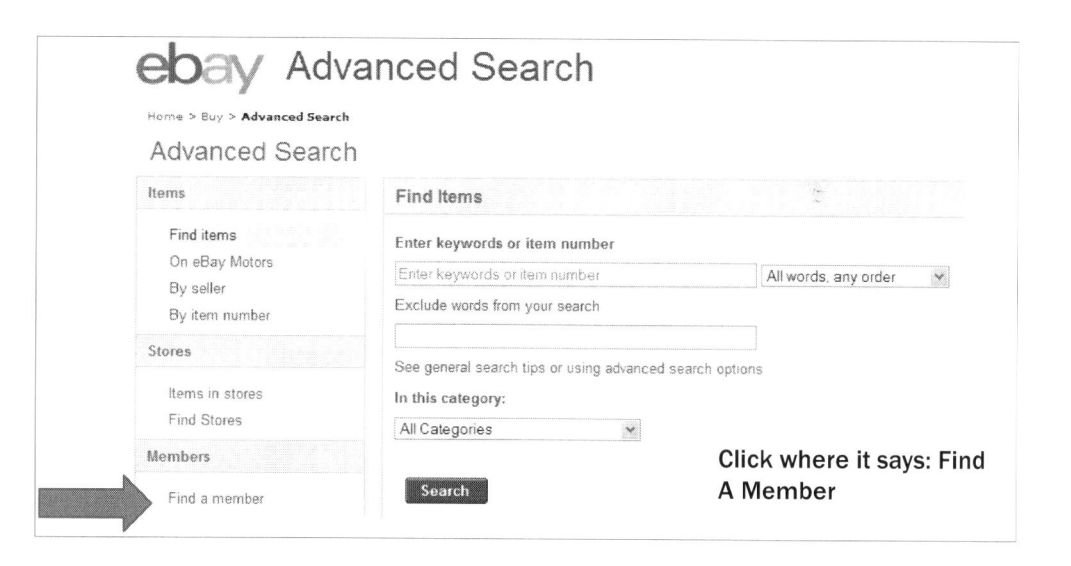

Notice on the top right the word "Advanced" – click on it

Advanced Search

Home > Buy > **Advanced Search**

Advanced Search

Items
- Find items
- On eBay Motors
- By seller
- By item number

Stores
- Items in stores
- Find Stores

Members
- Find a member

Find Items

Enter keywords or item number

Exclude words from your search

See general search tips or using advanced search options

In this category:
All Categories

Click where it says: Find A Member

When the next page opens, enter their user ID: ancientcaesar and the verification code that appears on the page and then hit the "Search" tab

Advanced search

Items
- Find items
- On eBay Motors
- By seller
- By bidder
- By item number

Stores
- Items in Stores
- Find Stores

Members
- Find a member
- Find contact information

Find a member

Enter user ID or email address of member

`ancientcaesar` ⬅

Enter a user ID to access a member's profile, items for sale and eBay Stores. limited information is provided when searching by email address. Learn more.

Enter verification code hidden in the image

483390 `483390`

Change the image | Listen to the numbers

[Search]

As you can see eBay finds this member – now click on their ID name – "ancientcaesar" and you will be taken to their listings on eBay

Find a member

`ancientcaesar`   [Search]

1 exact match and 0 close matches for member: ancientcaesar

User ID	Member for	Location
Exact match:		
ancientcaesar (19253 ☆)	15 years 2 months	KS, United States

My order of ancient coins came in from eBay. This photo came from the eBay listing and shows some detail but not much. I paid a little over $1 per coin. These two pictures show the front and back of the coins (10 coins total).

The eBayer who sells these coins is: stephengriffin6631 (eBay Name)

He and some others who have good products are: shopday2012 and tina0116g11.

When the coins arrived it was very difficult to discern any features because of the crust that accumulated over the years.

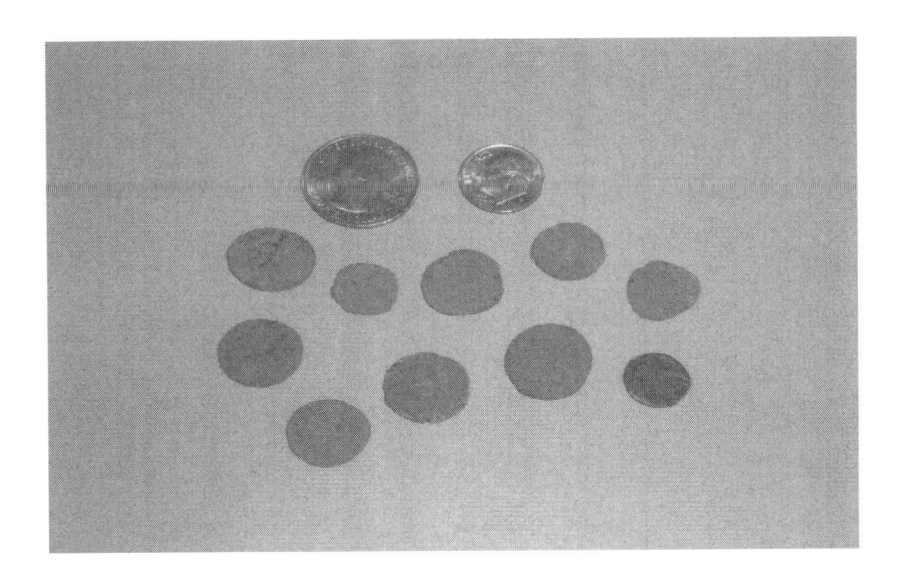

Note the relative size of the coins, and how encrusted they are. I took this picture as soon as they arrived. I was ready to start cleaning with my distilled water, plastic container and lid.

As soon as the coins were placed into the distilled water the crust started to loosen

This is the safest way to clean ancient coins but it is very time consuming

As often as the water dirties I will change it

The lid will cover the container so water does not evaporate out

Every few days I brush the coins with a cut off tooth brush (bristles cut down so it is not soft)

After a few weeks of distilled water soaking and tooth brushing, some details begin to emerge on this coin above: notice the ear and the profile and the hair style – is it braids?

Roman numerals are beginning to emerge

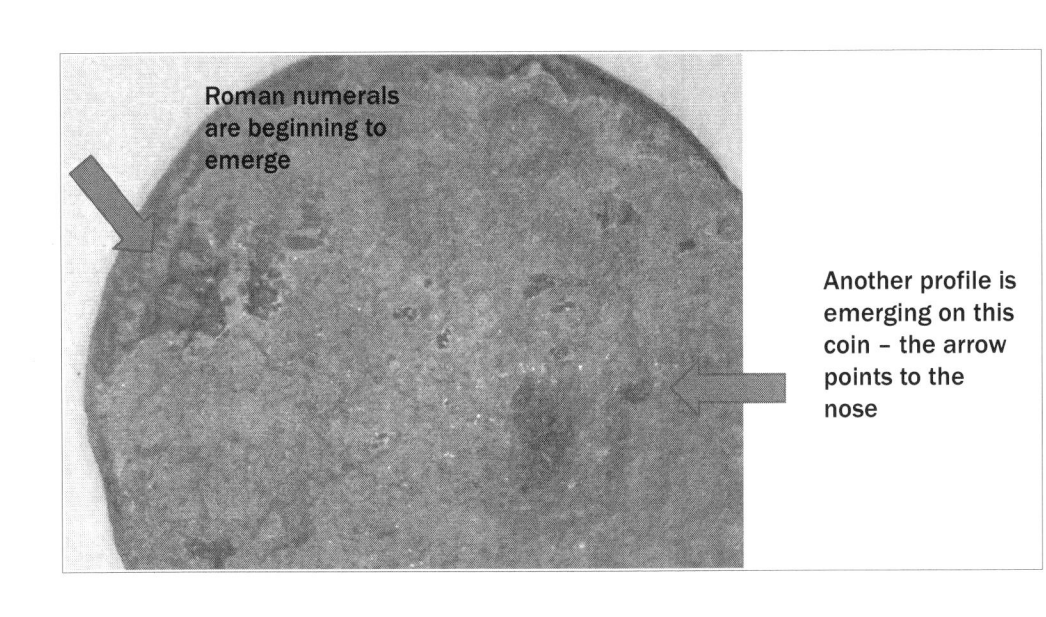

Another profile is emerging on this coin – the arrow points to the nose

Buying Coins

Buying coins from reputable dealers, like those mentioned with respect to the U.S. Mint authorized dealer program, helps prevent fraud. Many of the dealers we listed sell bullion coins and bullion gold and silver. They also advertise their buy back price; so buying from them helps insure that you can quickly sell back to them, and at the price they advertise at the time you want to sell. These dealers typically do not sell rare coins (other than pre-1933 gold coins, which as you now know are not rare). They do not sell collectible coins either, such as the coins we want for our coin collection.

Years ago buying coins was a very simple process: either you went to your local coin shop or you bought from a coin magazine or journal. Now you still have a few coin shops, and there are some coin magazines, but most buyers look for sources online. Many come to mind: eBay, Amazon, small coin dealer web sites, major coin auction sites, craigslist, local online classified sites, forums that sell coins and smaller coin auction sites. There are also some newer sites like Ubid, Ebid, Onlineauction and Delcampe. Most of the coins on these newer sites are either junk or fake.

While eBay has become the de facto standard for coin purchases, I do want to talk about other options. My experience with smaller coin auction sites suggests that you can often find good deals on them, but you do not have the forms of protection that eBay gives buyers such as buyer protection, easy pay system using PayPal, the ability to check feedback and search history of the seller, a good quality photo system so you can see the coin detail, a wide selection, easy and effective search methods and more.

However, with this in mind, you can often find a coin you really want and need for your collection on these smaller sites and sometimes on local classified.

Some sites to consider: www.vcoins.com. This site has some nice coins and dealers have to abide by a code of ethics. U.S., Ancient and Foreign coins are listed. You can sign up for their free newsletter.

Amazon has beefed up its coin listings with its new coin collectibles section: http://www.amazon.com/Collectible-Coins/b?ie=UTF8&node=9003130011

You can see that it refers to it as BETA. It has a search tab and many category selections.

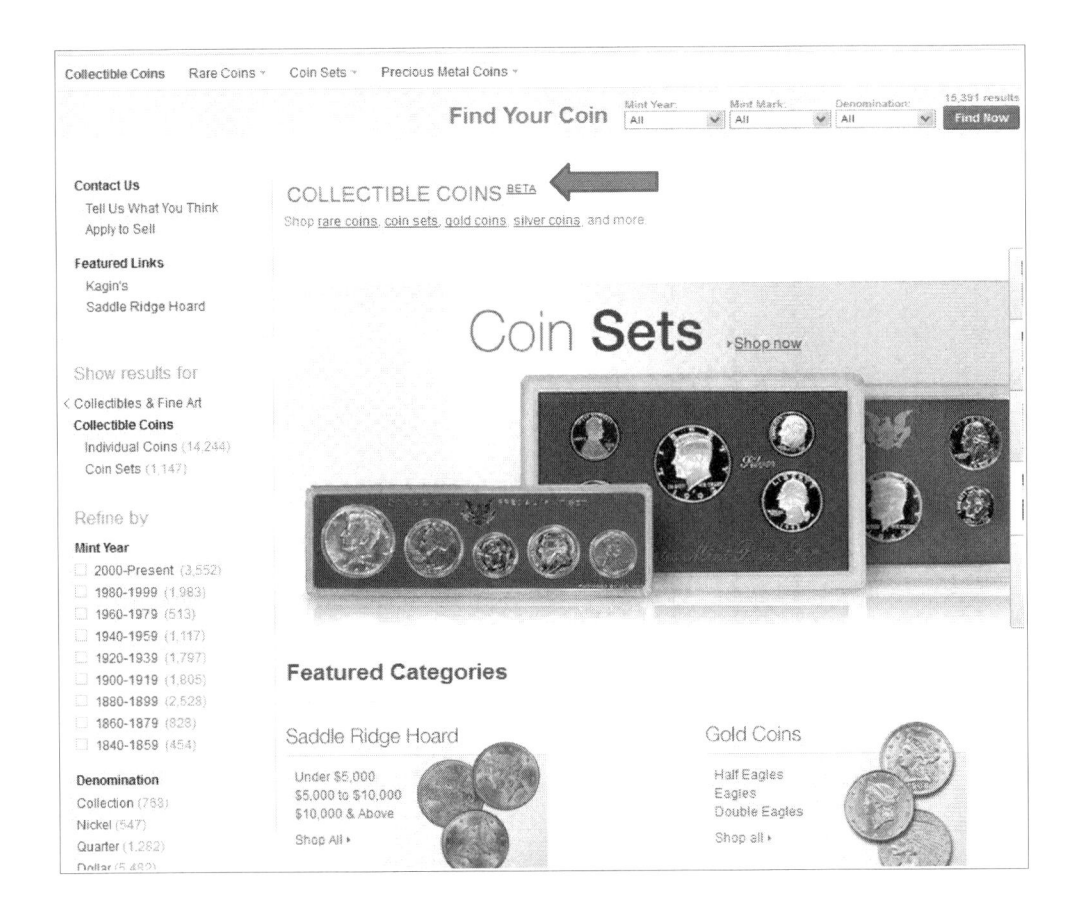

There are two coin auction companies/coin dealers that also need to be mentioned. These are the two most important coin companies in the world with respect to auctioning valuable coins. They also sell coins, typically expensive coins.

www.ha.com   Heritage Auctions is the world's largest coin dealer and coin auction house and probably one of the best. You can buy single coins and some at modest prices. This is a good place to find rare coins, and it is one of the best bets for selling your valuable coins.

http://www.stacksbowers.com/   Stacks Bowers is another large and well respected coin dealer-auction house. You can buy coins on this site.

http://www.coincommunity.com/   Coin community is a great forum and source for finding coins.

Your local coin club is also a great way to buy good quality coins from people you can trust. I have seen some good ads on Craigslist for coins, so keep that in mind.

It is important to spend a few minutes talking about a concept that you must come to understand. The term "Key Dates" is a term that is often used to describe the key or best coins in a series.

A "Key Date" is a coin or coins from a set of coins or series of coins, such as the Lincoln Head Penny series, starting in 1909 that is considered very hard to get and much more expensive than the other coins in the set. There are no pre-defined definitions for each set. Just look at the Red Book and look at a series and you will very quickly see the "Key Dates". The coins with the big prices are usually the "Key Dates".

When you start collecting you will soon notice that your coin folder fills up with the easy to find coins, but the key dates remain elusive. Many collectors can only fill in the Key Dates by buying them or trading for them. I mention this subject because of a technique that I have used and recommend to you. I call it "buying down".

I am not suggesting that you buy all your coins, but this technique should be part of your thought process in case you want to try it. It works like this:

I cannot tell you how many times I have seen The Lincoln Penny series, for example, selling on eBay in very good condition but missing the key dates. I consider the key dates for the Lincoln Series to be: 1909S, 1909S VDB, 1914D, 1922, 1931S. Sets like these (missing the key dates) in very good condition often sell for well under $200. Old pennies can be hard to find in change so if you want to jump start your collection, consider this approach. Buy the coins and then try to slowly find (buy) the key dates.

The downside to this is that you cannot see the coins close up (sometimes sellers have good pictures of each coin, but usually not). I trust sellers who sell sets like these.

Sets like these show up on eBay quite often.

Let's look at eBay again and mention some basic rules that will help protect you when purchasing:

• Coins priced over $50 should be slabbed or graded.

• Never buy coins unless you see very clear pictures of the front and back.

• Only buy from a seller that has a very good track record – read their feedback carefully.

• Look for bargains by searching for auctions that end at odd hours – such as in late night hours or on days when people are not online much – week days during the mornings, for example.

• Only buy from sellers that communicate well with you. I always write to my sellers and ask questions about the coins: How long have you had them? Where did you get them?

I do this not so much because I need these questions answered, but because I can tell by their answers if I want to do business with them – do they answer quickly and provide detailed information. I have seen eBay sellers who answer you in riddles – they try to be vague and often make no sense – they are hiding something.

If you find a coin that you want to purchase, I suggest you save it or put it in your watch list and only bid at the last minute. I never place a bid until the very end. If I am not available when the auction ends, I use a sniping tool to place the bid for me, and I decide how much I am willing to pay. The tool places the bid for you at the last minute, and bids up according to your limit. This way you spend the least amount of money possible and no more than your limit. What is a fair price to pay for a coin? Look it up in the Red Book and use their price as a guide. Don't worry if you do not win a bid. The same coin will show up again.

There are a few good auction tools out there:

https://www.ezsniper.com/index.php3 Ezsniper works well and you get three free auction bids and pay 1% after that for any auction that you win.

There are free sniping tools as well that have good reviews:
https://www.jbidwatcher.com/
http://www.gixen.com/index.php

Another tool that can help analyze a seller's feedback for you is:
www.auctionshadow.com

Selling Coins

We spoke about selling in an earlier chapter. It is an important topic. Selling has two parts to it. You can sell when you are in a hurry and need cash fast; therefore, price is not a key issue. Then there is selling for the best price. In this case you can hold out, you are not in a hurry. Local coin and gold shops and even pawn shops typically pay 50 - 70 cents on the dollar for precious metals, including coins with gold or silver in them. Jewelry stores do the same. Many shops claim they pay spot price, but if they do, they cannot make profit unless the price of the metal goes up. Be careful of this claim.

You can advertise on Craigslist and other local online sites, but this is dangerous if you have high priced items to sell. Coin web sites can be used to sell your products, but they seldom have the audience and safety features that eBay has. Your local coin club is another possibility, but this method takes time.

For best results, and as I stated before, eBay, and the dealer you buy from, (assuming they are reputable and authorized) are your best bet for getting the best price. Quality dealers will publish their buy back price. Ebay is a great way to sell, and you can always get spot price.

With respect to silver coins, like junk silver (90% and 40%) and numismatic coins, eBay is the way to go. Silver bars and rounds and gold bars and rounds can also be sold on eBay or to your dealer. It doesn't hurt to shop around and see what several authorized dealers will pay for your items. Oddball products, like foreign bullion coins and non-certified gold and silver may be problematic as far as dealers are concerned, so eBay may be your only option.

Ebay has such a large audience and so many coin enthusiasts that bidding can drive the price of your product up. Remember that the dealer you purchased from and eBay will cost you around 13% to sell your item. That means you will lose 13% when you sell back to the dealer and on eBay, assuming the price of silver and or gold has not changed.

Here are some key points to keep in mind with respect to eBay and selling in general:

- If you are selling coins that have precious metal in them, always sell when the price of that metal is on the upswing.
- Coins in great condition often sell for more money than coins in average condition, and if they have precious metal in them can sometimes get prices even higher than their metal content because of their high grade.
- With this in mind have better coins graded or slabbed – it will result in better auction results. (This only applies to coins that have real numismatic value and are worth over $100)
- Start and end your eBay listings on Sunday night around 6PM Pacific Time, more people are on eBay at that time.
- Free shipping attracts more bids and more potential buyers.
- A low starting price, such as 99 cents, attracts more bids in a big way.
- Auction listings work better than "buy it now" does – buy it now cost money and gets poorer search engine results.
- If you are worried about the price going high enough for your coin(s) you can include a reserve, but you pay for this and eBayers do not like reserves.
- Most coin auctions bid up to a good price, so you seldom have to worry about using a reserve price.
- Providing a very clear, beautiful picture makes all the difference in the world – use the USB digital microscope mentioned in the course – it is phenomenal.
- Answer communications quickly and thoroughly.
- Use very brief but very good descriptions.
- The description should never mention any rules or do's or don'ts – this is a big turn off.

- If there is a story associated with the coin(s) tell it – this makes the listing more personal, and eBayers like this.
- Ship very quickly and package your coin(s) properly – make sure they do not make any noise or move around – protect them with cardboard.
- Always include a copy of the order with the item (if possible), and hand write a note with a happy face – thank them.

The secret to success on eBay is getting traffic to your listing. If the coin you are selling is one of 100 similar coins, it can be quite challenging to get buyers to your ad. This applies mostly to rare coins, rather than silver or gold coins, which will always attract buyers. There are many dynamics associated with getting traffic, but one in particular is more important than the others and needs to be mentioned: The Title.

The 80 character title is what eBay uses as a way to draw buyers to your listing. As you can imagine, a well written title gets the best results. I want to draw your attention to a great free tool that can help you write an effective title. It is called Title Builder: www.title-builder.com

This is the main page from the web site:

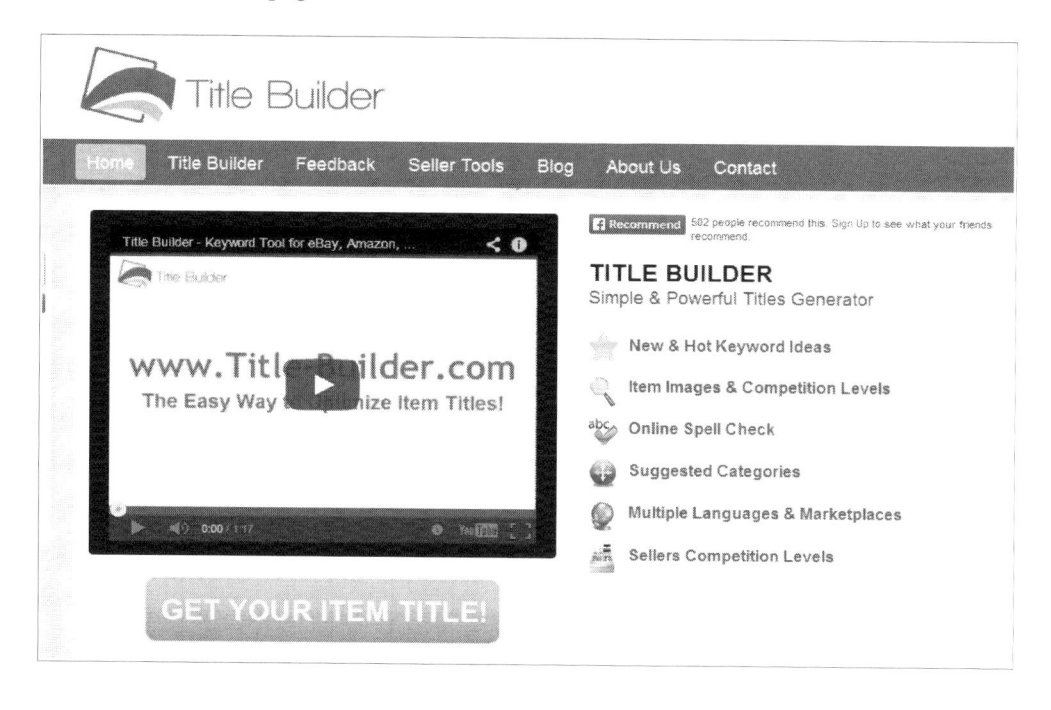

Just click on "Get Your Item Title" and you will see this:

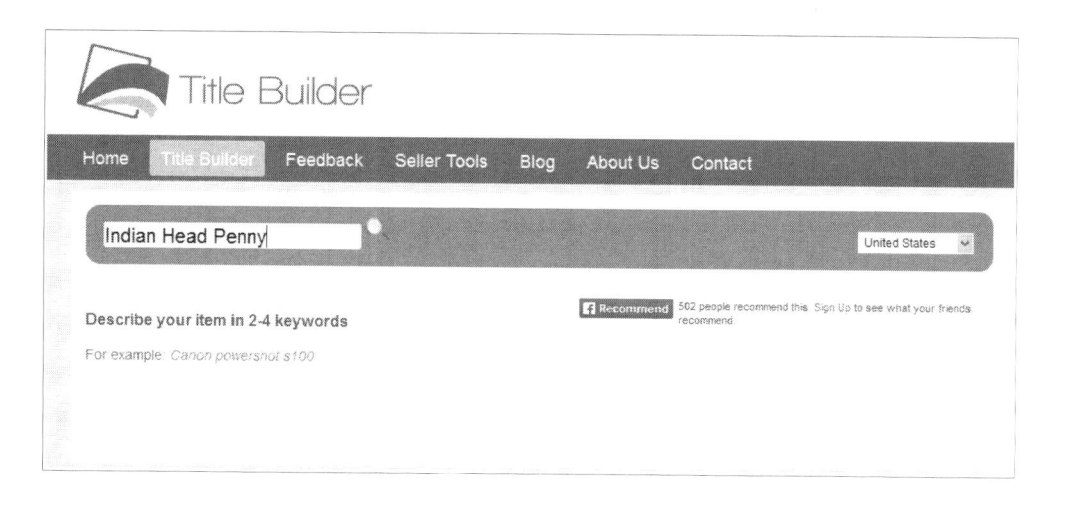

I entered the words "Indian Head Penny" and then pressed the enter key.

As you can see, Title Builder comes back with this rather long suggested title based upon the strongest words used in eBay when someone is looking for an Indian Head Penny. The words: Indian, head, penny and cent have the biggest bars, and therefore, carry the most weight.

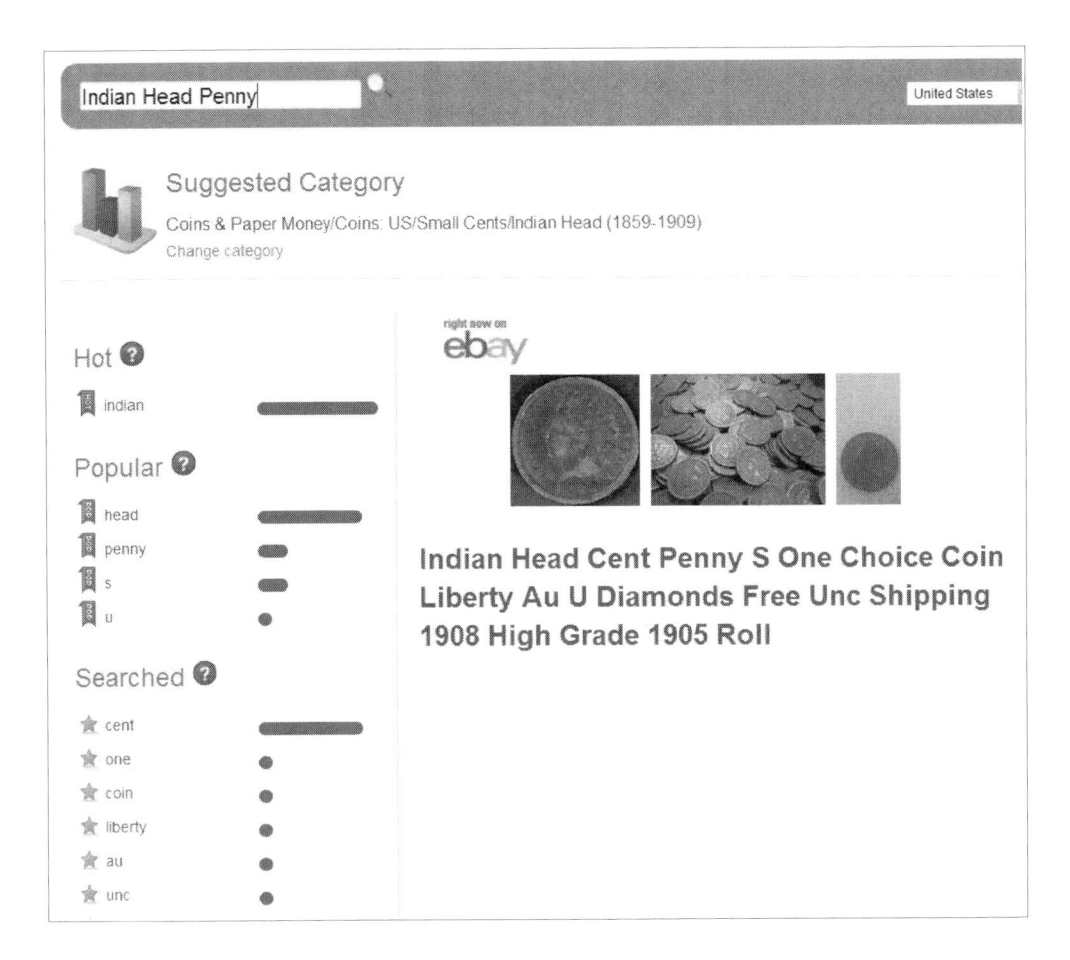

```
Indian Head Penny                                          United States

         Suggested Category
         Coins & Paper Money/Coins: US/Small Cents/Indian Head (1859-1909)
         Change category

                                  right now on
                                  ebay
Hot
  indian

Popular                    Indian Head Cent Penny S One Choice Coin
  head                     Liberty Au U Diamonds Free Unc Shipping
  penny                    1908 High Grade 1905 Roll
  s
  u

Searched
  cent
  one
  coin
  liberty
  au
  unc
```

So if you take the title created and boil it down to 80 characters, you end up with a strong traffic magnet.

Indian head cent penny s one choice coin liberty au u diamonds free unc shipping 1908 high grade 1905 roll

This is what I come up with: (I took out Au and Unc and U)

Indian Head Cent Penny Choice Coin Liberty Diamonds Free Shipping High Grade

(Note: If the 4 diamonds still show on the coin this implies great condition)

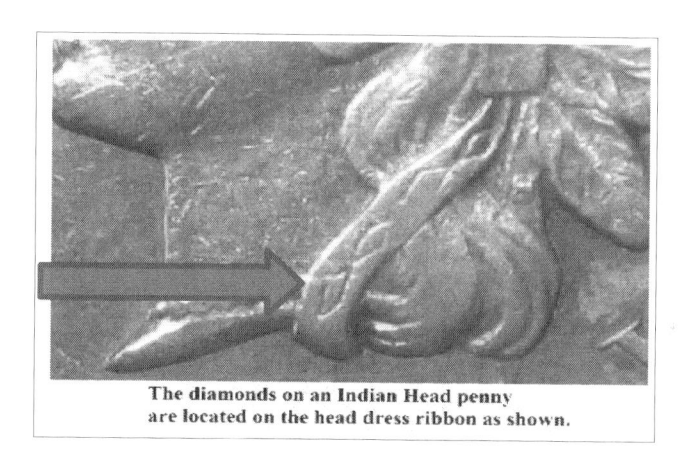

The diamonds on an Indian Head penny are located on the head dress ribbon as shown.

What's nice about eBay is that if the item does not sell you can relist it. In an emergency you can cancel your listing before the listing ends if you have to. If you have an extremely valuable coin please contact the two auction houses mentioned earlier – Heritage and Stack's Bowers and get their opinion on the coin(s) before attempting to sell. My course on eBay called: "Learn How Power Sellers Make Million On eBay" will provide more detailed information and is available on the web site: www.udemy.com.

Here is a list of the top 11 coin auction results of all time:

The following list is a chart of the most expensive coins. Most of these are auction prices. Several private sale prices over $2m are not in this list yet.

List of most expensive coins

Rank	Year	Type	Issuing country	Provenance	Price	Firm	Date of sale
01	1794	Flowing Hair Dollar	United States	Green, Contursi, Cardinal	$10,016,875	Stack's Bowers Galleries[1]	January 2013
02	1933	1933 Saint-Gaudens Double Eagle	United States	Farouk	$7,590,020	Sotheby's/Stack's[2]	July 2002
03	1787	Brasher Doubloon - EB on Breast	Privately minted		$7,400,000	Blanchard and Co.[3]	December 2011
04	1787	Brasher Doubloon - EB on Wing	Privately minted	Newlin, Davis, Perschke	$4,582,500	Heritage Auctions[4]	January 2014
05	1804	Bust Dollar - Class I	United States	Childs	$4,140,000	Bowers & Merena	August 1999
06	1804	Bust Dollar - Class I	United States	Mickley, Hawn, Queller	$3,737,500	Heritage Auctions[5]	May 2008
07	1913	Liberty Head Nickel	United States	Olsen, Farouk	$3,737,500	Heritage Auctions	January 2010
08	1907	Saint-Gaudens Double Eagle - Ultra High Relief	United States	Trompeter	$2,990,000	Heritage Auctions	November 2005
09	1787	Brasher Doubloon - EB on Wing	Privately minted		$2,415,000	Heritage Auctions	January 2005
10	1804	Bust Dollar - Class III	United States	Adams, Carter	$2,300,000	Heritage Auctions	April 2009
11	1907	Eagle - Rolled Edge	United States		$2,185,000	Heritage Auctions	January 2011
...	1343/4	Edward III Florin	Kingdom of England		$680,000	Spink[6]	June 2006

Investment Strategy - Conclusion

Precious metal investing is a complex subject. There are so many options available. With precious metal ownership you know that you can always cash in. The money is always there in time of need. For some, particularly those living on a very tight budget, buying a coin or two each month, such as a 1oz Silver Eagle is not a bad idea. Coin collecting is another way to start saving. As you learn and acquire coins your financial base will build. Rare coins provide a great rate of return, some argue that it is the highest rate of return for all asset classes, and are a good buffer against market volatility.

Running ads and looking for precious metals and coins pays off over time. Keep running your ads and you will be rewarded. Handing out business cards, placing fliers and speaking to groups, such as seniors will produce good results. About 15% of the senior population has some form of precious metal and coins and seldom know what to do with it. They usually end up selling for a fraction of their worth.

Others are challenged by the high end of the financial spectrum - involving millions of dollars and how to invest it. Should you buy physical gold or silver? Should you invest part of your portfolio in precious metals (just to provide a mental buffer), and if so, how, and how much? Getting sound financial advice from an established investment house is worth the effort and is necessary. If you need help ask friends who they invest with. There are many well established financial institutions that have good reputations and good financial advisers on staff.

Having a broad based stock portfolio with some, maybe 5%, precious metal exposure makes sense and if nothing else provides some piece of mind. The top performing precious metal ETFs and mutual funds support this reasoning. The stock market over the years has yielded the best results and solid companies that have delivered year in and year out provide more piece of mind than precious metal investments do.

Buying gold and silver as a hedge against inflation and future calamity is not sound and is not supported by the facts. Only in very extreme circumstances (as was the case in World War II), has this thinking paid off.

Please keep in mind the fact that reputable precious metal dealers, like those authorized by the U.S. Mint, such as APMEX, will continue to sell pre-1933 gold coins for inflated prices. This does not mean that they are unethical or in any way untrustworthy or even dishonest. On the contrary, these are the dealers you should be buying from, but don't buy pre-1933 coins unless the price is close to spot value. The marketplace has distorted the worth of these coins.

In 1912 a Persian philosopher traveled to the United States. In one of his presentations he stated: "Money is like a pile of sand in the desert. One minute it is yours, and the next minute the wind comes and blows it away"

If you have more than you need, remember those in need. Blessings to all.

Why did this 1794 Silver Dollar sell for $10.5 million and break all coin records?

(Answer at book's end!)

It is rare (unique - only one of a kind) and in great condition, but it sold for $10.5 million because that is what someone was willing to pay for it!

Printed in Great Britain
by Amazon